CORPORATE CORRUPTION

CORPORATE CORRUPTION
THE ABUSE OF POWER

MARSHALL B. CLINARD

PRAEGER

New York
Westport, Connecticut
London

Library of Congress Cataloging-in-Publication Data

Clinard, Marshall Barron, 1911–
    Corporate corruption: the abuse of power / Marshall B. Clinard.
       p.   cm.
    Includes bibliographical references.
    ISBN 0-275-93485-3 (lib. bdg. : alk. paper)
    1. Corporations—United States—Corrupt practices. I. Title.
HV6769.C558   1990
364.1'68—dc20   89-23088

Library of Congress Catalog Card Number: 89-23088
ISBN: 0-275-93485-3

First published in 1990

Praeger Publishers, One Madison Avenue, New York, NY 10010
A division of Greenwood Press, Inc.

Printed in the United States of America

The paper used in this book complies with the
Permanent Paper Standard issued by the National
Information Standards Organization (Z39.48-1984).

10 9 8 7 6 5 4 3 2

**To those corporations
that do not abuse their power**

CONTENTS

PREFACE

Ethics, like cholesterol, has increasingly become a major concern of the American people. This does not mean that the public has not long suspected, and often known, that conduct in high places has failed to conform to the credos of the Boy Scouts. Within recent years, however, there appears to have been a veritable explosion of exposures of ethical decline. Illegal dealings uncovered in security transactions, including widespread insider trading, have involved losses of hundreds of millions of dollars and, in some cases, have implicated the nation's largest brokerage firms. The banking and savings and loan institutions have been rocked with scandals. The sexual escapades and financial shenanigans of several prominent television evangelists have shocked even their own followers. Sordid reports of wrongdoing at the highest levels of our Congress and governmental administration have appeared, reminiscent of the Richard Nixon years that many believed had become history. Almost each day brings to light a new major ethical scandal.

Here we turn the spotlight on the conduct of America's giant industrial corporations, the prestigious *Fortune* 500, and their executives, to find out how they fare ethically. These corporations represent the industrial heart of our nation, the basic economic force that drives it. Their massive production capacities and their innovative powers have contributed immeasurably to the high standard of living that Americans now enjoy. However, far too many of them have abused the public trust, the people who consume their products, their own workers, their stockholders, the environment, and the Third World, which they often profess to help. They have abused and exploited the democratic process for their own ends, and in so doing have endangered the very democracy that permits our capitalist system to operate and flourish. Many have demonstrated an utter contempt for the government of the United States, and thus have defied the laws and the regulations established for the common good. Some of them have even defrauded the government out of hundreds of millions of dollars; it is the taxpayer who ultimately must foot the bill.

Corporate giants cause the deaths of thousands of workers and consumers, and hundreds of thousands of individuals suffer injuries because of corporate violations of health and safety standards and marketing of unsafe products. Corporations have illegally fixed prices on a grand scale. Many of them have seriously polluted the air and water, and have illegally and improperly disposed of hazardous waste products. A single corporate offense may run into millions of dollars of losses. In some instances, a single case has exceeded a loss of a billion dollars, nearly a third of the total cost of all U.S. burglaries in a single year.

This tale of corporate misconduct conflicts with the glowing image that advertising and other media portray of the corporations. However, relatively little of what this book describes appears in the general press or receives any prominence except, occasionally, in the business sections of our newspapers. The *Wall Street Journal* is a primary exception: It carries many detailed reports of corporate transgressions, many of which bear a direct relationship on a corporation's financial well-being. It has been a useful source of information, along with government reports, court documents, numerous research reports, and scholarly books.

For at least ten years I have been examining corporate behavior, the good as well as the bad. I have received two grants from the U.S. Department of Justice in order to make specific corporate studies, one under the Jimmy Carter administration, and the other under the Ronald Reagan administration. I have published three other books on corporate misbehavior. On two occasions I have testified before congressional committees dealing with corporate unethical practices and law violations. I have interviewed both top- and middle-management corporate executives. The cases of corporate misconduct included here represent only a sampling drawn from a large number in my files. In turn, they are probably a mere fraction of the actual cases.

Several persons have been of particular help to me in writing this book. Professors John Braithwaite and Peter Yeager carefully read an earlier version, and I have incorporated several of their suggestions. Jan Best worked unstintingly on the mechanics of putting my messy manuscript on a word processor and offered helpful suggestions. Marcia Stamell contributed several useful editorial changes. Mildred Vasan, acquisitions editor, William Neenan, production editor, and Nicole Balant, copy editor, have all been helpful in whipping this book into shape for publication. Finally, my wife and best friend, Ruth, has been an adviser and editor, as she has been with all my books. The story this book tells must be told.

Marshall B. Clinard

CORPORATE CORRUPTION

Chapter 1

THE ABUSE OF CORPORATE POWER

The power of large corporations is awesome. Today, transnational corporations dominate the Western world in much the same manner in which the Roman Catholic Church dominated medieval society. As the nation-state was the primary entity at the dawn of the modern age, so the giant corporations are all-powerful in the twentieth-century world.[1] Unfortunately for society, far too many giant corporations have abused this power in their relations with their workers, their stockholders, their consumers, and the public at large. They have also abused our environment, defrauded the government, and exploited the developing nations of the Third World. In their actions, they have even abused the very democratic process that has given them the opportunity to achieve this power.

Some might say that the *Fortune* 500 corporations are so essential for maintaining and improving our high standard of living and so vitally linked to our capitalist political system that it is un-American to criticize them. Although most people would take exception to this extreme view, it is unquestionably true that great corporations have contributed enormously to the industrial and commercial development of the United States. Through their continuing research and technological advances, they have enriched life for millions of people and eased human suffering. They have provided employment to tens of millions of persons and have immeasurably increased the wealth of the nation in many other ways, including the dividends paid to their millions of stockholders. By their very size, they are able to organize and coordinate production and distribution on a grand scale. Given the contemporary requirements for machines and complicated technology, only a large corporation can raise and deploy the requisite capital and equipment, as well as mobilizing the essential technological skills.

In fact, every modern industrialized Western nation has had to accept the dominating presence of the large corporation. It is not just a concomitant of modern technology; it is the very heart of an industrial society. As such, it must have big-business organization in the form of large, integrated plants that use mass-production methods. Big business is the basic condition of modern industrial society, regardless of the type of social organization or the political systems and beliefs that individual countries have adopted. Peter Drucker has aptly pointed out that the central problem of all modern society is not whether it wants big business, but what "we want of it and what organization of Big Business and of the society it serves is best equipped to realize our wishes and demands."[2]

CORPORATE POWER

The *Fortune* 500 corporations hold such vast aggregates of wealth and such immense social and political power that their operations vitally influence the lives of every American citizen from cradle to grave. Major corporations, directly or indirectly, control the work lives, and hence the health and safety, of a large part of the population. Some corporations control broad areas of the American economy. Thus, the policies they make greatly affect the quality of the goods they produce. The prices they put on their products influence inflationary trends in the country, and they can, and often do, manipulate public opinion through their increasingly effective use of modern mass media. Their actions also often affect our foreign relations. They even may jeopardize the democratic process through large political contributions and honoraria, which are often strategically placed to accomplish corporate objectives to the detriment of the general public welfare.

The top one-fifth of the *Fortune* 500 corporations have a greater share of all manufacturing profits than all the other 370,000 manufacturing firms combined. The 500 employ well over two-thirds of all workers engaged in manufacturing, they control over two-thirds of all industrial sales and manufacturing assets, and they earn about four-fifths of all profits. The combined work force of just two auto manufacturers, General Motors and Ford Motor Company, exceeds one million persons.

The 1988 annual combined sales of America's *Fortune* 500 corporations totaled nearly $2 trillion, as were their combined assets. Their total 1988 profits were $115 billion. General Motors' $121 billion 1988 sales made it the largest industrial corporation in the world and would rank it seventh among total government expenditures of all countries in the world. Ralph Nader once aptly pointed out that individual states are no match for the resources and size of our great corporations: "General Motors could *buy* Delaware, if DuPont was willing to sell it." Trailing behind monolithic General Motors in 1988 came Ford Motor Company with $92 billion in sales, Exxon with $79 billion in sales, IBM with $59 billion, and General Electric with $49 billion. Some giants continue to grow through mergers and acquisitions so that many already large corporations in oil and other industries have recently greatly increased both in size and power. In the 1980s, for example, Chevron bought Gulf Oil for $13 billion, and mammoth RCA, with $7 billion in assets, joined already mammoth General Electric to create an incredible "megamerger" with assets of $25 billion.

Approximately two-thirds of all corporate manufacturing industries are highly concentrated, and a few firms dominate most of the principal manufacturing sectors. Although no single firm dominates an entire major market, some come close. Western Electric produces virtually all telephone equipment, General Motors produces practically all diesel locomotives, and Campbell controls over 95 percent of the prepared soup market. Four firms control over 75 percent of a large number of industries. Some 90 percent of the cereal industry, for example, is in the hands of four corporations, and two of them, Kellogg and General Foods, dominate the industry. Twenty-five years ago there were 375 breweries in the United States. Today there are less than 30, and 4 corporations dominate the industry. This market concentration is commonly known as oligopoly, from the Greek word meaning few sellers. Through the oligopolistic process of weakening competition and reducing the number of sellers, these giants can exercise immeasurable power both over output and prices.

Three or four corporations generally dominate most industries; they are referred to as the "Big Three" or "Big Four." Market control by a few corporate giants largely enables them to set prices. Through this "administered" pricing system, corporate giants can individually decide what the price of a product or the amount of a price increase will be, often on the basis of what the market will bear rather than through the natural market force of free competition. A high degree of market concentration means that price leadership (or follow the leader) in pricing decisions can proceed without any necessary conspiracy in violation of antitrust laws.

As the activities of the giant U.S. corporations increasingly reach beyond the economic to the diplomatic, they take on the attributes of a nation-state. John Kenneth Galbraith once said that as the modern corporation acquires "power over markets, power in the country, power over the state, power over belief, it is a political instrument, different in form and degree but not in kind from the state itself."[3] The construction of transnational corporate plants in foreign countries and the movement of products are dictated by comparative wage scales, tariffs, and transportation costs, as well as by political and labor factors. Corporate managers weigh all these considerations on a worldwide basis. Transnationals like International Telephone and Telegraph Corporation (ITT) coordinate on a global level decisions on financial flow, pricing, marketing, tax avoidance, and research and development goals. On several occasions, American corporations have interfered politically in another country. In the 1950s, for example, United Fruit was instrumental in the overthrow of Jacobo Arbenz, the democratically elected president of Guatemala, whose fall from power was followed by thirty years of military dictatorship. During the 1970s, ITT played a significant role in the overthrow of Salvador Allendé, the elected president of Chile, in its attempt to protect ITT Chilean investments.

Not until the Industrial Revolution did the corporation emerge as a significant legal and economic unity. Legal incorporation in the form of a charter became a necessity. Charters made it possible to raise funds through the sale of corporate stocks and bonds, to provide a beneficial tax structure, and to secure the succession of property rights. As business opportunities continued to expand, the larger firms sought new avenues of development that had not been possible prior to the age of incorporation. As they attempted to dominate their sources of supply, as well as their markets, the large manufacturers first tried to gain control of factories in certain key industries by buying stock in other companies. This led, in turn, to the introduction of holding companies, as economies could result from a combination of mass production and mass distribution. Corporations made every effort to gain control over all stages of a given commodity's production, from the acquisition of raw materials to the distribution of finished products. In this way, they could be assured of an uninterrupted flow of goods into and out of their production and processing plants. By the mid-twentieth century, a relatively few giant firms had come to dominate most key industries.

Later, this process of growth through the expansion of a product line came to a near standstill as the market slowed down. At this stage, the most technologically advanced industries, such as chemical, rubber, and electrical, led the way into the second major growth stage of corporate expansion: diversification. Integrated firms began to diversify into other industries and product lines. Following World War II, corporate leaders often found it cheaper and faster to acquire other concerns or to form mergers rather than to build new factories and develop new companies from scratch, thus contributing to still more rapid growth in corporate size.

Today, most giant corporations are conglomerates. Although all of them have some leading lines of business, most have acquired a variety of other product lines. As a result, these massive conglomerates have power, political as well as economic, that extends well beyond that of the traditional large corporation operating in a single product line. ITT is a classic case of diversification through acquisition. Although originally a telecommunications firm which remains still the world's second largest manufacturer of telecommunications products, this commodity accounts only for approximately 20 percent of its present income. In 1960, ITT began its drive to become a giant conglomerate rather than a one-product company, and from 1960 to 1974 its sales grew by 1,375 percent. Assets rose from $1.1 billion in 1961 to more than $38 billion in 1988, largely as a result of its acquisition of large business concerns in varied areas such as electronic and automotive products, defense technology, semiconductors, vending machines, plastics, pulp and timber, hotels, consumer financing, and insurance. It is one of the world's largest manufacturers of pumps. ITT had annual sales of $20 billion in 1988. Among ITT's acquisitions have been the Hartford Fire Insurance Company and Sheraton Corporation of America. It has also acquired more than 50 foreign companies, and it now operates in more than 70 countries. ITT has more than 400,000 employees. Although a 1972 antitrust consent agreement forced the company to divest Canteen Corporation, Avis, Levitt, and a few other companies, ITT still directly touches the lives of millions of persons.

Although large corporations may have other goals such as, for example, the increase in corporate power and prestige, along with corporate growth and stability, their paramount objectives remain the maximization of corporate profits and the general financial success of the corporation, whether this be through sales, market shares, or increased assets. Regardless of how strongly corporate managers prefer to pursue other objectives and how difficult it may be to find profit-maximizing strategies in a world of uncertainty, any failure to satisfy these criteria will mean that ultimately the firm will vanish from the economic scene. As in all large organizations, corporations achieve their goals within a complex hierarchical context of social relationships and expectations. In large corporations, the social structure consists, on the one hand, of those with a great deal of power: the board of directors, and top executives like the chairman of the board, the president, the chief executive officer (CEO), and the vice presidents; while on the other side are those with much less power: middle managers, supervisors, and workers.

As a legal entity, a corporate organization uses capital provided by individuals who are called shareholders or stockholders. Although technically these stockholders own the corporation, it is the top managers who largely control it, often influenced by investors such as banks or by a strong board of directors. In this sense, shareholders can be treated not as real owners but as legitimate claimants to some fixed share of the corporation's profits, and to nothing more. The major day-to-day de-cision-makers of a corporation are hired employees, that is, management, whose principal remuneration is their salaries and bonuses, and who seek advancement either in their own corporate hierarchy or by move-ment to another corporation.

THE ABUSE OF CORPORATE POWER

Increasingly, our large corporations have been abusing the awesome power that they have amassed. John Gardner, head of Common Cause, has termed today's atmosphere in the corporate world "piratical" in its excessive predatory practices. All power, he has said, overreaches if it is allowed to, and the corporate world is overreaching. Supreme Court Justice William O. Douglas, in a 1948 dissenting opinion, had this to say with reference to corporate power: "Power tends to develop into a gov-ernment in itself. Power that controls the economy should be in the hands of elected representatives of people instead of an industrial oli-garchy." Attorney General Robert F. Kennedy put it bluntly in a 1961 interview: "Too much power scares me, whether we find it in a trade union or in a corporation."

ABUSE OF THE DEMOCRATIC PROCESS

This abuse of power shows itself in many ways. Particularly disturbing have been the efforts of the corporations to conscript the political process for their own benefit through their large financial contributions, both legal and illegal.[4] Although corporate political influence became more pronounced under President Ronald Reagan, it has long exercised a heavy hand over the White House, the Congress, and the state govern-ments. Former top corporate executives often hold many of the most powerful cabinet and top agency positions in the executive branch of government. Politicians listen when large corporations speak. They have enormous advantages in influencing political decision-makers. They can maintain individual lobbying activities that smaller firms can conduct only in groups. They can enlist the political support of subsidiary cor-porations and suppliers who are dependent on them. The former Sen-ator Phillip Hart (D-Michigan) once said, "When a major corporation from a state wants to discuss something, you can be sure it will be heard. When that same company operates in 30 states, it will be heard 30 times." On one occasion, General Motors sent a letter to 1.3 million shareholders, 13,000 dealers, and 19,000 suppliers asking them to support its even-tually successful campaign to postpone congressional action on auto safety and emission standards. Corporate political power expands enormously when huge corporations merge with other large firms.

The average cost of running for the House of Representatives in 1988 was $259,043, and for the Senate, $2,882,071, according to *Common Cause*. The winning candidates in the House spent $358,992 on the average; winning Senate candidates averaged $3,945,806. Following the Watergate scandal, Congress passed laws that prohibited corporations from making "political bribes" through direct political contributions in federal elections. However, corporations, like other powerful interest groups, were quick to take full advantage of their new right to organize Political Action Committees (PACs) and make indirect contributions to members of Congress whom they wished to influence. While PACs were also sponsored by unions and other trade groups, the largest contributions often were made by large corporations. In 1988 corporations also evaded the law by making substantial contributions to national elections through state organizations. It is a common practice, moreover, for members of Congress to pocket "honoraria"; typically these run from $1,000 to $2,000, but sometimes the total received from various corporations may exceed $25,000 for speeches or articles for corporations or industry-wide groups, or simply in return for showing up with executives and lobbyists at a corporate breakfast, luncheon, or tour of corporate premises. Honoraria are illegal for all other government officials, but members of the House legally can earn up to about 30 percent of their salaries—and senators 40 percent—in honoraria.

In 1987, honoraria totaled $6.7 million to representatives, and $3.1 million to senators. Senator Robert Dole (R-Kansas) received the highest amount, $106,000, while the average senatorial honorarium totaled $31,000. The average in the House was $15,600, where Ways and Means Chairman Dan Rostenkowski (D-Illinois) led the pack with $245,000. The largest corporate donors of honoraria were Northrop, MacDonnell Douglas, United Technologies, General Electric, and Lockheed, all of which are giant defense industries. The Tobacco Institute was the fifth largest provider of honoraria to members of Congress. A 1988 *Wall Street Journal*/NBC News poll found that nearly two-thirds of those surveyed favored outlawing the lucrative and rapidly growing practice.

Corporate America regularly buys a large piece of both political conventions, particularly the Republican. Most of these contributors are interested in swaying government policy and gaining special access to federal officials. Atlantic Richfield, for example, was among the highest contributors ($100,000) to the 1988 Republican Convention. The Republican platform committee approved one of Richfield's primary corporate goals, the opening of 1.5 million acres of the Arctic National Wildlife Refuge to oil and gas exploration. Other heavy contributors were Chevron, RJR Nabisco, and Dresser Industries.

ABUSE OF THE WORKERS AND LOCAL COMMUNITY

Large corporations put communities and their workers in the United States and throughout the world in a continuous struggle to acquire new corporate plants or to hold on to those they have. For years, they have closed their plants in the United States with little or no advance warning, and they have seldom made an effort to assist the workers whom they lay off or the local community, which may long have contributed to the corporation's well-being.[5] In fact, in one case a worker learned of his plant's closing over his car radio as he was returning home from a bank where he had just signed a $50,000 mortgage on the purchase of a new home. As for the local community itself, a plant's closing means reduced tax collections, an impairment of community services due to reduced tax revenues, increased social welfare payments, and tax increases to compensate for corporate tax losses. Faced with a large lawsuit, in 1988 the Chrysler Corporation came up with a unique solution to ameliorate the effects of the closing of its large Kenosha, Wisconsin, plant. When Chrysler acquired American Motors, the state of Wisconsin waived certain pollution standards, and partly because of this waiver, Chrysler had assured the state that it would keep the plant open for at least five years. In addition to a settlement of $250,000 paid to the workers and to the community when the plant closed before then, there were also provisions of a contribution to Kenosha of six acres for a municipal golf course, supplemental employment benefits of $100 a week to the laid-off workers for as long as 24 weeks, and health and life insurance for as long as two years. In addition, Chrysler also set up a $20 million trust fund to help meet housing, educational, and welfare needs of the families affected by the plant closing.

Corporations also abuse their power when they arbitrarily close plants and relocate to Third World countries, such as Mexico, the Philippines, and countries in the Caribbean, where they can pay workers less, where working conditions are far below U.S. standards, and where unions are either nonexistent or impotent. When they make these moves, they generally fail to consider fully their responsibilities to their workers or how the relocation affects the American economy. Often they simply pick up and leave for a Third World country, leaving behind unemployed workers and a community economically devastated by a shrinking tax base.

Almost all Western European countries, as well as Japan and Canada, have laws that require prior notice of plant closings to workers and the community. Fortunately, in 1988, over the overwhelming opposition of large corporations and the Reagan administration, Congress finally passed plant closing legislation that would require 60 days advance notice of plant closings if more than 50 workers are to be laid off. President Reagan, who opposed this legislation, allowed it to become law without signing it.

ABUSE OF THE STOCKHOLDERS

Most large corporations abuse their power by largely disregarding the shareholder in the corporate accountability process. They generally regard their electorate as passive stockholders whom they woo only intermittently. There is little corporate democracy. Management personnel largely preempt decision-making, although there is input from the board of directors. Shareholders have little real say about the nomination of elected directors; nor do they have much to say about corporate policies, and decisions at annual meetings are usually a sham. Seldom do shareholders receive full disclosure of socially significant corporate operations, such as environmental considerations or law violations. Corporations give millions of dollars of their stockholders' money to arts, educational and philanthropic groups without consulting them. Moreover, the nature of the gift and the selection of the recipient generally reflect the personal tastes of the top corporate officers and the board rather than the majority of the stockholders.

Corporations pay excessively high financial compensation to their top corporate executives without stockholder approval and usually with little or no shareholder financial consideration. Financial remuneration of chief executives often has had little relation to corporate performance. For example, among 131 *Fortune* 500 corporations studied in 1988, there was absolutely no relation between change in performance and change in the pay of the Chief Executive Officers (CEOs).[6] In fact, there was hardly any difference in performance between the 10 corporations that paid their CEOs the least and the 10 who paid relatively the most. The total financial remuneration of chief executives of 40 of the 100 largest U.S. corporations in 1988 rose 43.8 percent over 1987, while the sales for these corporations rose only 11.7 percent and net income rose 16.3 percent.

In 1988, the average salaries of 68 chief executives of the 100 largest industrial corporations was $1.2 million, up 14 percent over 1987. Additional financial remuneration came primarily through bonuses and stock options. The latter give the top executives the right to buy a certain number of shares at a set price sometime in the future. In 1988, the top executives of 40 of the 100 largest corporations received stock options that were 1.5 to 1.6 times their annual salaries. Total financial compensation paid the chairmen of the boards of Firestone and ITT in 1987 exceeded $4 million; Chrysler's chairman and chief executive officer, Lee Iaccoca, received $20 million. The chief executive officer of Squibb received $14 million in financial remuneration, and the chief executive officers of General Electric and Unisys received $12.6 and $10 million, respectively. In 1988, the chairman and chief executive officer of Bristol-Myers received $14.1 million; of Ralston Purina, $12.9 million; and of Digital Equipment, $10 million.

The average American chief executive earns about 40 percent more than a chief executive in Japan, more than twice as much as a British chief executive, and over three times as much as an Australian chief executive. In 1979, the average compensation paid top U.S. corporate chairmen was 29 times greater than the income of the average manufacturing worker; by 1985, their salaries had risen to 40 times greater. Salaries of top Japanese executives rarely exceed eight times the wage of a blue-collar worker. In recent years, the rate of pay for corporate chief executives has been rising much faster than that of either the white- or the blue-collar workers, faster than inflation, and even faster than profits. In 1987, for example, chief executive officer salaries and bonuses increased 11.5 percent, while salaries of corporate white-collar workers rose 5.5 percent.

In addition to the high salaries and bonuses, corporations provide other compensation to their top executives, all without the consent of the stockholders. A "golden parachute" of possible additional millions awaits the executive should his or her position be terminated, as in the case of a takeover by another corporation or through a merger. When Sperry merged with Burroughs in 1987 to form Unisys, Sperry's chief executive officer received a golden parachute of $6.6 million. The CEO of Gulf Oil received stock options worth $6.7 million when Chevron purchased Gulf. When Signal and Allied corporations merged, the outgoing president received what might be termed a "platinum" parachute: He received salary and other financial benefits of the new president, which totaled over $1 million, whether he chose to work or loaf. In 1988, Squibb Corporation paid its chairman and chief executive officer $400,000 for "accumulated deferred vacation time" over several years, on top of the $1.5 million he received in salary and cash compensation. At the stockholders' expense, top corporate executives generally may have the privilege to use, free of charge, corporate limousines, jet aircraft, and yachts. They generally receive free medical check-ups, and they often may use corporate facilities for vacations.

Many claim that the financial compensation of top management of large corporations, such as the chief executive officer, is warranted because they have the crucial responsibility of steering the multi-billion-dollar corporations that employ thousands of workers. Others question, however, to what extent the duties of these top executives merit such enormous compensation. They feel that it is debatable whether top corporate officials are better qualified than are the managers of federal or large state government departments that also administer billions of dollars and manage even larger numbers of employees. For example, the salary of cabinet members is $99,500 and the director of the Environmental Protection Agency (EPA) receives $75,000, all with no bonuses or stock options. The Chief Justice of the U.S. Supreme Court, who is also responsible for the large federal court system, receives a very large government salary of $115,000. The governor of New York gets $100,000, while the governor of California's salary is $49,100. The city managers of New York City and Los Angeles get slightly over $100,000. The head of the giant University of California state academic system receives $165,000, and the salary of the president of the World Bank, who oversees a staff of 5,600 and an annual budget of $746 million, is $150,000. Even the pay of the president of the United States, $200,000, is miniscule in comparison to that of many top corporate executives. Still, some may argue that a top corporate executive reaches the top after a Darwinian weeding process of survival of the fittest and has thus demonstrated exceptional competence for the job. This has not always been the case, however, as some are merely survivors of corporate political maneuvering through their own careful cultivation of the right persons at the right time.

ABUSE OF THE CONSUMER

Unethical practices of numerous *Fortune* 500 corporations exploit millions of consumers as they add billions of dollars to their profits.[7] Price-fixing, which eliminates competition, is comparable to stealing from consumers. So much corporate advertising either misleads or deceives that many watchdog groups, both private and governmental, must constantly scrutinize corporate claims for their products. As an example, in 1989 the Campbell Soup Company agreed to abide by advertising guidelines in action brought by nine states to settle health claims made in its "Soup is Good Food" campaign. Among the various claims challenged was that Campbell misled consumers by highlighting the calcium content of its tomato and other soups when most of the calcium would actually come from the added milk. The Minnesota attorney general said that this case "should put all food companies on notice that they won't get away with false claims about their products."[8] Packaging that deceives and conceals the true size of consumer products also occurs on a grand scale. Deceptive pictorial and television advertising is common, as are questionable endorsements, "tests," "surveys," and "research of consumer products." Even dogs have a tough time. A federal judge in 1989 found two of the leading manufacturers of dog food, Ralston and Alpo, guilty of having engaged in "serious deceptive advertising practices."[9] Ralston came in for particularly harsh criticism and was fined $10.4 million for claiming that its Purina Puppy Chow would help puppies avoid the common painful canine hip dysplasia when they matured. Judge Sporkin found that Ralston's internal research was without scientific basis. Consumer warranties as well as guarantees are often likewise deceptive. For example, consumers must be prepared to deal with an auto industry that is saturated with unethical practices. Authorized auto dealers often utilize unethical sales practices, furnish fraudulent service operations, and maintain secret warranties. The unethical oil-pricing methods that rip off consumers result in staggering profits for the oil companies. The giant pharmaceutical industry plays a significant role in the promotion of a "drugged society"; they often sell ineffective drugs, mislead consumers in their advertising, and sell life-saving drugs at excessive prices. Even Congress in 1988 finally became involved in attempting to limit the amount of corporate exploitation of children by television commercials aimed directly at them. President Reagan vetoed the bill.

On occasion, corporate consumer fraud may go too far to escape severe punishment, as in the case of Beech-Nut Nutrition Corporation, a large subsidiary of the giant Nestle Corporation. For more than 50 years, parents have depended on this well-known corporation to provide natural, healthful baby foods. Between 1977 and 1983, however, Beech-Nut breached this trust in what *Consumer Reports* termed the "food scam of the decade" in its May 1989 issue. During this period, Beech-Nut was able to extract as much as $60 million from consumers with largely sugared water sold as apple juice and advertised as "100 percent fruit juice," when actually it contained little or no apple juice. One chemist termed this apple-flavored concoction "a fraudulent chemical cocktail." In 1987, Beech-Nut pleaded guilty to federal charges that it had intentionally sold adulterated and misbranded juice in 20 states, Puerto Rico, the Virgin Islands, and 5 foreign countries. The company paid a $2 million fine, the largest in the Food and Drug Administration's history. The Justice Department later prosecuted two Beech-Nut executives, one of whom was convicted on 359 counts and the other on 448 counts of having violated FDA laws, as well as conspiracy and mail fraud charges. They received prison sentences of a year and a day and fines of $100,000. A new trial was ordered, however, in 1989 on grounds of a jurisdictional issue.

ABUSE OF THE ENVIRONMENT

Before federal and state governments instituted concerted programs during the 1970s, most major corporations exhibited an utter disregard for the environment. Today, in spite of government controls, the corporate world still pollutes air, water, and soil on a wide scale. The result has been serious damage to human beings, wildlife, and the land and water. Even after controls were instituted, at times corporate abuse of the environment has become so great that the public has become outraged. Perhaps the most serious case was the catastrophic 1989 Exxon Valdez oil spill that wrought havoc over 800 miles of pristine Alaskan shoreline and killed tens of thousands of animals and birds.

Today, the proper disposal of hazardous wastes ranks high among the concerns of the American public. Of increasing concern are the violations of regulations designed to control the disposal of serious hazardous waste products by our major corporations. Chemical and oil corporations produce the bulk of the dangerous wastes, but there are others as well. In the past, few large corporations were overly concerned about the disposal of their waste products, with many of them simply getting rid of the wastes by the least expensive means and with little or no concern for the possible serious effects on people or on the present and future environment. Even today, many continue this same pattern of disposal.

ABUSE OF THE THIRD WORLD

The boundaries of nation-states have become meaningless in the dynamics of multinational corporations. Multinationals can affect a wide range of another country's sensitive areas, including employment, worker safety, income distribution, environment, and taxation. This is particularly true in the developing countries, where corporate giants often use their considerable power to circumvent even national laws. Their extensive economic power, with its social and political correlates, often enables them to defy the host country's tax and other laws. In the less developed countries of Latin America, Asia, and Africa, moreover, they may market products that the U.S. government has restricted or banned in the United States. Pharmaceutical corporations, for example, promote and freely distribute drugs that are rigidly restricted or even banned. Drug companies that operate in Third World countries often fail to advise either medical doctors or patients about important restrictions on their products' use and possibly dangerous side effects. Major chemical corporations export banned pesticides to developing countries where they can cause injuries and death. Operations of giant corporate agribusinesses, in their Third World plantations and cattle ranches, often result in the disruption of local food-production and employment patterns. Corporate operations in beef, rubber, and palm oil, as well as lumber, have greatly contributed to the rapid destruction of the tropical rain forests with their centuries-old trees.

Moreover, in their aggressive drive to maximize profits, transnationals often exhibit a total disregard for the political well-being of a country. More than 450 large U.S. corporations, mostly *Fortune* 500s, have engaged in extensive bribery of foreign government officials, including prime ministers and other top officials. Corporate bribery abroad, as in Iran under Shah Reza Pahlavi during the 1970s, has provided ample ammunition for political extremists in many countries to direct verbal blasts at the United States and harm its citizens. Corporations have also done extensive business with nefarious right-wing dictators. Until public and political pressures against their operations rose to a crescendo in the United States, American corporations operated without a twinge of conscience in South Africa.

CORPORATE CRIME

An authority on illegal corporate behavior asks, "Why is it that despite the high numbers of victims, when people think of crime, they think of burglary before they think of monopoly (if they think of monopoly at all), of assault before they think of harmful pharmaceuticals, of street crime before they think of corporate crime?"[10]

Such corporate law violations include illegal restraint of trade, such as illegal price-fixing, fraud in government contracts, submitting fraudulent data to government agencies, unfair labor practices, false advertising, bribery, illegal kickbacks, unsafe working conditions, violations of laws protecting consumers, violations of laws protecting the environment, and income tax evasion. Although the public increasingly fears the possibility of murder or assault, it seldom realizes that the activities of large corporations kill or injure far more persons than do individuals. The tobacco industry's cigarettes alone result annually in nearly 400,000 consumer deaths and hundreds of thousands of health disorders, many of them severe. The production and distribution of unsafe products, as in the case of unsafe autos and prescription drugs, kill and injure innumerable consumers; unsafe working conditions kill and injure many workers; the illegal exposure to chemicals results in death and injury to thousands of plant workers; and corporate pollution of the air and water, as well as the illegal disposal of corporations' waste products, injures thousands of citizens each year. Congressional investigators have found that in some cases top executives have knowingly concealed the fact that certain unsafe products and hazardous environments have brought injury, sickness, and even death to thousands of people.

Due to the relative infrequency of criminal prosecutions for corporate violations, the public has developed the perception that much of corporate violations are of a "non-criminal" type, and thus not serious in nature. This widespread perception tends to shield violators from the "criminal" label that invariably stigmatizes all persons who are prosecuted under the criminal law. Corporate power has seen to it that in the event of a law violation, legislatures have provided besides or in lieu of the criminal law a wide range of administrative and civil penalties. These include warnings, injunctions, consent orders, and non-criminal monetary payments. Even where the criminal penalty is available, it is infrequently invoked because of the greater amount of investigative and prosecutorial effort and time its use entails. Consequently, the seriousness of a corporate violation is not necessarily related to the type of penalty invoked. For example, a large-scale study of sanctions imposed for corporate law violations found that administrative penalties were employed in two-thirds of serious corporate law violations, and that slightly more than two-fifths of the sanctions imposed for serious or moderately serious violations consisted simply of a warning to the corporation not to commit the offense again.[11] It is for these reasons that the only realistic definition of corporate crime must include any corporate violation punished under either administrative, civil, or criminal law. This position has been adopted by many as the only way to bring the law violations of corporations into the same perspective as those of ordinary criminal offenders.[12]

Many government investigations, both federal and state, have revealed extensive law violations in such industries as oil, autos, and pharmaceuticals. Even though only limited enforcement staffs have been available to uncover corporate violations, over one two-year period, the federal government charged nearly two-thirds of the *Fortune* 500 corporations with law violations; half were charged with a serious violation.[13] One out of ten of the *Fortune* 500 companies received a court sanction for a major law violation between 1970 and 1979.[14] According to a 1982 *U.S. News and World Report* study, more than one out of five of the *Fortune* 500 companies had been convicted of at least one major crime or had paid civil penalties for serious illegal behavior between 1970 and 1980.[15] Estimates of the cost of crimes range as high as $200 billion a year as compared to the estimated annual losses from street crimes of $3 to $4 billion. The cost of a single incident of corporate crime may run into the millions or even billions of dollars, as in Exxon's $2 billion illegal gasoline overcharges. Fraud and other law violations in the defense industry have cost taxpayers billions of dollars. By comparison, the loss incurred in an average burglary in 1987 was $1,014 an average robbery $631, and an average theft $404.

A close inspection of major corporations often turns up dirty linen that contradicts their claims of integrity. For example, General Electric has long maintained that it is an exemplary corporation interested in the public good and devoted to the excellence of its products. Although its advertising motto is "GE Brings Good Things to Life," General Electric actually has a long history of unethical and illegal practices, according to an in-depth study done by John Woodmansee.[16] In 1988, the *Multinational Monitor* named General Electric one of the ten worst corporations because of its practices. During the past 70 years, the government has charged General Electric with price-fixing and other monopolistic practices in producing light bulbs, turbines, generators, transformers, motors, relays, radio tubes, and heavy metals. The Department of Justice has brought at least 67 suits against General Electric, and it has been convicted several times of price-fixing, bribery, and procurement fraud. In 1959, the courts convicted the company and its executives of massive price-fixing in heavy electrical equipment. In this price-fixing scandal, which also involved Westinghouse, Allis Chalmers, and ITE, the companies divided the market with "sealed bids" whose contents they had agreed upon in advance. The judge fined General Electric $437,000 and sentenced two of its top executives to 30 days in jail. As far back as 1962, the Department of Justice remarked on "General Electric's proclivity for frequent and persistent involvement in antitrust violations." The company also made large illegal contributions to the Nixon 1972 campaign and engaged in extensive bribery of foreign officials. In 1974, the courts charged the company with widespread illegal discrimination against women and minorities in its hiring policies, and General Electric agreed to a $32 million settlement. In 1981 the government convicted General Electric and two former high executives in connection with a $1.25-million bribe paid to a Puerto Rican official to obtain a $93-million power plant contract. In 1985, General Electric became the first contractor to be indicted and found guilty of charges of defrauding the government for overcharging on defense contracts. The corporation had tried to minimize cost overruns on defense contracts by illegally transferring charges from one contract to another. It had also falsified time cards that defrauded the government on defense contracts. Commenting on the corporation's abuse of power, the federal judge who imposed a fine of $1.04 million on the corporation said, "All of America has depended on General Electric, just like a newborn baby is dependent on its mother," to perform defense work in a "trustworthy" manner, which it had utterly failed to do. In 1988, General Electric paid $3.5 million to settle four lawsuits brought by the federal government and four whistle-blowers under the False Claims Act for fraud in military contract work. Moreover, General Electric is one of the nation's prime environmental polluters. It has been involved in many cases of toxic waste dumping, some of a serious nature. Of the 195 toxic waste sites targeted for Superfund money by the EPA, General Electric was found to be responsible for 22, the largest number of any major corporation.

More than two decades ago, the President's Commission on Law Enforcement and Administration of Justice reported that corporate crimes seriously affect the moral climate of American society. A *Fortune* editor once wrote, "How much crime in the streets is connected with the widespread judgment that the business economy itself is a gigantic rip-off?" Derelictions by corporations and by their top executives, whom the public generally regard as community leaders, set examples that erode the moral basis of the law. When corporations disregard the rules of the game by which the free enterprise system operates, particularly the basic tenets of free and open competition, they endanger the system itself. Among corporations the economic drive for profit, power, and productivity is not in itself criminal; it is likely to become so only when these objectives dominate all other considerations. Price-fixing offenses victimize the consumer as well as the law-abiding corporations. Income tax violations deprive the government and all those who depend on it for needed revenue. The many scandalous law violations of the defense industry and their sordid bribery of Department of Defense officials has been no demonstration of American patriotism. As shocking cases such as these have come to light, the public has increasingly looked on these corporate crimes as serious offenses. A 1978 national survey that ranked 204 offenses for seriousness revealed, for example, that the public considers many corporate offenses equal to, or even more serious than, many ordinary crimes such as burglary and robbery.[17] A more recent study, in 1982, has shown that during the previous decade, the public generally perceived corporate offenses as more serious today than in the past.[18] Particularly growing in strength were public reactions toward corporate offenses that have resulted in death or injury, as, for example, from defective autos, and toward corporate price-fixing.

NECESSITY FOR GOVERNMENT INTERVENTION

A number of *Fortune* 500 corporations have long been able to compete successfully while at the same time demonstrating a high degree of social responsibility and compliance with the law. They belie any stereotype that all large corporations are lawbreakers or that they exhibit little concern for ethical behavior and social responsibility. Among them are Procter and Gamble; Hershey Foods; Hart, Schaffner and Marx; 3M; Digital Equipment; Bendix; Kellogg; Pitney Bowes; Hewlett-Packard; Johnson and Johnson; Reynolds Metals; and Maytag Corporation. One corporation particularly well known for its ethical practices is the 145-year-old Procter and Gamble Corporation, which has a long-standing reputation of working closely with consumers to clarify its product advertising and to improve the quality and safety of its products. This corporation, along with many others, has amply demonstrated that large corporations can be socially responsible while continuing to grow and show substantial profits each year. Procter and Gamble's profits surged 18 percent to $1.21 billion in 1989. The Chairman of Johnson and Johnson, James E. Burke, recently said: "In the process of making money, we damn well better understand we have a responsibility to society."[19] The corporation demonstrated this sense of social responsibility in its handling of the 1982 Tylenol tampering incident, in which several persons were killed by cyanide poisoning introduced into bottles of its product Tylenol. The Food and Drug Administration tried to persuade the chairman of the board of the corporation not to recall because it believed that such a move would frighten the public.[20] Because the corporation felt that the public should be protected immediately, however, it recalled 31 million bottles of the product. They also alerted physicians and set up toll-free numbers for consumer inquiries. As a voluntary measure, the corporation installed tamper-proof packaging before government regulations were put into effect. Another demonstration of social responsibility was the case of Reynolds Aluminum Corporation, which began a recycling program shortly after World War II when no other aluminum company considered recycling to be economically feasible. Reynolds led the movement, which later spread nationwide.

Outside pressures have forced other corporations to assume a degree of social responsibility. Most large corporations would not have protected the public, the consumer, the worker, or the environment of their own volition. Through collective bargaining and with the support of legislative changes, unions have brought pressure to bear on corporations to improve plant working conditions and safety standards, to provide better health insurance coverage, and to eliminate discrimination in the hiring and firing of workers. Environmental and consumer groups have exerted pressure on the government to control corporate excesses. Improvements in auto safety, for example, have come about largely due to influences from outside the auto industry. Much product safety legislation has resulted from the pressures and the power of strong consumer groups, while corporate manufacturers have generally resisted changes. Various government agencies, at both the state and federal levels, have put pressure on corporations to produce safe products, present honest advertising, curb unfair competitive practices, assure the safety of workers, and control pollution.

Corporate greed and the unethical behavior of some corporations, along with their inability to regulate themselves effectively, have necessitated government regulation. This federal intervention has become

essential to protect the public. To discourage excessive industrial concentration leading to monopolistic control and excessive prices, Congress
enacted the Sherman Antitrust Act in 1890. As early as 1906 Congress
enacted laws to protect consumers from impure and unsafe foods, drugs,
and cosmetics. For example, it first mandated the labeling of the nutritional content of certain packaged foods in 1972. About half of all packaged foods display nutritional information. A product must provide this
information if its label makes a nutritional claim. Finding this inadequate
and voluntary labeling unsatisfactory for other foods, the FDA in 1989
moved to make mandatory nutritional and ingredient labeling on all
packaged foods. It also proposed setting standards for such terms as
"light" and "natural" and clarifying health claims. Congress established
the Federal Trade Commission in 1914 to help prevent unfair competition such as price-fixing and to deal with unfair and deceptive trade
practices such as false and misleading advertising. It can even be argued
that one of the principles of such government regulations is to protect
the less sophisticated consumer from victimization. Congress also established further regulatory measures to regulate the financial aspects of
corporate abuse.

During the 1960s and 1970s, as citizens became more fully aware that
corporations' conduct was endangering people's civil rights, their safety,
and even their physical environment, they began to demand even greater
corporate regulation. As a result, the federal government created several
new types of agencies. The purpose of the Equal Opportunity Commission, created in 1965, was to enforce previously enacted laws to prevent discrimination on the basis of race, sex, religion, or national origin.
With the creation of the National Highway Traffic Safety Administration
in 1966, it became possible for the government to intervene in auto
safety problems that the industry had ignored but that had resulted in
thousands of needless deaths and hundreds of thousands of injuries.
The Occupational Safety and Health Administration came into being in
1970 to regulate the safety of the workplace and to protect the work
force from harmful chemicals and other substances. The government
also created the Environmental Protection Agency in 1970 to protect
the national environment including controlling air and water pollutants.
In 1972, Congress passed further legislation designed to prohibit corporations from giving direct contributions to political candidates in federal elections, contributions that often constituted bribes made to
influence favorable votes. After studies revealed massive injuries to consumers from the use of unsafe corporate goods, the government created
the Consumer Product Safety Commission in 1972 to ban the sale of
unsafe and defective products. The purpose of the Foreign Corrupt
Practices Act, passed in 1977, was to prevent wide-scale corporate bribery
of foreign officials by American corporations.

In addition, most states have created agencies of their own to regulate such harmful corporate behavior as consumer fraud and price conspiracies. On several occasions, states have even banded together to take joint action against a powerful corporation. In 1987, for example, 41 states, acting jointly, forced a settlement from Chrysler Corporation to pay more than $16 million to buyers of cars whose odometers had been tampered with before sale.

Congress wisely gave newly created federal administrative agencies their own rule-making powers to help them avoid the onerous task of passing innumerable specific laws, many of which are so politically controversial that enacting them into law would have been overly time-consuming, if not impossible. In the event of a violation, several major types of actions against a corporation are available: warnings, product recalls, consent agreements and decrees, injunctions, monetary penalties, and criminal penalties against corporate officers. The wide options of administrative and civil actions, in addition to criminal proceedings, have made it possible for government agencies and the courts to show excessive lenience in cases of corporation violation, which they have in many cases.

In 1909, the Supreme Court held that corporations are "persons" within the meaning of the Fourteenth Amendment. Christopher Stone has explained that by means of this device, laws that either explicitly or implicitly speak in terms of "no person shall" were smoothly transferred to corporations.[21] The similarity in treatment between acts of individuals and those of an entity like a corporation has arisen in part because many acts of corporations are acts that could be committed by individuals, such as engaging in tax fraud, producing injurious goods, polluting the environment, or bribery. However, the evidence that the courts must evaluate is often far more complex and technical in the case of a corporation than in an individual's case.

Government intervention has undoubtedly been significant in preventing a great deal of corporate abuse. In addition, it has clarified the rules of proper corporate conduct. At the same time, however, the presence of these rules has not been accompanied by widespread acceptance and compliance. The *New York Times* reported on June 9, 1985, for example, that "not since the mid-1970s when a series of foreign bribes and illegal political contributions shocked the body politic have there been so many deep gashes in corporate America's armor." In order to correct corporate abuses, the corporate world does not need self-regulation and deregulation so much as more government regulation and stricter enforcement of those regulations already in existence. The growth of unmitigated economic and political power has corrupted many large corporations. In particular, the abuse of power by the giant auto, oil, pharmaceutical, and defense industries, all of which lead in law infractions, clearly demonstrates this need.

Chapter 2

DETROIT ROULETTE

Every 10 minutes, 24 hours a day, 365 days a year, an American is killed in an auto crash; every 10 seconds another U.S. citizen is injured. Over the years, the auto industry has strenuously resisted every effort of the government to reduce this terrible human toll of 60,000 lives each year. Powerful automakers have resisted regulations requiring safety glass, collapsible steering columns, bumper crashworthiness, dual brakes, seat belts, and air bags. Even with government regulation, the mayhem continues. Each year, it is necessary to recall millions of U.S. autos for safety-related defects. The automakers have thwarted safety recalls, violated labor and fair-trade laws as well as environmental regulations, illegally switched engines, disconnected odometers, and failed emission tests.

The auto business, from the manufacturers down to the dealers, is saturated with rip-offs, rackets, and law violations. One writer has referred to the business environment in the auto industry as a "criminogenic market structure," with sales methods that virtually force those in marketing to commit fraud and other unethical practices.[1] Auto manufacturers often set conditions that contribute to dealers' violations of ethical and legal standards. Imposed on the dealers is a pricing system that necessitates high volume and generally low unit profit. Such a policy results in high profits for the manufacturers and a profit squeeze on the dealers, who must meet certain sales quotas. Manufacturers often award prizes to dealers who underspend their auto-warranty repair budgets, thus emphasizing sales and not service. To keep ahead of the game, dealers may engage in fraudulent services such as charging for labor not actually done or repairs not made. John Z. DeLorean, formerly a top executive with General Motors for many years, claims that "a car dealer is judged by how many cars he pushes out of the showroom doors and not how he services them in the back."[2]

When an auto company encounters a major defect that occurs after the written warranty expires, it frequently establishes an adjustment policy with the dealer to pay for the repairs. In cases where the manufacturer never notified the consumer, the policy is called a secret warranty. The Washington, D.C.-based Center for Auto Safety estimated that at any one time there are more than 300 secret warranties that cover virtually every car on the road. Purchasers do not know about the warranty, which means that some owners get free repairs, others get only free parts, and others get nothing at all depending on how loudly the customer complains or whom he or she knows. In 1985, for example, the Center for Auto Safety reported that General Motors had a secret warranty covering repairs up to 75,000 miles for defective auto transmissions in 2.4 million 1980–1982 X-, A-, and J-cars. Many owners reported that these transmissions lost power, leaked transmission fluid, and caused the front wheels to lock up with mileages as low as 15,000 miles. In one documented case, a Pennsylvania woman had five rebuilt transmissions installed in her 1981 Buick Skylark in the first 50,000 miles free of charge, while the Dallas, Texas, Buick Division told a man that the reimbursement request for his 1980 Skylark's transmission failure at 41,000 miles had to be denied. Obviously, such practices keep down the enormous cost of a total warranty or general recall of the autos.

Unethical practices really begin when dealers first meet the public in their display rooms. Dealers are the authorized distributors for the auto corporations, and the dealership can be terminated for practices not approved by the manufacturers. In few sales areas must purchasers be more on their guard. The unethical sales practices in the used-car market are so extensive that in 1985 the Federal Trade Commission issued nationwide rules on used-car warranties and specifications designed to protect consumers from deceptions totaling hundreds of millions of dollars.

All new cars must have factory-priced stickers attached to the vehicle. The sticker price represents little more than a standard the manufacturer has established for a "free market" negotiation. The first figure on the sticker is usually the manufacturer's suggested base price. It includes the car's standard equipment and the dealer's charge for cleaning the car before its sale, which is pure profit. Ordinarily, the dealer does not reveal what he paid the manufacturer for the car, making it impossible for the consumer to calculate the dealer's profit margin. Purchasers who pay this list price should have their heads examined. Next come long lists of options, also subject to negotiation; options on one car may be standard equipment on another. The next to last price on the sticker is the destination charge, also called freight and handling; no customer should expect a break for living near a manufacturing plant. If there is a trade-in, the hassle to get a square deal has only begun. Those later purchasing the used car can expect to play games to achieve fair representation and pricing. Dealers may sell repossessed used cars for more than they allowed the customers on them, plus sales costs, without returning the excess to the owner, a practice the Federal Trade Commission has ruled to be unfair and deceptive, as well as "immoral, unethical and unscrupulous."

Sometimes unfair dealer practices can go too far. After receiving over 1,000 complaints, the attorney general of New Mexico in 1988 secured a restraining order against Frontier Ford, a large Albuquerque dealership, after charging the company with using unfair and high-pressure tactics in violation of New Mexico's Unfair Practices Law. The attorney general claimed that Frontier Ford had intimidated customers into signing sales contracts, harassed customers with several sales agents until the customers were too tired to resist signing contracts, sold used cars as new and at new-car prices, convinced customers to sign contracts containing false information, forged signatures of customers and co-signers on loan documents, misrepresented car options and equipment so customers would buy them and banks would make loans, and charged far in excess of advertised prices, sometimes as much as $2,000 above manufacturers' suggested retail prices. The case was settled in 1989 for a total of $1.2 million, with half of the amount to make restitution to many of the complainants and half going to the New Mexico state fund.

A study of the *Fortune* 500 firms covering the years 1975–1976 found the motor vehicle manufacturing industry to be responsible for one out of six cases that the federal government charged with law violations, and one out of five of the more serious violations.[3] The industry had nearly four times its share of all law violations, and it accounted for one out of six penalties imposed on the *Fortune* 500 firms and one in five of the most serious cases. Convictions included the manufacture of unsafe or polluting vehicles, violations of labor and fair-trade protection laws, numerous violations of environmental safety laws, and deliberate fraud as, for example, in record keeping and the submission of false pollution test records to the government. Only the oil industry had more violations of government regulations.

Examples of serious law violations are numerous. In 1985, the government fined the Chrysler Corporation $1.5 million, one of the largest fines ever imposed under the Environmental Protection Agency Clear Water Act, for extensive water pollution near three of its plants. In the "engine switch" case of 1977, General Motors dealers sold at least 128,000 higher-priced Oldsmobiles in which they had fraudulently installed much cheaper Chevrolet engines. As a result of this fraud, the state of Illinois filed a consumer fraud suit against General Motors on behalf of

39 other states. The suit charged that General Motors advertised "the superiority of its brand name and trademarked Oldsmobile automobile . . . and the performance qualities of its Rocket V–8 engines. Consumers purchased the 1977 automobiles believing them to contain Oldsmobile-produced engines." After the serious damage had already been done in this case, General Motors agreed to a Federal Trade Commission order that each General Motors division henceforth disclose which specific division of the company had made the auto's engine.

One of the most publicized cases of auto industry fraud was the 1970 Ford Motor violation of emission testing requirements of the Clean Air Act. The government charged Ford with making false statements to the government about emissions in order to secure the certification of its 1973 engines. Many of the tests were found to be invalid because of engine tampering during the test. Moreover, Ford routinely performed a large number of misleading tests and inspections. The General Accounting Office found that Ford had fixed the test cars 442 times without informing the EPA. A former Ford executive claimed that the violations had been carried out due to pressures put on middle managers to get the engines certified. Had the engines not met the test standard, "It would have been impossible for Ford to meet its ambitious production and earnings goals that year."[4] Because of the violations, Ford agreed to pay one of the largest monetary settlements ever extracted from a corporation, a total of $7 million, plus a criminal fine and other civil damages. The court also ordered Ford to keep precise written records of emission testing procedures for 10 years.

Almost every year one can expect the disclosure of some new fraudulent practice in the auto industry. A new disclosure involved Chrysler in 1987: the first odometer tampering case brought against a major U.S. automaker. The government charged Chrysler and two of its executives with a conspiracy to sell as new more than 60,000 trucks and cars built during 1985 and 1986 that company executives had used as test vehicles with disconnected odometers. In addition, at least 40 vehicles had been involved in accidents; some of the damaged cars had allegedly been repaired and then shipped as new models. The Department of Justice said that these practices dated back more than 38 years and may have involved millions of cars. The government accused Chrysler of having conspired to commit mail fraud, wire fraud, and odometer fraud, and Chrysler faced a maximum fine of $100 million. Chrysler first tried to defend these acts by claiming that these policies were similar to those of their competitors, a claim denied by the other major automakers. Concerning selling cars that had been in accidents, Chrysler stated that fewer than 40 cars in 10 years had been in accidents and that they had been completely repaired. This claim was contrary to government findings that shortly after a 1984 sale of one of the test cars involved in an accident, the rear bumper had dropped off. Finally, in July 1987 Lee Iacocca, chairman and chief executive officer of Chrysler, stated publicly that "We were dumb. . . . [But] the only law we broke was the law of common sense."[5] Chrysler extended warranties on the affected vehicles and agreed to replace some cars that were damaged during testing and sold as new. Later, under pressure from many owners, Chrysler agreed to pay $500 to any owner whose car could be certified by Chrysler's records as having had the odometer disconnected. The company estimated this would involve at least 32,000 car owners and payments of $16.4 million. Chrysler was indicted in federal court in St. Louis for selling more than 60,000 cars and trucks, some of which were driven as many as 400 miles with the odometer disconnected. In December 1987, Chrysler agreed to settle the criminal charge by pleading "no contest."

DISREGARD FOR SAFETY

Richard Grimshaw was riding with Rita Gray in her Pinto in 1972 when it stalled on Interstate 15 near San Bernardino, California. They were hit by a vehicle traveling about 35 miles per hour. Within moments, their car was engulfed in flames. Rita Gray died two days later; Grimshaw survived, although he had burns over 90 percent of his body and lost his nose, left ear, and much of his left hand. In all, over 500 similar Pinto burn deaths and thousands of injuries occurred. Tests run by the National Highway Safety Traffic Administration in 1978 revealed serious defects in the Pinto's fuel tank, which was located only six inches in front of the rear bumper, and the structural parts surrounding the tank. In the event of a rear-end crash, the fuel tank could easily be punctured and the fuel tank filter pipe could be pulled away. As a result of these defects, many serious burn accidents had occurred. However, eight months passed and much arm twisting by government agencies was needed before Ford ordered a massive recall of 1971 to 1976 subcompact Pintos. Ford took this recall action not so much as a result of the injuries and deaths, but because it wished to avoid additional damaging publicity. It later developed that an original $11 expenditure per car, including lining the gas tank with a rubber bladder, would have largely prevented the problem. An early internal cost-benefit memorandum indicated that Ford considered this small additional cost per car too high to implement. Civil suits against Ford totaled more than $1 billion; one judgment alone was for $3 million.

In a landmark case in 1980, Ford Motor Company went on trial in an Indiana community for reckless homicide stemming from the deaths of three women in a Pinto crash.[6] A grand jury unanimously returned indictments against the company on three counts of reckless homicide.

The prosecution stated that the Indiana statute defined reckless homicide as the act of a "person who recklessly kills another human being," and that the criminal code defines a "person" as a "human being, corporation, partnership, etc." Because a corporation cannot be put in jail, a maximum fine of only $10,000 for each count was the only penalty possible for reckless homicide. However, for Ford, the fourth largest corporation in the world, the stakes were much higher. Ford feared that media coverage would tarnish its image and thus affect investors and the public trust, and that there would be long-term effects on sales, including those of other Ford models. Finally, Ford also feared even stronger federal auto safety rules.

After a lengthy trial and four days of deliberation, the state of Indiana lost the case, not because the Pinto was not a "reckless auto," but, according to one juror, primarily because the state had not proved that Ford had failed to make some effort to recall the Pinto prior to the accident. The Pinto case showed, however, that corporations can be prosecuted for homicide, and that they can be prosecuted criminally for failure to warn those who use their products of safety hazards known to the corporation.

Partly as a consequence of automakers' disregard for safety, between 44,000 and 60,000 persons have been killed annually in highway crashes in the last 25 years, more than the total American casualties of the entire Vietnam War. Auto crashes are the major cause of death for Americans under the age of 34; they are the largest single cause of paraplegia and a primary cause of head injuries. Motor vehicle crashes cost the nation more than $57 billion each year. It is impossible to estimate the cost of the personal pain, physical disability, and emotional trauma for the victims and their families.

The auto industry has never accepted responsibility for protecting motorists. During the 1950s, Alfred P. Sloan, the famous General Motors tycoon, rejected the use of safety glass in windshields. Sloan claimed that the improvement would not stimulate car sales but would actually reduce sales by increasing costs to the consumer. He put it bluntly: "Accidents or no accidents, my concern in this problem is a matter of profit and loss."[7] As a result of this attitude, auto safety continues to be a serious problem. An early exception to this general view of auto safety was a new auto manufacturer of the 1940s, Preston Martin Tucker. The Tucker Torpedo was safety-minded, using seat belts, a pop-out windshield with shatterproof glass, a padded dashboard, and other safety innovations now commonplace. The greed and envy of Detroit's large automakers eventually destroyed Tucker and his dream safety car.

An examination by an authority on auto design, Joel W. Eastman, showed that between 1900 and 1960, the industry as a whole largely ignored safety.[8] When accidents did occur, manufacturers blamed them on the driver or on road conditions. According to Eastman, auto manufacturers stretched this line of reasoning to argue that since their products were not responsible for accidents, they were under no specific obligation to design automobiles to this possibility, but merely to make them safe under normal operating conditions. Even today, the industry often takes a similar position; in particular, it would like the public to believe that driver irresponsibility is the primary cause of accidents rather than any faults of the auto manufacturer. However, it is far easier to "package" drivers more safely to begin with than to change their driving habits or personality. Moreover, auto manufacturers believed that engineering improvements were of no particular value in selling autos. In fact, the industry thought that even raising the subject of safety in their advertisements would prove detrimental to sales. Automakers have long claimed that "auto safety doesn't sell." They have believed that new-car buyers are not nearly as interested in a car's crashworthiness as in its styling, comfort, and overall running reliability. For example, in the 1970s a witness testified before a Senate committee on auto safety that "The automobile purchaser is paying twice for the privilege of owning a car whose front and rear ends are designed to look like French pastries in the ads and showrooms and to act like antique porcelain or aluminum foil in even minor collisions." Another authority on autos, David Halberstam, has concluded that Japanese cars have sold well because of American ineptitude and Japanese perseverance. "Detroit's attitude," he said, "seemed to be that if the customer was truly a good American, he would stop complaining and do the right thing, which was to buy a new car."[9] Meanwhile, the Japanese were poring over consumer auto-safety publications like *Consumer Reports* which American car manufacturers dismissed as "the product of do-gooders." Japanese cars became known for their safety features. Only recently have some manufacturers tried to sell safety the way they have sleek styling or fancy wheels.

Throughout its history, the auto industry has emphasized yearly style changes. Ford's Model T was a famous exception, as it was successfully marketed for years with few changes. However, the trend literally leaped forth as manufacturing became concentrated in a few large plants. Alfred P. Sloan, Jr., of General Motors, led the industry in introducing annual model changes, hoping to accelerate the replacement cycle, increase the corporation's market share, and guarantee a large profit on each car. Glossy advertisements encouraged the public to believe that the purchase of a new car every two or three years was necessary for keeping in style. This concentration on annual model and style changes led to serious safety deficiencies that included impaired steering controls and inferior tires and wheels. Visibility was also affected as windshields and back and side windows were more stylishly slanted, curved, or angled. An automobile design authority has concluded that while the strategy produced enormous profits, "the new models on which the money was made were less economical, less efficient, and in many ways less safe than the vehicles they replaced."[10]

When annual model changes failed to produce the desired sales growth, the industry beefed up auto speed and power. The public then began to believe that autos were meant to be driven at high speeds, in an individualistic, competitive manner. The increase in horsepower necessitated a heavier engine, which often created an imbalance in the safety relationship of power, weight, and braking capacity. Autos were now capable of speeds that greatly exceeded the legal limits, resulting in injuries and deaths. Detroit ignored safety in its desire to sell "powerful" cars.

The government declined to regulate the industry until 1966, when annual highway deaths first topped 50,000. It is generally agreed that government intervention has saved at least 10,000 lives annually and prevented thousands of injuries. The National Highway Traffic Safety Act made it possible, for the first time, to require that new cars be equipped with seat belts, collapsible steering columns, penetration-resistant windshields, padded instrument panels, dual brakes, and other safety equipment.

With the advent of the Reagan administration, the automakers saw a chance to get off the hook and to press for more deregulation in safety and pollution, and thus to increase their profits. As the administration was getting underway, an August 14, 1981 *Wall Street Journal* article gave a preview of what the auto industry was after: "Most of all, the automakers want to substantively roll back certain car and truck pollution rules, completely revamp emissions enforcement, junk a requirement for automobile crash protection devices for passengers, and dilute existing standards for bumpers." The auto industry was really saying: "The public be damned; we need more profits."

The Reagan administration's drive to roll back auto safety regulations went into high gear for two years. Rules to require automatic restraints such as air bags in future cars were done away with, the issue of new regulations was largely taboo, and the enforcement of auto defect and safety rules declined sharply. The administration even rescinded tire treadlife grading; a federal appeals court called it "flouting" the law and ordered it reinstated. The auto industry pressured the government to cut in half requirements on auto bumpers, that is, to reduce the speed of crash that does not do damage to the vehicle from 5 to 2.5 miles per hour. This surrender, according to Ralph Nader, cost motorists $400 million per year in added insurance premiums and repair costs.

Beginning in late 1983, the auto industry and its Reagan supporters ran up against an aroused public, and they began a slow retreat. The courts, Congress, and various consumer groups quickly intervened to bolster auto safety regulations. Government officials who were still somewhat unenthusiastic about auto safety regulations were replaced by more fervent regulators. In fact, by 1985, a Ford spokesperson commented: "We're working overtime responding to a real sprint in the number of inquiries from the agency." However, the situation never returned to the active days of Joan Claybrook, the Carter administration's firebrand auto-safety regulator, who dealt with the auto industry by issuing numerous safety regulations and enforcing them.

The automakers' resistance to the introduction of air bags is a classic example of their callous disregard for the safety of their customers, the American driving public. Air bag components and their operation are simple. In a frontal or front-angle crash, with an impact equivalent of hitting a wall at 12 miles per hour or more (the approximate speed at which almost all injuries occur), crash sensors trigger the inflation of a nitrogen bag. Nitrogen gas fills the fabric pillow to cushion the impact on the front seat occupants. Peak inflation of an air bag occurs at one-twenty-fifth of a second, faster than the eye can blink. Air bags offer better protection than a seat belt because the air bag better diffuses the impact at higher speeds. They are more essential for safety in smaller cars than in larger vehicles, they work well in multiple crashes, and they also protect children in the front seat. Air bags do not inflate inadvertently; they inflate only in a crash. The rider is always protected, as the bags work automatically. They are not like the usual seat belt, which riders frequently refuse to use.

If one puts a money value on one's life or health, air bags are not expensive. A full front-seat air bag, which some call a cushion system, cost about $700 in 1989, but with mass-production, the cost could probably be lowered to about $300 or near what an automatic seat belt system costs. They are less costly than auto air conditioners. All American auto insurance companies stand squarely behind the air bag as the best safety device.

As long ago as 1952, the first of a series of patents was filed for automatic air bags; by 1968, the patents were sufficiently advanced to attract the interest of government auto safety experts. Thousands of tests have documented the effectiveness of the air bag. For about 15 years, some 12,000 cars, mostly 1974–1976 General Motors models and some Fords and Volvos, have been operating with air bags that were installed experimentally, and have traveled 1.2 billion miles. According to a study by the National Highway Traffic Safety Administration (NHTSA), these cars have been involved in about 270 crashes in which the air bag was deployed, and the 385 persons involved sustained either none or at the most minor injuries. The effectiveness of the air bag in these crashes has been dramatized in several cases.

Dr. Arnold Arms, an elderly doctor, fell asleep while driving home from visiting numerous patients. His 1975 Oldsmobile Regency hit a large transit bus head-on at about 25 miles-per-hour. But, as he later explained, "My car was completely demolished; however, I was able to get out . . . without any injuries, due solely to the effective use of my air bag as I was not using a seat belt."[11]

However, the auto industry long resisted the installation of air bags in new cars, which could have saved at least 9,000 lives and prevented 120,000 injuries annually, according to studies made by Professor William Nordhaus of Harvard University. The U.S. Department of Transportation estimated that their use would save 10,000 lives and prevent 50,000 serious injuries. In light of all this evidence, the history of the automakers' vigorous opposition to the air bag is astonishing.

Before the Reagan administration, government agencies supported a move toward compulsory air bags. This support began in 1969 with a proposal by Transportation Secretary John Volpe that new cars be equipped with automatic front seat restraints. At the behest of Lee Iacocca, then president of Ford, and other Big Three automakers who claimed that the cost would be far too great, President Nixon postponed setting the standard. Four years later, it was rescinded outright. It looked like the end, but in 1977, under the Carter administration, a new government order gave the auto manufacturers four to six years "lead time" to meet the performance requirements for automatic occupant protection in 30-mile-per-hour frontal crashes. The government gave manufacturers the choice of using air bags or automatic seat belts; larger car models would have to comply by 1982, and all cars by 1984.

After more than a decade of exhaustive testing and debate, it looked as if we were on our way to greatly reducing auto deaths and injuries. Mortgaged as it was to corporate interests, including the auto industry, the Reagan administration lost no time, rescinding the air bag crash protection of the 1977 order in 1981. With the support of the auto industry, the administration reasoned that a decrease in regulations would lower auto prices and thus make them more competitive with Japanese and European imports. Furthermore, they claimed, automatic seat belts would be cheaper and more practical than air bags.

Again, it looked as if air bags were dead. However, the auto industry counted its pennies too soon. A broad coalition of consumer groups, insurance companies, and other groups, working through State Farm Insurance Company, one of the largest auto insurers, brought suit before the U.S. Court of Appeals in 1982 to rescind the order. The court overturned the air bag revocation order on the grounds that the Department of Transportation had failed to "heed the goals that Congress asked it to meet," namely safety. It called the revocation order arbitrary and capricious, not supported by "one iota of evidence." In spite of all the accumulated evidence in favor of air bags, the Reagan administration then decided to appeal to the Supreme Court where it thought it had a favorable audience for its policy of deregulation. It received a shock when the Supreme Court unanimously upheld the Appeals Court in 1983. The court ruled that the agency had exceeded its prerogative and that the air bag was "an effective and cost-beneficial lifesaving device." The Supreme Court recognized the auto industry's obstructionist role: "For nearly a decade, the automobile industry waged the regulatory equivalent of war against the air bag and lost—the inflatable restraint was proven sufficiently effective." It ordered the U.S. Department of Transportation to require automatic restraints (air bags or automatic seat belts) in all new cars or to provide sound justification for not doing so.

Shortly before the court decision, and because of political pressures and the view that the Reagan anti-safety approach hardly brought votes, Secretary of Transportation Elizabeth Dole decided to have air bags installed in 5,000 government-purchased Ford Topaz cars. In 1983, she sought to comply with the Supreme Court decision but equivocated by setting a new compliance date of 1990 instead of the original 1984 for mandatory automatic restraints.

To the amazement of many, and after all those years of resistance, in 1987 Ford began to offer optional air bag equipment on some 1987 models, but only on the driver's side. Their newspaper advertisements stated what had long been known:

In a serious frontal crash (as serious, for example, as hitting a parked car at 25 miles-per-hour or more), the air bag inflates in less than the blink of an eye. And deflates immediately. Yet, in that brief time, it can help cushion you from forces that might otherwise cause severe injuries.

Ford planned to install air bags in one million 1990 cars. General Motors, after years of opposing them, planned to offer driver-side air bags in 550,000 of their 1990 models. In mid-1988, Chrysler became the first American auto company to make air bags standard equipment on some of their passenger cars, and by 1990 they would become standard on all of their cars. In the announcement, Board Chairman Lee Iacocca declared in full page ads that "air bags represent the state of the art in car safety systems," and that "You won't hear any more beefs about air bags from me." U.S. and import manufacturers expected to sell about 2.9 million air-bag-equipped passenger cars during the 1990 model year.

Nonetheless, the auto industry had on its conscience thousands of deaths and hundreds of thousands of injuries that without doubt could have been prevented had the air bag voluntarily been adopted earlier throughout the industry or had the industry not vigorously opposed government efforts to impose such a requirement. Finally, it is well to recall that the installation of air bags was not entirely voluntary. Auto

makers were under NHTSA order to provide some form of mandatory
automatic restraint by 1990.

MASSIVE SAFETY RECALLS

Each year, auto manufacturers recall millions of autos for safety-
related defects. Most of the recalls have been termed voluntary, as if the
automakers had decided to protect the public. It is true that few recalls
are made in response to a direct government order, but they are far
from voluntary. Usually, the federal government, through the NHTSA
or the EPA, asks the manufacturer "voluntarily" to recall certain autos
when reports from consumers, or the government's own tests, show a
safety defect. The government agencies prefer this method over the use
of the difficult and time-consuming court order to gain compliance. The
automaker usually goes along with the "arm twisting" because "voluntary" sounds better to the public; it also reduces the likelihood of consumer liability suits.

Rarely is a Japanese or other foreign car recalled. When there have
been recalls, the defect has with few exceptions been minor. A 1984
Consumer Reports auto safety survey of 400,000 readers who owned autos
found that only 6 percent of the U.S.-made cars scored better-than-
average repair records, compared with 88.7 percent of the Japanese cars
and 50 percent of the German and Swedish cars. These differences occur
partly because of Japanese and European automakers' broader views of
what constitutes quality and their efforts to see that manufacturing and
testing standards are high. U.S. automakers have been slow to accept
quality that reaches beyond the fit of a car door or the paint finish. All
this contrasts with the vision of Henry Ford, who first designed the auto
assembly line and had a vision that he would build a motor car for the
multitude that would "be constructed of the best materials, by the best
men to be hired, after the simplest design that modern engineering can
devise."[12]

Since the creation of the National Highway Safety Administration in
1966, more than 100 million cars have been recalled because of safety
defects. From 1980 through 1986, there were 876 recalls involving
28,799,883 domestic vehicles. In 1985, there were 137 safety-related
recalls of 4,996,186 vehicles; in 1986, 139 recalls involving 1,730,657
vehicles; in 1987, recalls involved 8.9 million vehicles, and in 1988 recalls
involved 4.2 million vehicles. In 1988 General Motors recalled 371,000
Chevettes for transmission problems. In 1989 Ford recalled 518,000
Escorts for engine fires, and General Motors recalled 1.7 million vehicles
for safety defects in their cruise control systems. From 1984 to 1987,
Ford recalled 7.5 million vehicles, or 55 percent of its U.S. sales during

this period. General Motors recalled 42 percent, and Chrysler 12 percent. In 1987, Ford recalled 3.6 million cars at one time for a serious safety defect in the fuel line connection.

The following are typical examples of the serious safety factors involved in recalls in the 1980s. The cases are primarily from the 1985–1987 reports of the Washington, D.C. based Center for Auto Safety:

- The NHTSA in 1985 asked General Motors to recall an estimated one million cars, including 1982–1983 Cadillacs, Buicks, and Oldsmobiles, that could develop door fires, possibly trapping the cars' occupants. Power door locks could short out as a result of electrical fires. One woman in her company-owned Coupe de Ville had this experience on an interstate highway: "All of a sudden, I smelled a burning smell and saw smoke forming inside the power-window control panel." She pulled off the highway and tried to get out of the passenger side, but she heard the ominous click of the doors locking automatically. She panicked as smoke filled the car. In a matter of minutes that must have seemed an eternity, she was finally able to unlock another door manually and thus escape. The sheriff reported that the fire, which melted the driver's seat and the control panel, was caused by an electrical short in the power lock system.

- In 1987, Ford issued two separate recalls amounting to 3.6 million 1986–1987 vehicles to repair fuel system problems that had led to fuel leaks, fires and injuries. One covered potential fuel line disconnections on 3.4 million 1986–1987 fuel-injected cars. This could cause engine fires by spraying gasoline throughout the compartment. One victim reported that after he removed the gas cap from his 1985 van, "boiling gasoline gushed out, burning my eyes, mouth, nose and groin, melting the contact lenses in my eyes." This was Ford's second largest recall, and covered 56 percent of car production during the previous two model years.

- Ford makes the basic chassis on which virtually all ambulances are based. In all, about 180 ambulances with Ford E–350 chasses caught fire between 1986 and 1988. More than 200 of them developed problems that could have led to fires. Reports kept coming into NHTSA that fuel spurted out of the fuel tank when the filler cap was removed, causing fires and serious burns. One van burst into flames in West Virginia while rushing a patient to the hospital. Another ambulance in North Carolina had its side blown off by an exploding gas tank. One ambulance that had delivered a patient to an emergency room erupted in flames while parked outside, and another caught fire while an emergency crew was treating a heart attack victim. These events prompted the president of the International Association of Fire Chiefs to say that "Ford is worried about the overall costs as opposed to safety." At first Ford tried to duck the issues of design and production defects by blaming the spurting fuel problem on the extended idling of ambulances, overfilled gas tanks, and on other factors. Ford made two recalls, one covering as many as 16,000 ambulances.

- In 1989 the government announced a formal investigation covering 1.9 million General Motors cars after complaints that a defect in the cruise control system could cause a driver to lose control of the car. The National Highway Traffic Safety Administration said that the investigation was opened to prepare for a possible court-ordered recall of several models of 1984 to 1988 Buicks, Cadillacs, Chevrolets, Oldsmobiles, and Pontiacs that are equipped with cruise control. The agency said that it has received 144 complaints, involving 18 accidents and 7 injuries, in which a small plastic ring slipped out of a part of the vehicle's cruise control system at highway speed without warning, causing the throttle to be held partially open. In announcing the investigation, the agency said that "under certain conditions, the driver may be startled and lose control of the car, and the brakes will be less effective." General Motors refused the government's request for a voluntary recall.

- A retired social worker got out of her Ford while waiting for a neighbor. She left the motor running as she walked to the rear of the car. It lurched into reverse gear, backed over her, and then hit a tree. The neighbor found the woman dead. By the end of 1980 alone, NHTSA had attributed 6,000 accidents to the faulty transmission; 1,700 persons had been injured and 98 killed. Deaths and injuries continue, and by 1988, the government estimated that the total had reached 300 deaths and over 5,000 injuries. By 1984, 2,000 lawsuits involving the transmission defect, representing claims of over $1.3 million, had been filed against Ford. Outstanding damage claims at the beginning of 1988 were $598 million. In the late 1970s, the NHTSA had planned a massive recall of the 19 million Fords, Mercurys, and Lincolns with these possibly defective transmissions. The Reagan administration, however, caved in under Ford's claims that a recall would cost them more than $100 million at a time when the auto market was financially depressed. In a 1980 government agreement with Ford, all the company did was to send warning letters and dashboard warning stickers to 23 million Ford owners. Still, as of 1988, seventeen years later, there had been no recall. The *Wall Street Journal* reported on April 14, 1988 that "no other auto-safety conflict has ever run so long or been so bitter. The number of deaths blamed on unexpected backing-up by these vehicles now exceeds that of such celebrated cases as Pinto gas-tank fires, defective Firestone 500 tires and Audi 'sudden accelerations' combined. Safety regulators and consumer advocates, once allies, continue to squabble over the government's unprecedented about-face long after most people thought the matter was over with. Ford, having paid untold millions in thousands of cases, continues to fight suits over new incidents."

When auto manufacturers make no concerted efforts to build safe cars, while at the same time opposing government-mandated actions to assure car safety, they are contributing to the deaths and injuries of thousands of consumers, as well as to extensive and costly vehicle repairs. It is tragic that consumers have had to pay with their lives, their health, and their financial resources for the monetary benefits gained by the auto companies. By 1989, however, there were strong indications that the deregulation phase commenced under President Reagan might finally be over and that, instead, consumers might find the auto industry more interested in safety and environmental regulatory measures that are vital in protecting both human beings and the environment. The auto industry had finally succumbed, in part because auto buyers have been bombarded with increasing amounts of information about the safety records of various makes of cars. The news came from consumer groups, government agencies that publish the results of crash tests, of which the auto manufacturers were probably already aware, and insurance companies that charge more to insure cars with poor safety records. Foreign auto manufacturers, often the first to introduce high-tech safety systems, have also played a part. As a consequence, American manufacturers are not only adopting air bags but perfecting such long-neglected features as anti-lock brakes, electronic collision-avoidance systems, fighter jet–style instrument panels, and four-wheel steering. The latter would make cars more maneuverable and stable at high speeds by allowing all four wheels to turn, not just the front two. In fact, the auto industry may be moving from resistance to increased cooperation with the government. Clarence Ditlow, director of the Center for Auto Safety in Washington, D.C., commented: "I couldn't say they [the automakers] have gotten religion. But they have come up the learning curve on how to deal with regulation."[13]

Chapter 3

THE GREAT OIL RIP-OFF

The very size of the oil industry makes its highly unethical activities affect millions of Americans. The American oil industry is the largest as well as the richest in the world; it does $200 billion in business each year. In 1988, three of the top 10 U.S. industrial corporations were oil companies. Exxon, with sales of over $79 billion, was the third largest industrial concern in the United States and also the world. The largest in order of sales are Exxon (Standard Oil of New Jersey), Mobil (Standard Oil of New York), Texaco, Chevron (Standard Oil of California), and Amoco (Standard Oil of Indiana). The industry giants own huge supertankers larger than aircraft carriers, offshore drilling rigs as tall as skyscrapers, Alaskan and other pipelines longer than superhighways, and huge refineries resembling something out of *Star Wars*. Anthony Sampson, a leading oil expert, describes these powerful giants:

Their boards could allocate hundreds of millions to bring into being a new oil field, a new harbor, or a new trade route.... Their skyscraper headquarters... seemed to evoke a new world where nations themselves were obsolete.... Their incomes were greater than those of most countries where they operated, their fleets of tankers had more tonnage than any navy, they owned and administered whole cities in the desert.[1]

The oil giants have increased their wealth and power in part by engaging in serious unethical and illegal practices. In fact, the industry has a continuous history of law violations that include, particularly, antitrust laws and illegal overcharges of consumers. It has made large-scale illegal political contributions at home; it has also been involved in extensive foreign bribery. Several major oil corporations have stolen oil royalties from federal as well as American Indian lands, and, for a long time, they have been major polluters of the nation's air and water. Its power over members of congress and state government officials is so awesome that it often threatens America's democratic processes on important issues. It makes staggering profits by price-gouging American consumers.

A HISTORY OF LAW VIOLATIONS

No U.S. corporate industry has abused the American public more or has had as bad a record of unethical and illegal behavior for a longer period of time than the oil industry. During 1975–1976, for example, the federal government charged oil corporations in 1 out of every 5 cases it brought, and 1 out of every 10 cases involving serious and moderate violations.[2] In all, 22 out of the 28 oil companies violated the law at least once; 20 had 1 or more serious violations. The oil industry has been the target of countless congressional committees and government agency investigations. Year in and year out, the government has charged oil companies with serious unethical practices and law violations, and has brought numerous suits against them for monopolistic practices, price-fixing, and illegal price overcharges. American oil companies have also been involved in similar cases in Canada and in other countries.

For the most part, however, these big oil companies have had little to fear concerning the eventual outcome of these law violations. They have the funds and talent to frustrate the American legal system, and they know that if they hold out long enough their case will probably be dropped, as has occurred many times. For example, in 1973 the Federal Trade Commission (FTC) began legal proceedings against the eight largest oil corporations, charging them with a wide range of anticompetitive practices that included permitting one company to set the prices for the others to follow. In 1980, the FTC issued a 394-page document asserting that "parallel" increases and maintenance of crude oil prices by the eight concerns raised "a powerful inference of conspiracy." After seven years of legal battle, in 1981 the government finally dropped the antitrust suit, giving as its reason the excessive delays caused by corporate stalling tactics. These tactics included filing 500 pre-trial motions, and continuously challenging the government in court on procedural grounds. The Federal Trade Commission concluded that if the case were not dropped, it could continue for 15 or 20 years without a final judgment.

These legal battles are not new to the oil industry, as it had serious ethical and legal problems a hundred years ago with the founder of the industry, John D. Rockefeller, and his Standard Oil Company, which by 1880 controlled some 95 percent of U.S. oil refining. The company bribed politicians, used strong-arm tactics against rivals, and even maintained its own espionage system in its attempts to expand its oil empire. It soon became a hated monopoly, aptly described by a line in a Eugene O'Neill play: "Down with all tyrants! God damn Standard Oil!" Congress enacted the Sherman Antitrust Act in 1890 primarily to try to control Standard Oil's exorbitant profits and power. By 1911, the government had ordered the breakup of Standard Oil, and the "Three Sisters" were created: the Standard Oils of New Jersey, New York, and California, known today as Exxon, Mobil, and Chevron. Rockefeller and Standard Oil's lack of scruples, the secrecy that surrounded them, and their deceptions had created increasing public and governmental distrust of the entire oil industry. This distrust continues today. Sampson believes that Rockefeller left an indelible mark on the industry.

Even after the original monopoly was broken up and the family became aloof from the business, the methods and attitudes of the old man inspired his successors. . . . He established the separateness of the industry, defying governments and societies, vulnerable only to the most extreme legal sanctions. His lack of scruples and his mendacity provoked a continuing distrust of the oil industry, by the public and politicians, that was never to be allayed.[3]

Politicians and the public alike have condemned the industry giants that dominate the worldwide distribution of oil supplies. "Honest" Harold Ickes, the famed crusty secretary of the interior during World War II, had to deal with those rapacious giants. He once remarked that "an honest and scrupulous man in the oil business is so rare as to rank as a museum piece." In the debates on the 1986 tax reform bill, Senator Russell Long (D-Louisiana), a long-time friend of the oil industry, strongly defended certain tax favoritism to the industry. He shouted, "This industry is not plagued by prejudice, it is plagued by hatred." In 1971, the president of the American Petroleum Institute acknowledged that "quite frankly, the oil industry has developed the reputation over the years of being a robber, cheating and despoiling the environment."[4]

PRICE-FIXING

It is obvious to American gasoline consumers that the major oil companies generally charge almost identical prices. Price-fixing appears to be Big Oil's way of life. A pattern of suspect and illegal (namely antitrust) agreements has existed between large multinational oil companies since the end of the nineteenth century, and the evidence strongly suggests a long-standing industry culture that promotes price-fixing relations between firms today.[5] As an example, in 1980, when supplies of gasoline were plentiful and demand was down drastically, every major oil company raised its wholesale gasoline price.

There is evidence that, on occasion, representatives of oil companies meet in various states to exchange retail price information in efforts to stabilize the market; on other occasions they contact competitors. On December 17, 1984, the *Wall Street Journal* carried a lead article based on federal court antitrust records that showed during the 1970s "major oil companies [were] working in concert to prop up retail prices in gasoline in states at the expense of consumers." During one West Coast gasoline glut, for example, various corporate officials traded information about the size of refiner discounts given to gasoline distributors. Furthermore, to preserve secrecy, some major oil companies kept no written records of these competitor contacts. They set up a system that allowed officials of other major companies to contact them by telephone without dialing their offices directly, thus leaving no printed record of the contact. In 1969, the Supreme Court ruled that this direct communication between corporations was illegal but many of the major oil companies continued to hold face-to-face meetings to discuss pricing. The state of California claimed that these conspiratorial actions over many years cost consumers, the state, and independent oil producers hundreds of millions of dollars. The state attorney general asserted in 1984 that "the exchange of information within the petroleum industry was so pervasive, regular and commonplace" that it resembled a "single company."[6]

California had charged Atlantic Richfield (Arco) and six other major oil companies, in 1975, with having agreed to underpay the state of California and the city of Long Beach for crude oil pumped from state-owned tidelands during the 1970s and 1980s. According to the California state comptroller, price-fixing agreements had netted the seven corporations a total of $300 million. In 1984, Atlantic Richfield agreed to a settlement of $22.5 million. When Senator Howard Metzenbaum (D-Ohio) learned of all this in late 1984, he asked for a congressional and Department of Justice investigation of "the pervasive and prolonged anticompetitive behavior of some oil companies." Senator Metzenbaum charged that "collusion, price-fixing and artificial shortages were a way of life" in the oil industry, adding that "it would be foolish to assume that the industry has become a model of free market competition." A federal district judge threw out the California suit due to insufficient evidence, but in 1989 a San Francisco federal appeals court revived the state and federal law suits against the six big oil companies. The suits, which are for over $800 million, were to be tripled if the antitrust allegations were later proven.

In 1979, the West German government castigated the large U.S. oil companies for all substantially raising gasoline prices by the same amount, contending that if there were real industry competition, the price increases would not all have been the same. In 1981, the Canadian government issued a 1,750-page report revealing that major oil companies had overcharged Canadian consumers by $10 billion as a result of their price-fixing tactics from 1958 to 1973.[7] The report stated that Imperial Oil (70 percent of which was owned by Exxon) led the oil industry in price-fixing and restraining competition.

ILLEGAL OVERCHARGES

Violations of federal price controls on gasoline, heating oil, and other products that were in effect from 1974 to 1981 cost American consumers billions of dollars, only a fraction of which was ever recovered through government efforts. Almost all the largest oil companies, as well as many second-echelon companies, violated the law.

It all began with the Department of Energy's imposition of price controls on oil products in 1974 because of the Arab oil embargo that accompanied the Israeli-Egyptian war. This embargo had created a great shortage of petroleum supplies, and had led to much price-gouging and general consumer exploitation by the oil companies. After the much-needed price controls had gone into effect, nearly all the large oil companies were repeatedly charged with price violations.

The large oil corporations pulled off a massive heist of billions of illegal dollars, in part by lying about the kind of oil they were producing, transporting, and refining. As price controls had sent prices skyrocketing in the United States, oil was divided into two price categories: price-controlled "old" (oil that had already been discovered and was being used) and "new" oil. New oil prices were uncontrolled, on the assumption that this freedom from controls would stimulate new drilling and production. The price difference between controlled old oil and the uncontrolled new oil was as much as $30 per barrel at the world price. By illegally switching old oil and labeling it as new, the profit potentials were enormous.

Major oil companies were holding large stores of low-priced old oil. Some companies that were producing and refining the cheaper old oil simply claimed fraudulently that they were producing expensive new oil when actually they were not. Working hand-in-hand with the big oil companies, resellers aided this operation. According to government reports, resellers transferred about 250 million barrels of low-priced oil to the high-priced category during the price-control period. In other cases, the major companies sold controlled old oil that was combined with new oil at the higher price of the uncontrolled oil. As a result, the major oil companies were getting illegally high prices and profits for their controlled old oil.

Price controls ended in 1981. Estimates have been made that price overcharges from 1974 to 1981 cost consumers as much as $25 billion. The Department of Energy charged Shell, Atlantic Richfield, Texaco, Standard Oils of California and Ohio, Conoco, and Marathon with having violated federal price rules and regulations on a variety of petroleum products totaling $5.2 billion, or an average overcharge of five cents a gallon. The Department of Energy filed similar charges against Cities Service, Gulf, Chevron, Getty Oil, and Amerada Hess.

A special federal appeals court in 1985 ordered Exxon to pay $2 billion, the largest fine ever levied on a corporation, for violations of oil price regulations. In their enormous Hawkins oil field, Exxon had begun by falsely shifting about half the field production of old oil into the higher-priced, unregulated new oil category, and then, by 1979, had escalated it to include almost all the field's production. The Hawkins field daily production in 1985 was 30,000 barrels, making it then the thirteenth most productive of U.S. oil fields. The federal judge in the case ordered the government to distribute the fine to state energy conservation programs as it would be impossible to identify the defrauded consumers. An Exxon executive vice president said that the ruling was inequitable and unfair.

In 1985 the Department of Energy investigated the assertion that Arco was involved with the notorious Marc Rich Company, which had been party to a variety of fraudulent oil transfer deals.[8] Marc Rich Company had pleaded guilty in 1984 to 38 felony counts in connection with concealment of taxable income from oil trading operations from 1980 to 1981, and had later paid the government a settlement of $150 million. A government investigator assigned to the case said that attempts to prove that certain oil transactions had been structured to evade price regulations, such as Arco's relation with Marc Rich, was like trying to follow trails in the jungle. "You don't know how to use them without a guide."

Large as these settlements seem, they constituted only a modest part of the illegal profits. One consumer leader stated, "The oil industry has come out on top, showing it pays to violate the law." Later, almost every major oil company made settlements with the government. Standard Oil of Indiana (Amoco) agreed to a $690-million consent decree to settle all overcharge violations between 1974 and 1981. In 1988, Texaco agreed to pay $1.25 billion as part of a final settlement agreement with the Department of Energy for oil price overcharges between 1973 and 1981. The government estimated that its claims could have totaled more than $2.1 billion.

The government realized that it would be impossible to locate and reimburse millions of consumers for money virtually stolen from them. Consequently, as James McGovern, an expert in the oil area, put it, "The oil companies, which saw themselves as corporate Medicis promoting the virtues of the free market, became sponsors of a social welfare program."[9] Amoco agreed in a court settlement to pay $71 million of the $690 million into a federal escrow account for disbursement to persons suffering the most from rising energy bills, mainly low-income families. In addition, they agreed to pay $29 million for direct reimbursement to past buyers of heating oil and diesel fuel, mainly public utilities and bus lines. Other provisions of the settlement included forgoing certain production price increases and reducing some consumer product prices two cents a gallon for 18 months. The really shocking part of the settlement, however, was that the government actually allowed Amoco to pay itself $411 million by investing in projects that later would return a profit to the corporation. These projects included $105 million to modernize a refinery to produce more gasoline, $178 million for domestic oil exploration, and $218 million to accelerate production from old fields. This was done presumably for the purpose of increasing the amount of available domestic oil.

THEFT OF OIL ROYALTIES

A House subcommittee in 1986 found that some large oil corporations, like Amoco, were underpaying their royalties to the Department of the Interior, the collection agency for federal on-shore and American Indian oil lands, by almost $1 billion annually, or an average of 21 percent during the period from 1979 to 1985.[10] Under the Mineral Leasing Act, oil companies are required to pay Native Americans an oil royalty rate of $16^2/_3$ percent. The collection of these royalties is the responsibility of the Mineral Management Service of the Department of the Interior, which must rely almost entirely on sales data reported by the oil and gas companies. Oil companies may accurately report the amount of oil produced yet still fail to pay the full royalties, or they may fail to report all the oil produced, thus making it appear that they owe less in royalties than they actually do. Senator Daniel Inouye (D-Hawaii), chairman of the Select Commitee on Indian Affairs, claimed in 1988 that, according to Interior and Government Accounting Office reports, $5.8 billion worth of oil and gas had been illegally siphoned off since the early 1970s from American Indian and public lands.[11]

When the violations were discovered, primarily through government audits, the Shoshone and Arapaho Indians brought suits against Amoco and Sohio oil companies in 1982.[12] The Indians claimed that these companies had defrauded them of tribal royalties on almost 500,000 barrels of oil, or over $4 million worth, over a 13-year period. The U.S. Department of the Interior supported the Indian tribes' charges, and

Amoco partially conceded them as "accounting errors." The tribes' petitions maintained that, among other things, Amoco had opened new wells and lifted large quantities of crude oil without either reporting the production or paying royalties on the oil. The tribes claimed that Amoco underestimated the production of oil by a number of methods, including the installation of at least two clearly illegal bypasses of the metering device and installing resettable oil counters.[13] Senator John Melcher (D-Mont.) of the Senate Select Committee on Indian Affairs said that the "oil companies are calling many of the shots and doing whatever they please in the oil fields."

Oil leases on federal lands present similar problems. The inspector general of the Department of the Interior testified before a congressional committee in 1982 that oil royalties from federal lands are underpaid by about 3.5 percent, a loss of about $90 million a year. Amoco, Gulf, Conoco, Cities Service, and other companies have partially reimbursed either American Indian landowners or the federal government.

POLLUTING THE ENVIRONMENT

The major oil companies have a long history of environmental irresponsibility, in spite of all the propaganda they dish out in their television commercials and other public relations releases. One study of the *Fortune* 500 corporations found that over a two-year period the oil industry had committed half of all environmental violations and more than a third of the serious and moderately serious violations.[14] It led all others in violating water pollution control laws. The oil companies committed over 70 percent of all water pollution violations that had occurred, chiefly in the refining operation and from serious oil spills.

Oil pollution of the water ruins the environment, kills wildlife, particularly fish and birds, and deposits a residue of muck on the shorelines. Frequently, the big oil companies drill for oil, particularly offshore, with little regard to environmental consequences. For example, Texaco pleaded guilty in Los Angeles in the 1980s to charges of having failed to conduct safe offshore drilling; the company was fined $750,000. Consequently, oil companies have been the targets of most of the powerful environmental groups, including the Sierra Club and the National Resources Defense Council. Without the efforts of these and other interested groups to block offshore leases, to assure that Alaskan wildlife is not threatened by pipelines, and otherwise to protect the environment, one can well imagine what might have happened.

A particularly calamitous oil spill involved the runaway offshore wells of the Chevron Oil Company in 1970 that spewed oil into the Gulf of Mexico for three weeks at the rate of 600 to 1,000 barrels a day. This spill threatened Louisiana's shrimp fishing grounds, the oyster beds, wildlife refuges, and the coastline with a 52-square-mile slick. So serious was it that Walter Hickel, then secretary of the Department of the Interior and once considered a reliable friend of the oil industry, accused Chevron of hundreds of deliberate violations of federal regulations, including the failure to install safety-valve "storm chokes" in drilling rigs that would have prevented the blowout. According to a vice president of Chevron Oil Company, the safety valves "result in more work overtime to clean the wells. It costs money. Somebody at Chevron thought they could increase production and save money at the same time."[15] Hickel angrily demanded that a grand jury be convened to take the "strongest possible action" against the lawbreakers and to investigate the drilling practices of all 50 oil companies operating in the Gulf area. A federal grand jury subsequently indicted Chevron on 900 separate criminal counts of "knowingly and willingly" violating the law.

As another example, in January 1988 Ashland Oil delivered a devastating blow to residents along the Ohio and Monongahela rivers downstream from Pittsburgh through three states. In one of the worst inland oil spills ever, nearly a million gallons of diesel oil spilled into the river when a large Ashland Oil storage tank crumpled as it was being filled. City after city along the two rivers declared an emergency as drinking water supplies became contaminated. In some areas, drinking water was not available at all, water usage was strictly controlled, and some businesses had to curtail operations. Thousands of birds and fish died. Ashland Oil had moved and reconstructed a 40-year-old steel tank without a written permit, and the company had also failed to comply with prior federal water-testing requirements on the tank. In addition, the company had failed to construct a sufficient barrier around the tank in order to trap any leakage. The spill had several repercussions. A task force of five Pennsylvania state agencies concluded that the mishap "could have been and should have been averted." They claimed that Ashland Oil was "apathetic to pollution problems, ignorant of actual events, unwilling to take any engaged role." Following a civil suit brought by the Justice Department, Ashland agreed to reimburse the federal government for $680,000 in costs incurred in the cleanup. It also agreed to a comprehensive cleanup of the facility area. Finally, in September of 1988, a federal grand jury indicted Ashland Oil on two misdemeanor counts of violating environmental laws. The company later entered a plea of no contest.

Exxon is guilty of having caused the nation's most disastrous oil spill when its tanker, the *Exxon Valdez*, went off course and struck a reef in the pristine waters of Prince William Sound, Alaska, in March 1989. More than 240,000 barrels, or over 11 million gallons, of crude oil spilled over a 1,600-square-mile area, contaminating more than 800 miles of shoreline of one of the world's richest wildlife areas. The thick crude oil devastated commercial fishing and killed tens of thousands of Alaskan wildlife. The man whom Exxon had permitted to captain the huge tanker had a known history of alcoholism that included several arrests for drunken driving. Nine hours following the incident, a blood test revealed he had an unacceptable level of alcohol. In difficult waters, he had turned his boat over to an uncertified third mate. A grand jury later indicted the captain on charges of reckless actions. Although it is the world's largest company, Exxon responded late and ineffectively to this serious accident. Even with huge profits accruing from Alaskan oil, Exxon had prepared no real contingency plan to deal with potentially large spills that might devastate Alaskan waters, and the Coast Guard termed the plans that Exxon did make on government orders after the accident "very thin." At subsequent hearings, Alaska's examiner charged that Exxon's representatives were conducting a misinformation campaign, saying, "It's beyond me how officers of a big corporation like this can tell things they flat know are lies but they're doing it repeatedly." As the immensity of the spill became increasingly evident, consumers, environmentalists, and politicians vented their anger on Exxon, initiating boycotts of Exxon products. Commenting on the boycott, Ralph Nader said that Exxon should not be allowed to forget the spill and that the boycott would send the oil giant a message. A Massachusetts state senator told a Boston boycott rally, "We are beginning the war of words and actions against any oil company that doesn't understand its responsibility to protect the environment." Exxon admitted that consumers had returned more than 18,000 credit cards.

Also involved in the *Exxon Valdez* disaster was the Alyeska Pipeline Service Company, the consortium of seven large oil companies, including Exxon, set up twenty years ago to placate congressional fears about Alaskan environmental safety. Its job was to run the pipeline and various safety operations designed to prevent damage to the environment. The state of Alaska has estimated that during this time the oil companies had taken $45 billion in profits out of Alaska. Following the *Valdez* spill, on July 6, 1989, the *Wall Street Journal* ran a front-page article that revealed Alyeska's dismal environmental record:

The pipeline operator's track record, as shown in internal documents, state records, talks with regulators, public testimony and interviews with current and former employees, paints a picture of a consortium that has long pursued a policy of cutting corners on environment and safety. Over the years, Alyeska has gradually and quietly scrapped many safeguards and never even built others that it told Congress it planned. Several past and present employees say they occasionally fabricated environmental records. Alyeska has fought proposed new regulatory controls in long, expensive legal wars of attrition that have enabled it to dump pollutants into the environment far in excess of what regulators now consider safe. It allowed its defenses against a major accident to fall into disrepair. And many Alyeska statements—both before and after the spill—appear now to have been misleading at best. Alyeska's attitude, critics charge, made an environmental disaster more likely to occur than it need have been and made the *Exxon Valdez* spill worse than it need have been.

An official of the American Petroleum Institute referred to pollution problems prior to the enactment of federal laws in this way: "We didn't have any concern or curiosity at that time."[16] Since 1972, regulations prohibit oil refineries from emitting into the air sulfur and other chemicals that exceed certain fixed standards, and they prohibit the discharge of oil in navigable waters. In addition, the companies must also report all spills and clean them up properly. The industry's water and air clean-ups have increased in direct ratio to the tightening of federal pollution laws, but still their compliance record has not been good. Efforts to control air pollution have encountered stiff opposition from the oil industry, which regards them as unwarranted interference with acceptable refining methods and profits.

STAGGERING PROFITS

The oil industry cannot claim that its illegal and unethical acts are due to poor profits; although ups and downs do occur, overall profits are huge. In sheer size of the profits, oil companies are generally the leading profit-makers of all U.S. industrial corporations; occasionally, their profits are staggering. Between 1978 and 1980, for example, oil companies accounted for almost half the total profits of the *Fortune* 500. Even when profit percentages decrease, profits still remain enormous. In 1988, the large oil companies had a 63 percent median increase in profits over 1987. Only occasionally do they report a loss.

Oil prices do not always follow supply and demand. Generally speaking, when oil supplies are low, prices go up; while if there is an abundance, the prices remain up. Typical newspaper headlines point out the contradiction: "Cost of Gasoline Continues to Rise Despite Glut of Oil," and "Gasoline Prices Climb Despite Lag in Demand." During summer vacation time, Americans can almost always count on increased gasoline prices, regardless of available supplies; the consumer is over a barrel, an oil barrel. By the fall of 1988, crude oil prices had crashed to their lowest levels in more than two years, but in spite of the plunging prices, profits of big American oil companies soared. Commenting on this situation, a lead *Wall Street Journal* article, on October 3, 1988, reported:

Despite plunging prices, Arco's profit is surging. So, in fact, are the profits of Exxon Corp., Mobil Corp., and nearly every multinational oil company. Despite the collapse of oil prices, the profits of the nation's 18 largest oil companies will leap by about one-third this year to nearly $20 billion, far exceeding the profits of every major airline and automaker combined.

The oil industry can get away with supply "shortages" because it controls the books. Estimates of oil reserves, availability, and production are not subject to independent verification. The government derives its estimates from the oil production reports of one self-interested source: the American Petroleum Institute, the chief representative of oil interests. One can say about the oil companies' reserve estimates that, like the miracles of biblical times, a few loaves of bread could be turned into a feast. Today oil companies need only a stroke of the pen to multiply their oil and gas reserves. The industry guides the measurement of its reserves by rule of thumb. One oil analyst said:

No other industry of comparable importance gets to operate with such secrecy. If the government wants to know how many cars General Motors has in inventory, the government need only send an agent around to storage lots and count them. But if it wants to know how much oil and gas Exxon and Mobil, for example, are sitting on, it must ask Exxon and Mobil. Whether or not the statistics it receives are accurate is anybody's guess.[17]

Public outrage over excessive oil industry profits reached its apex in 1979. With the excuse that the political crisis in Iran had reduced oil supplies, prices were raised and industry oil profits increased an average 76.5 percent over the previous year, as compared to 21.2 percent for other major corporations. Some individual corporate profits were even greater: Texaco's profits in that one year increased 211 percent, Mobil's 130 percent, and Exxon's 118 percent. The companies claimed an oil shortage, yet a poll of the American public indicated that two-thirds of them believed the shortage to be a hoax inspired by the desire for even higher profits. The public and Congress wondered if it were ethical for the oil producers to continue to raise gasoline prices when profits continued to soar. President Carter in 1979 called such oil profits "excessive, undeserved and enormous." Their capital budgets were at record levels and far exceeded their profits. Oil companies had more financial resources than they could profitably spend. As a result of public, congressional and presidential outrage, in 1980 Congress enacted the windfall oil profits tax, amounting to $227 billion over a 10-year period, to siphon off some of these riches.

The oil industry spends millions of dollars in media advertising in their efforts to convince the public that their profits are not only decent but actually are inadequate to explore and develop more oil resources that will be essential in coming decades. However, oil companies do not put the major part of their profits into the development of greater domestic oil supplies. According to a 1982 study by the Washington, D.C.-based Citizen-Energy Labor Coalition, the nation's 16 largest oil companies have diverted billions of dollars to purchase non-oil companies. For example, at the time of the study, Exxon owned subsidiaries that produce golf clubs, electric typewriters, word processors, tape cassettes, and automotive parts; Standard Oil of California owned 65,000 acres of agricultural land in the San Joaquin Valley; and Tenneco had cattle ranches in Arizona and California. Mobil in 1974 purchased Montgomery Ward, the fourth largest retail concern in the United States. Getty Oil owned an 85-percent interest in an entertainment and sports TV network. Big oil corporations have even joined the ranks of the nation's top real estate owners. They build houses, hotels, resorts, and a variety of commercial projects. In 1982 an Exxon subsidiary, Friendswoods Real Estate Development in Houston, had 31,000 homes intended to house 200,000 people with 2 million feet of retail and office space. Apropos of all this, President Carter told a Kentucky town meeting he addressed in 1979: "What they have done in the past is to buy restaurants and motel chains; they bought department stores; they have taken profits off oil and gasoline and not put it back in the ground to develop more energy for you and me."[18]

Oil has become an industry that people learned to hate when large acquisitions of other businesses go hand-in-hand with price increases, gasoline shortages due to claimed inadequate refining facilities, and exploding profits. The magnitude of oil profits also allows top oil executives to live in far greater grandeur than potentates of old, for as the oil companies become richer, so do the executives. For example, in 1986, the president of Mobil, William P. Tavoulareas, received a salary and bonus of $1.2 million, a 27 percent increase over 1985, while the company's chairman, Raleigh Warner, received $1.1 million, also up 27 percent. In addition, they received indirect compensation by exercising stock options, awarded in previous years, of $2.4 million and $967,666, respectively.

HOW THEY GET AWAY WITH IT

One wonders just how the big oil companies get away with their arrogance and excessive profits. One also wonders why the government does not forcefully step in to rectify the situation. Certainly many courses of action are available. The government could: (1) file antitrust suits against them that would more effectively curb price collusion; (2) order that they cease further acquisitions of non-oil-producing businesses; (3) reinstate price controls on petroleum products, as there is relatively little real interest in crude domestic oil exploration; (4) designate oil as an essential commodity similar to gas and electricity where the government can better regulate profits and operating practices; (5) set up a government agency to import oil, which several Western countries do; and, (6) as a last resort, the government could nationalize the oil industry on the production and import level, on the grounds that the misbehavior of the oil giants has become intolerable and that military and domestic needs are too essential to permit the present situation to continue. For example, during World War II, when Secretary of the Interior Harold Ickes became fed up with the oil companies, he proposed the formation of a government corporation, Petroleum Reserves Corporation, to buy out control of Saudi Arabian oil from U.S. companies.

From time to time, bills are introduced into Congress to put some of these suggested solutions into effect, but none has been successful. The oil companies have always counterattacked with an advertising media blitz, increased the activities of their extensive lobbying organization, and upped strategic political contributions.

The big oil companies continuously beef up their public relations efforts because of the threats to their increasingly damaged public image. For example, Bob Hope has assured television viewers that Texaco is "faithful to our trust", and Exxon and other oil companies increase their considerable support to higher education and to the arts, all in an effort to create a public-spirited "good guy" image. Mobil Corporation sponsors several programs of the Public Broadcasting System and spends more money than the other oil companies on its advocacy ads, in some years as much as $3 million. Its ads appear mainly in newspapers, and proclaim Mobil's position on almost every aspect of the oil industry. Others also use advocacy ads: A sample Gulf newspaper ad typified the arguments used to counteract measures that would control oil industry abuses.

Price controls over fuels should be eliminated . . . public lands should be made available for mining and drilling. . . . We must permit off-shore drilling . . . [and] strip mining must be permitted. . . . A free market price system would encourage conservation. . . . Increased prices will stimulate more production.

Oil companies use a number of methods to influence opinion-makers about their points of view as, for example, in the seminars they often hold to bring together their own company executives with academics. In particular, several corporations use the Public Broadcasting System to give an image of the artistic and cultural benefits that they offer to the public. In fact, they have sponsored so many programs on PBS that some have suggested that PBS really stands for "Petroleum Broadcasting System." Mobil presents such programs as "Masterpiece Theater" to reach an audience of influential persons. Partly with this same goal in mind, Mobil also has given support to the Whitney and Guggenheim museums.

The oil lobby stands as the most awesome force in Washington for exerting political pressure; it is almost like a subgovernment. To achieve its objectives, it exerts great pressures on the White House, Congress, and state legislatures. Oil companies give millions of dollars to congressional candidates to make them indebted to the oil industry. Well over $100 million is spent on lobbying of one kind or another, and lobbyists are always on the alert to frustrate legislation detrimental to the oil interests. Some 500 newspaper, radio, and television stations regularly receive press releases from the industry mouthpiece, the American Petroleum Institute. They regard their lobbying activities as essential to the well-being of the oil industry because the government can exercise great control over its future. James McGovern, an oil expert, has pointed out that this industry is unlike other American industries in one crucial respect: Its operations are primarily directed not at sales to customers, who have no choice but to buy the industry's products at any price, but at state, local, and federal governments, especially the federal government, as well as the general public.[19] What Washington does, or does not do, has a direct and vital impact on the industry and its very survival in its present form. Above all, the oil industry is concerned about taxes, environmental restrictions, the leasing of federal lands for exploration, price controls, proposals to break up or nationalize the big oil companies, and a national energy program.

The large oil corporations employ highly skilled lobbying staffs in Washington, and these lobbyists present their views and arguments to representatives, senators, and many other government officials. They furnish all kinds of pro-oil propaganda that claim to show members of Congress, for example, how certain proposed pieces of oil legislation can affect their home districts. They also zero in on the executive branch. Senior oil executives lobby on Capitol Hill where they call on key White House staff members and officials of the Department of Energy, the very agency that regulates the industry. The results of their lobbying efforts are evident from the fact that the Reagan administration slashed the Department of Energy enforcement staff by 60 percent and almost succeeded in eliminating the department altogether. These actions almost destroyed the efforts of the government watchdogs whose job it supposedly is to protect the consumer from Big Oil exploitation.

In addition to lobbying by the individual corporations and their large political contributions, the major clout of the industry comes from the American Petroleum Institute, the right arm of the oil industry.[20] Founded in 1919, it has an annual budget of more than $40 million, making it one of the richest lobbies in Washington, D.C. Its staff exceeds 500 people, most of whom work in Washington, while others are in New

York, Dallas and in 34 "state councils." The institute represents 314 corporate members, mainly the giants or so-called "majors." Other organizations represented include independents, jobbers, refiners, pipeline operators, and truckers.

Oil and natural gas interests are the most lucrative source of political contributions to members of Congress. In a study underwritten by eight newspapers, free-lance journalist Edward Roeder spent four months in 1980 unlocking oil contributions made to the 1978 election campaigns of the 96th Congress.[21] He found that oil industry PACs, executives, and lobbyists gave $3.9 million as direct contributions to winning candidates. Republicans received 50 percent more contributions than Democrats. Nearly $600,000 went to the 20 members of the Senate Finance Committee, the oil industry's protector and the spawning ground for many tax breaks for the industry. The top winner was Senator John Tower, Republican of Texas, with a total of $363,000 from identifiable oil interests. The story was the same in the House, but on a smaller scale, where the industry helped out all but 116 representatives for a total of $1.6 million.

The oil interests expect, and get, plenty for their money. Roeder's analysis of Big Oil's political contributions to the 96th Congress and the votes in both the House of Representatives and the Senate showed a close relationship between crucial votes for oil interests and the monetary contributions members had received on issues ranging from the Alaska Lands bill to home-heating-oil price controls. Roeder concluded that "in both houses of Congress, on vote after vote, there has been a consistent correlation between votes and oil industry contributions." When representatives voted to prohibit development in large portions of the Alaskan wilderness, oil interests opposed the bill because it would close off the lands to exploration. The representatives who voted against the oil interests had received an average campaign contribution of $1,855, while those who cast pro-oil votes had received $7,055, four times as much. In a crucial Senate vote on oil depletion, those who voted against had received an average of $3,326, and those voting pro-oil, $46,545, which was fourteen times greater.

However, this is not the whole story. The relationship between the oil industry and the government agency that regulates it, the Department of Energy (DOE), is usually a cozy one. In fact, many of the agency's senior and middle executives came from the oil industry. At times, the relationship has become sordid, as in the case of John Iannone.[22] Iannone worked as a consultant to the Federal Energy Administration, the predecessor of the Department of Energy, from 1974 to 1976. In this position, he was instrumental in persuading the Federal Energy Administration to raise the price of gasoline, which resulted in profits of $600 million to the industry. When he later left the government, he became associated with the American Petroleum Institute, yet he continued to spend time at the Department of Energy during the Carter administration. He was able to supply the American Petroleum Institute with secret government plans before they became public, which was of great value to the oil interests' lobby. For example, he obtained copies of more than 20 vital draft rule-making and internal memoranda and various studies before they were made public. Iannone might still be spending time in the Department of Energy had he not trumpeted his achievements in an internal report to the American Petroleum Institute, a copy of which was leaked to Ralph Nader. Ensuing congressional hearings found that Iannone was not alone in this work; other American Petroleum Institute personnel were also reporting on the Department of Energy's sensitive internal operations as well.

All of this double-dealing and abuse of corporate power has worked to the financial advantage of the oil industry. In some of its great victories, the industry significantly gutted the windfall profits tax, achieved decontrol of oil and natural gas, and staved off every attempt to break up the vertical monopolies of the major oil corporations. The head of Energy Action, an oil industry watchdog group, said, "It is a damned impressive record. It is even more impressive when you realize that the things they pulled off are opposed by the vast majority of the American people."[23]

Chapter 4

THE DRUGMAKERS

In December 1984, the multinational pharmaceutical corporation Smith-kline, with $2 billion annual sales at the time, pleaded guilty, and three of its executives pleaded no contest, to federal criminal charges of having suppressed information about adverse drug reactions in their reports to the Food and Drug Administration (FDA) on Selacryn, a drug widely used to control high blood pressure. The FDA later linked the drug to hundreds of cases of liver damage, including jaundice and hepatitis. During the eight months the company marketed Selacryn, 60 of 265,000 persons using the drug died and 513 suffered liver damage. The government charge also listed 20 counts of failure to give adequate warnings to consumers on the labels about the drug's known danger to the liver. This is not an isolated case.

There has been a veritable explosion of so-called miracle drugs produced by pharmaceutical companies during the twentieth century. Much of it began with the discovery in 1928 of penicillin by the British scientist Sir Alexander Fleming. As a result of these great advances, many former killer diseases are now curable. As a result of the pharmaceutical industry's great strides, the lives of millions of people throughout the world can now be saved, prolonged, and enriched. These great, often life-saving contributions to the health of Americans and others do not mean, however, that pharmaceutical companies have the right to abuse their power to help mankind. Although the miracle drugs of the twentieth century have produced immense profits for the industrial giants that dominate the industry, the quest for ever-greater profits has led many of them to engage in a range of unethical and illegal practices. Some companies have encouraged the unnecessary use of drugs; others have sold vital drugs at exorbitant prices; still others have promoted worthless drugs; and some have improperly tested, manufactured, and sold unsafe drugs. Several of the pharmaceutical giants have also engaged in foreign bribery in order to gain an advantage in the highly competitive pharmaceutical market. Finally, some have been charged with illegally conspiring to fix high prices for certain life-saving drugs.

Despite government efforts to protect the safety of consumers, major pharmaceutical companies have racked up a far worse record of federal law violations than any other industry except oil and automotive. A far-reaching study of *Fortune* 500 violations found the pharmaceutical industry to be involved in 1 out of every 10 cases of violations, and 1 in 8 cases of serious or moderately serious violations.[1] Serious violations included making unsafe products. As compared with other industries, the pharmaceuticals had 2.5 times their share of all violations, and 2.3 times more of the moderately serious or serious violations. One out of 10 of all the penalties the government imposed on large corporations for serious violations were levied on the pharmaceutical industry. One corporation alone had violated federal laws 21 times in a 2-year period.

PROMOTING A "DRUGGED" SOCIETY

In terms of sales in 1988, the five largest American pharmaceutical companies are the following: Johnson and Johnson, $9.0 billion; Bristol-Myers, $5.9 billion; Merck, $5.5 billion; American Home Products, $5.5 billion; and Pfizer, $5.3 billion. Other large pharmaceutical companies with sales over $4 billion were Abbott, Smithkline-Beckman, and Lilly (Eli). Each year, consumers spend more than $10 billion on over-the-counter (OTC) drugs. Because of their extensive advertising, drug companies encourage an excessive use of drugs. Under the pharmaceutical companies' influence, Americans have become habituated to letting legal drugs, as well as street drugs and alcohol, help them solve their problems. Our society has become so dependent on legal drugs that many drug abuse specialists believe that a basic cause of the increasingly widespread use of prohibited drugs like cocaine is the public's habit of "taking something" to relieve the anxieties and depressions caused by normal everyday living. People apparently find it easier to pop a pill than to face up to their personal problems.

The excessive promotion of over-the-counter drugs has made many people believe that there is a pill for every illness as well as a chemical answer to every physical, emotional, and social discomfort. The drug companies' massive advertising campaigns, in response to these beliefs, promote medicines that, they claim, will relieve almost any pain, tension, or discomfort. Any pharmacy or supermarket shelf, as well as most family medicine chests, offers testimony to the success of their mass media campaigns. The taking of too many drugs is particularly a problem among America's elderly. A former editor of the prestigious *New England Journal of Medicine* delivered a scathing indictment of drug advertising on television.

> The promoter, in coaxing or authoritarian tones, advises you to put your faith in the health or comfort-promoting effects of a "special ingredient," a product with "extra strength" or an agent "most recommended by doctors," but the nature of the potent miracle drug is not revealed. It might be snake oil, sassafras, or Dr. Pangloss' magic powder. Such ads are designed to outsmart too-trusting or unwary prospects.... Drugs affect health, the most precious of human possessions. Yet over-the-counter products are marketed on television by methods similar to those used to promote underwear, house paint and laundry soap. Indeed, as described by one television ad creator, television commercials observe a basic routine: "Thirty times a night you'll see it. Seven seconds of the problem, 14 seconds of solution when somebody tells the poor slob with the problem how the product can solve it, seven seconds of reward, and a closing two-second shot of the package."[2]

The makers of the painkillers Anacin, Bayer, Bufferin, and Excedrin conduct massive advertising efforts to capture over $800 million in sales of the $1.8 billion spent on over-the-counter painkillers. There is no scientifically sound basis on which to distinguish pronounced possible therapeutic differences between these products, nor are they therapeutically superior to any plain five-grain generic aspirin that sells for about one-fifth the cost. All these products contain aspirin (or a combination of aspirin and acetaminophen, as in Excedrin) as their only effective ingredient for relieving pain. As several health experts put it, "by spending $150 million on advertising, their makers convinced people to pay $800 million for aspirin and acetaminophen that should have cost two or three hundred million dollars."[3] A federal court of appeals upheld a Federal Trade Commission ruling that the Anacin ads in which the manufacturers claimed this product to contain "the pain reliever doctors recommend most" was misleading. Because the ads did not disclose that the pain reliever being referred to was aspirin, they were attempting to convince consumers that Anacin relieved pain more effectively than aspirin.

As they seek to gain more of this lucrative painkiller market, drug companies have for years sued each other repeatedly over the others' claims. American Home Products, for example, sued rival Johnson and Johnson in 1987 for claiming that Extra Strength Tylenol's (acetaminophen) slogan, "You can't buy a more potent pain reliever without a prescription," is false and misleading. Federal Judge William C. Conner ruled in this fiercely contested suit that the Tylenol slogan was definitely misleading. In his 65-page opinion, the judge then prescribed a dose of truth for the public to ease the pain of such analgesic ads. He admonished: "Don't be fooled by headlines and pictures; . . . beware of every word, even the smallest one, in an ad; . . . claims about the number of doctors recommending a drug don't mean much; . . . and repeating an advertising slogan doesn't make it true."[4]

Parents who have developed the habit of taking pills for their discomforts and tensions may also play a significant role in our "pill-popping" culture. Their children likewise learn to look to drugs to help them avoid unpleasant aspects of their lives, and some may drift into the use of illegal drugs such as marijuana, cocaine, amphetamines, and barbituates. John Braithwaite, in *Corporate Crime in the Pharmaceutical Industry*, elaborates further on the comparisons between the pharmaceutical corporations that "push" such legal drugs as Valium and Darvon, which can lead to addiction and drug dependency problems, and those that sell illegal drugs. "People who foster dependence on illicit drugs such as heroin are regarded as among the most unscrupulous pariahs of modern civilization. In contrast, pushers of licit drugs tend to be viewed as altruistically-motivated purveyors of a social good."[5] For example, sales of the highly profitable and addictive prescription tranquilizer Valium have been phenomenal throughout the last two decades. Valium's manufacturer, Hoffman-LaRoche, advertises this drug extensively in medical journals, and the company's promotional agents visit thousands of physicians. In 1980 alone, Americans filled over 33 million prescriptions for Valium, a total of 1.8 billion pills, on which they spent $293 million, or four-fifths of a million dollars each day.

Pharmaceutical firms spend as much as one-fifth of their huge budgets on advertising directed at doctors and pharmacists. The pharmaceutical companies subtly convert doctors into "pushers" of their drug products. On the average, doctors prescribe one or more drugs three out of every five times a patient visits their offices. Unfortunately, according to a 1986 survey of the National Center for Health Statistics, physicians still largely prescribe drugs by trade names. The generic name is used on the medical record only about one in five times. Doctors face a bewildering array of brand names—20,000 for 700 prescription drugs—and so many drugs come on the market each year that most physicians rely heavily on pharmaceutical representatives, known as detail men or reps, who now number about 25,000 in the United States. Pharmaceutical corporations regularly send their representatives to doctors' offices and hospitals to induce them to prescribe their products. Detail men may earn a bonus based on how much of their products the doctors prescribe. As they distribute samples and explain the advantages of their products over those of their competitors, they try to convince physicians to prescribe them. Physicians who receive the most visits from drug detail men generally prescribe the most drugs.[6] According to Senate hearings, Merck detail men were given these written instructions about selling their anti-arthritic Indocin during the 1970s:

"Tell 'em again, and again, and again."

"Tell 'em until they are sold and stay sold."

"For these entities he is presently prescribing steroids, aminopyrine-like buta-zones, aspirin, or limited analgesics like Darvon and the almost worthless muscle relaxants."

"You've told this story now, probably 130 times. The physician, however, has heard it only once. So, go back, and tell it again and again and again and again, until it is indelibly impressed in his mind and he starts—and continues—to prescribe Indocin. Let's go."

"Let's stand on our little old two feet this month and sell the benefits of Indocin."

"Take off the kid gloves. If he wants to use aspirin as base line therapy, let him use it. Chances are the patient is already taking aspirin. He has come to the physician because aspirin alone is not affording satisfactory, optimal effects."

"Now every extra bottle of 1,000 Indocin that you sell is worth an extra $2.80 in incentive payments. Go get it. Pile it in."[7]

Most physicians feel that this method of promoting pharmaceuticals is not ethical. It is even dangerous, as some of the more unscrupulous or overly zealous reps may give doctors biased or even incorrect information about their products. Rarely do they mention adverse effects or articles in medical journals questioning their use. For example, Senate investigators discovered that Merck's instructions to its sales reps had suggested dosages of their highly toxic Indocin in excess of the dosages approved by the Food and Drug Administration.

Some detail men have expense accounts to entertain physicians and thus become better acquainted with them and may even make physicians indebted to them. Pharmaceutical companies also often give personal gifts to physicians, a subtle form of persuading them to use their products and also to influence other physicians. In some cases, the value of the gifts that the sales reps distribute is related to the volume of company products either prescribed, or likely to be prescribed, by the physician. Hearings conducted by Senator Edward Kennedy (D-Mass.) in 1974 uncovered the fact that 20 pharmaceutical companies had given $12.8 million in gifts to members of the health-care profession. Among the gifts to doctors were freezers, tape recorders, stethoscopes, and even golf balls with the name of the drug manufacturer stamped on them.

Drug companies may even give direct monetary rewards to physicians for prescribing their drug products. They may pay doctors for so-called tests of the drug, whereby the doctors simply use it for their patients and then report the results. Assuming that the use of the drugs appears to be favorable, doctors may receive fees to give speeches on the merits of a drug to other doctors; companies may even pay the doctors for favorable articles published in journals. Drug companies may also further influence physicians to use their products by paying their expenses to attend resort meetings about a drug. For example, in 1988 Ciba-Geigy held such a weekend meeting in the Caribbean to discuss their drug Voltarin.[8] Selected doctors presented only favorable information.

INEFFECTIVE DRUGS

The average American spends over $40 a year on over-the-counter drugs; a family of four spends more than $100.[9] They choose the products from an estimated 300,000 so-called "different" OTC drugs. However, most of the drugs they buy fail to work as advertised. The ingredients in fewer than a third of the 343 well-known over-the-counter drugs surveyed in 1983 by the Washington, D.C.-based Public Citizen Health Research Group's were both safe and effective for their intended use.[10] Their study was based on the current status of ingredients contained in the FDA's ongoing OTC Drug Register. The ingredients were evaluated by FDA Advisory panels. Among the top-selling products which lacked evidence of safety and effectiveness were Dristan, Preparation H, Listerine, Absorbine, Jr., Sleep-Eze, and Sinutab. The Food and Drug Administration has allowed many ineffective and unsafe over-the-counter drugs to remain on the market for an average of 20 years in spite of the strengthened 1962 Food, Drug, and Cosmetic Act that charged the Food and Drug Administration authorities with their removal. The FDA did review the therapeutic category of over-the-counter drugs (such as cough and cold remedies or nighttime sleeping aids) to ascertain if the ingredients contained in the 300,000 brands really were safe and effective; few drugs were removed. Even though a large proportion of the drugs now on the market have been proven to be ineffective, they are still marketed due to government lethargy and timidity as well as the orchestrated pressures on the Food and Drug Administration by drug companies that are anxious for the drugs to remain on the market.

Drug manufacturers seem to assume that a mixture of several ingredients impresses consumers more than a single substance. Most drug products therefore contain a combination of two or more ingredients. Their safety and efficacy thus depends not only on how safe and effective the individual components are in treating specific symptoms but also how safe and effective the drugs are when used in combination. Many over-the-counter and prescription drugs, particularly cough and cold remedies, may contain as many as five different ingredients, some of which may be only partially effective. For example, Americans have spent hundreds of millions of dollars on curing the nighttime symptoms of sniffling, sneezing, coughing, aching, and head-stuffiness, which ads assure them can be alleviated with a medicine called Nyquil. Like many other best-selling drugs, Nyquil contains an ingredient that the Food and Drug Administration says lacks effectiveness. Furthermore, Nyquil uses a shotgun approach of four ingredients; like other "improved" products, this remedy treats multiple symptoms, rarely all present at the same time, with costly multiple ingredients.

Prescription drug sales total $30 billion annually. The Public Citizen Health Research Group also found in 1982 that 607 frequently used prescription drugs lacked evidence of effectiveness.[11] These widely used drugs include those prescribed for heart pain and disorders of the digestive tract, the circulatory system, and the skin, as well as drugs used for coughs, colds, and allergies. Based on prescriptions filled in 1979, the expenditure for each drug ranged from $24 million to $67 million in retail sales. Among the top ten less-than-effective drugs were Donatil (Robins), prescribed for digestive disorders; Isordil (Ives) for heart pain; Librax (Roche) for irritable bowel disorders; and Ornade Spansules (Smithkline) for allergic conditions and common colds. The well-publicized 1973 Senate hearings on the pharmaceutical industry had reached a somewhat similar conclusion about the efficacy of prescription drugs. They found that one out of every eight prescriptions filled, costing more than $1.1 million, was for a drug not considered effective by government standards. The chairman, Senator Gaylord Nelson (D-Wis.) said, "Drug companies need to be exposed and censured and the law needs to be tightened to control their advertising."[12]

UNSAFE DRUGS

Some "miracle" drugs have potentially dangerous side effects that can maim and kill. Among many examples, in 1985, only a year after Dow Chemical discontinued the sale of Benedictin, which had been prescribed for morning sickness since 1958, the company agreed to settle $120 million in 700 damage suits that charged that the drug had caused birth defects. Present safety standards for drugs began in 1906 with the passage of the first U.S. law to establish drug purity standards. Thirty-two years later, the Food, Drug, and Cosmetic Act of 1938 required the regulation of all prescription drugs and proof of their safety before they could be marketed. Drugs introduced prior to 1938 were not bound by these requirements of evidence of effectiveness as long as their manufacturers did not alter their composition, the dosage form, or the labeling. The Elixir Sulfanilamide case in the 1930s actually precipitated the passage of this law. This elixir, manufactured by a Tennessee company, claimed to "build up health," and contained a solvent that kept sulfanilamide, a widely used drug, in liquid form. The solvent, di-ethylene glycol, was transformed into kidney-destroying oxalic acid. The elixir was responsible for at least 107 deaths. In 1962, Congress toughened the Food, Drug, and Cosmetic Act to require mandatory tests for all new prescription drugs to assure the FDA of their safety and effectiveness.

The safety of a drug depends basically on three things. First, the drug company must submit evidence that it has been properly tested and the Food and Drug Administration must approve it before the company can market it. Second, the drug company must report to the FDA any adverse results from the use of the drug. Third, the pharmaceutical company must produce the approved drug according to acceptable safety standards. Drug testing must include evidence submitted by qualified experts based on an often elaborate program of tests on animal and clinical (human) subjects. The tests are designed to protect drug consumers, not only in terms of safety but also in proven effectiveness of the prescription drug in treating the illness for which it is intended. However, as Braithwaite has pointed out, among pharmaceutical companies there is often a "difference between the need for commitment to integrity and quality at operating levels of the organization and the need for top management to be able to suspend that commitment for decisions of major financial impact."[13]

Potentially dangerous drug products may even reach the market because of illegal and fraudulent testing practices. Drug testing is generally carried out for pharmaceutical companies by special laboratories that they engage, although sometimes the corporation does the testing itself. The record of accurate and fair testing is not good. According to a 1976 study made by the Food and Drug Administration and the General Accounting Office, 75 percent of the 238 clinical investigations of drug products had failed to comply with the law. In 25 percent of these cases the testing facility had not maintained adequate records on the patients' conditions prior to, during, and after the testing; in 28 percent of the cases they had not adhered to the study design; and in 12 percent of the cases they had failed to supervise the work properly. Faulty safety testing practices include hiding from the Food and Drug Administration certain side effects, many of them serious; maintaining inadequate records of tests; submitting reports on fictitious subjects and subjects to whom the drug was never administered; giving drugs to inappropriate subjects who were not representative of the population affected; reporting results of clinical work that was not actually performed; and hiring doctors to report on the effects of drugs who may have then either manipulated or falsified clinical data.

When pharmaceutical companies hire outside laboratories to perform the necessary tests prior to Food and Drug Administration approval, they may put indirect or direct pressure on the laboratory to provide them with favorable test results. Some corporations see a possible enormous profit in a new drug they are anxious to market, and so they may tend to choose a laboratory that is more interested in the profit it might continue to make if it can turn out favorable test results than in the scientific accuracy of its testing. The submission of unfavorable results may mean the loss of lucrative contracts in the future. Writing in 1984, Braithwaite found, for example, that Food and Drug Administration officers were of the opinion that certain contract drug testing laboratories had flourished by fabricating data and cutting the corners of careful scientific standards.[14]

Two former vice presidents of Biometric Testing, one of the largest testing companies, pleaded guilty in 1979 to charges of having conspired to falsify reports on animal tests in order to prove a drug harmless when the animals had not actually been tested. Another major offender in performing improper drug tests was Industrial Bio-Test Laboratories, one of the firms that tests products for some of the world's largest pharmaceutical and pesticide producers. Industrial Bio-Test had conducted between 35 and 40 percent of all toxicology tests for drug companies.[15] Their laboratories reported on thousands of clinical tests they had performed, but the Food and Drug Administration claimed that 80 percent of some 900 tests submitted to them contained invalid data, some of which had been deliberately falsified. The Food and Drug Administration charged that the laboratory's tests on Naprosyn, an anti-inflammatory drug, were so false that it ordered the drug, manufactured by Syntex Corporation, off the market. After new tests, it was later approved. Rats involved in the first test were so improperly handled that no judgment could be made about Naprosyn's safety. Several animals were recorded as having died on more than one date; weights were recorded on live animals that were actually dead on that date. When government investigators zeroed in on Industrial Bio-Test for a grand jury investigation of the charges, the company shredded laboratory records. In 1984, the Food and Drug Administration informed the major drug companies that any data collected by Industrial Bio-Test would, in the future, be subjected to careful Food and Drug Administration checking.

The most shocking case of a manufacturer involved in drug testing fraud was the nightmare caused by fraudulent testing of Mer/29 by the large pharmaceutical company Richardson-Merrill and its subsidiary, Merrill.[16] The Food and Drug Administration approved this drug in the early 1960s, intended to reduce blood cholesterol levels, on the basis of evidence submitted to it by Richardson-Merrill, and more than 300,000 patients subsequently used the drug prior to its withdrawal not many months after its approval by Food and Drug Administration order. Within a short period of time, complaints of serious side effects began to come in, including changes in the blood and reproductive organs, and serious damage to eyes and skin, as well as baldness. It turned out that when test monkeys, dogs, and rats became ill or died, test supervisors ordered testing personnel to change the test data and even to substitute healthy animals for the sick group. They also altered test records. Monkeys tested for only 8 months were reported as having been on the drug for 16 months. Also falsified was the amount of Mer/29 dosages given to the monkeys; many control monkeys were not used as controls at all. The company's drug approval application stated that the monkeys had not lost weight, when in fact they had; they also stated that certain monkeys had suffered no liver or gall bladder damage, when in fact they had. In some cases, irreparable eye and reproductive-organ damage to dogs was covered up. The corporation cover-up on the animal testing results was followed by cover-up of adverse results of the drug use on human beings. The company received many reports from doctors of such problems as eye disorders and swellings. On company orders, the doctors were told, without evidence, that the effects about which they were complaining were due to the administration of some other drug along with Mer/29. The Department of Justice prosecuted Richardson-Merrill and its subsidiary, Merrill, along with several of their executives. All later pleaded no contest to a variety of criminal charges. The court fined the corporations $60,000 and $20,000 respectively, and the executives received sentences of six months probation. Almost 500 civil suits followed, and the settlements in these cases totaled approximately $200 million.

During the 1970s the government charged G. D. Searle, a leading pharmaceutical corporation, with widespread fraud and incompetence in its own drug-safety testing program, particularly that involving the testing of Aldactone, Flagyl, and Norpace. Many fraudulent incidents occurred in the tests; test animals reported in good condition were actually dead, rats listed as dead were later listed as being alive, then dead, then resurrected once or even twice more. In Searle's other tests, an animal was used more than once, which would automatically invalidate test results. Some test animals with gross lesions were not examined. Searle researchers removed tumors from other test animals during the course of the study but the animals were still included. When reports on tissue slides of test animals were contradictory, Searle submitted only the favorable test reports, and record-keeping was generally inept. The Food and Drug Administration felt that Searle should be criminally prosecuted for its pattern of irresponsible drug testing. Although the Department of Justice brought a grand jury action against Searle, the grand jury decided not to indict Searle or any of its executives. The company felt itself vindicated, and one of its executives said, "While there might have been a little dishonesty here and there, basically it was a problem of incompetence and poor record-keeping among our research staff."[17]

After the Food and Drug Administration has approved a drug, it requires all drug companies to inform them of any reported adverse effects from drugs they are marketing. For example, if doctors report to the drug company that patients have become sick or died, it is the company's responsibility to notify the FDA. Drug companies do not always, however, file such reports. For example, Eli Lilly failed to report serious, and even fatal, side effects from the anti-arthritic drug Oraflex. When the Food and Drug Administration approved Oraflex for U.S. marketing in May 1982, the company claimed such good results, both in safety and efficacy, that within six weeks of its approval, half a million Oraflex prescriptions had been sold. It was later discovered that the company had known from Lilly's United Kingdom subsidiary that at least 25 persons who were taking the drug in Great Britain had died, but it had not reported either these or some other adverse reactions that had occurred elsewhere to the Food and Drug Administration. The U.S. Department of Justice reported, for example, in a June meeting of Lilly officials with the FDA that although "Lilly knew of approximately 50 unpublished liver and kidney reactions that had occurred in the United Kingdom, the company did not tell the FDA about any of the unpublished overseas reactions and discussed only those that had been published in the medical literature."[18] The Food and Drug Administration charged that the company had also withheld reports of at least 8 deaths and 10 other cases of near-fatal liver or kidney damage that had occurred in the United States during the testing period.

Several liability suits were filed against Lilly. In 1983, a Georgia federal grand jury found the company responsible for the death of an elderly woman who took Oraflex; the court ordered Lilly to pay $6 million in damages to the woman's son. During the trial, the former executive vice president of Lilly Research Laboratories testified that the company did know of the deaths in Europe, but he claimed that the cause of these fatalities was not entirely clear, and that Lilly was required to report only "severe unexpected events" to the Food and Drug Administration. When Lilly withdrew Oraflex in late August 1982, there had been reports of 49 Oraflex-related deaths and 916 near-fatal injuries in the United States. In August 1985, Lilly pleaded guilty to 25 misdemeanor counts rather than the felonies of failing to notify the U.S. government as required by law; the company was fined $25,000 and the chief medical officer received a fine of $15,000.

Many drug companies have poor records in the safe manufacture of approved drugs. In fact, the industry has 5.6 times its share of product manufacturing violations when measured against all *Fortune* 500 corporations, and 5.8 times more serious cases such as the unsafe manufacture and mislabeling of drugs.[19] For example, drugs may contain a less expensive ingredient than indicated on the label or may contain more dangerous levels of drugs than the label states. Human drug recalls during fiscal 1986 were 330; 1987, 437; 1988, 237 and 1989, 257, according to Food and Drug Administration reports.

In the past, the Food and Drug Administration has found bottles of Vitamin B_1 mislabeled as B_{12}, erythromycin mislabeled as a painkiller, 1/4-grain phenobarbital tablets mislabeled as 1/2-grain, and 5 mg. warfarin tablets (for control of blood clotting) mislabeled as 2 1/2 mg. tablets.[20] One liver preparation approved only for veterinary use was mislabeled and marketed for injection into human beings. Food and Drug Administration tests picked up nitroglycerin tables (for control of anginal heart pain) containing as little as 16 percent of the labeled amount of the drug and reserpine (for hypertension) with 25 percent. The Food and Drug Administration tests similarly have disclosed ophthalmic eye ointments contaminated with metal particles, drugs with mold, and hormone solutions with unidentified fever-producing contaminants. One lot of an antihistamine solution was shipped by the company in bottles that reportedly exploded because of the gas produced by contaminating bacteria.

PRICE-GOUGING

Throughout most of the past 30 years, the pharmaceutical industry has ranked first or second in profitability of all U.S. industries. They have become the most profitable of all corporate giants. In 1988, the pharmaceuticals' return on sales was 13.5 percent, or almost three times greater than the return on sales for all industries as a whole. In 1988, the median return on their equities was a tremendous 23.6 percent. In 1987, a House Subcommittee on Health and the Environment reported that prescription drug prices had risen 8 percent in 1986, four times the rate of the overall consumer price increase. For example, the price of the popular heart drug, Inderal, rose an average of 14 percent a year from 1984 to 1986. The chairman of the subcommittee, Henry Waxman (D-Calif.) said that "what is going on is greed on a massive scale."[21] He added, "They have taken advantage of the public. They have raised their prices as much as the market will bear."

Profits are extremely high when prescription drugs are produced under patents that give their manufacturers a legal price monopoly. Furthermore, the company can extend this legal price monopoly beyond the normal 17-year patent-protection period through the practice of evergreening. In this commonly used procedure, a company files a new patent application that modifies the originally patented formula, if only in a minor way. Evergreening adds several more years to the monopoly protection, and makes a successful drug even more profitable.

Drug prices are higher when a few companies control the market. For example, more than a hundred companies sell Vitamin C, but almost the entire output of Vitamin C is produced by three manufacturers: Merck, Pfizer, and Roche. In 1973, four pharmaceutical companies were providing the following percentages of market sales for these medications: sedatives, 61 percent; analgesics, 66 percent; antibiotics, 69 percent; antihistamines, 76 percent; tranquilizers, 86 percent; and anti-arthritics, 96 percent.[22] The peculiar nature of the industry also shelters manufacturers from much price competition on consumer prescription drugs because it is the physician, not the consumer, who actually decides what medication to prescribe. Seldom do physicians make their decisions on the basis of cost except when they prescribe generic drugs.

The drug industry claims that it has high research costs, yet only a fraction of the sales dollar is actually spent on research. For example, a House Subcommittee on Health and the Environment survey of 25 drugmakers found that between 1982 and 1986 price increases for existing drugs had produced additional revenues of $4.7 billion, while research and development expenditures were $1.6 billion.[23] The survey also found that much of the money spent on research and development has actually gone for so-called "copy-cat" versions of already successful drugs.

In contrast to the United States, the governments of most developed and many developing countries control drug prices, basing prices on a formula that incorporates the costs of the raw materials, research, production, distribution, and a set profit margin. As a result, there are enormous cost differences for identical drugs sold in the United States and elsewhere in the world. In 1989, five-milligram tablets of Valium cost approximately $.38 apiece in the United States and sell for $.01 in India, where the government regulates drug prices. One authority on pharmaceuticals has concluded about the situation in the United States that "since the market and courts have failed to regulate pharmaceutical prices effectively, and since self-regulation of pricing would be to put Dracula in charge of the blood bank, the only course is for greater government price controls of pharmaceutical products."[24]

In addition to government-set prices, another alternative for reducing costs to consumers is an increase in generic drug usage. These non–brand name products sell for one half or more the price of a brand name equivalent. The price difference is largely due to the elimination of the costly advertising campaigns the drug companies use to promote their brand name products. An FTC study has shown that in 1984 doctors prescribed generic drugs about 15 percent of the time, at savings of from $130 million to $236 million. One third of all prescriptions written in the United States in 1989 are filled with generic drugs, which usually sell for two-thirds to one-half the name brands.[25] In fact, West Germany, where U.S. companies account for 20 percent of pharmaceutical sales, passed a law in 1988 that reduced the prices of patent-protected drugs to the level of those of generic or unbranded drugs.

Many giant pharmaceutical companies savagely fight the use of generic drugs, which now have annual sales of about $2 billion and are steadily increasing. Actually, the generic drugs are subject to the same Food and Drug Administration regulations as brand name drugs. Moreover, several corporations that make brand name products also manufacture generic drugs, on which profit margins are lower. They include Squibb, Warner-Lambert, American Cyanamid, and Ciba-Geigy, companies that together account for some 25 percent of the generic market in 1989. A scandal involving some generic pharmaceutical companies broke out in 1989 and resulted in strong FDA action and the revocation of approval for 30 generic drugs made by three companies. The FDA accused the drug companies of bribing its inspectors and of doctoring their records. Of the estimated 300 generic drug manufacturers, however, only a fraction were involved in fraud or potentially fraudulent activities. A lead *Wall Street Journal* article reported that these and other problems were a legacy of the Reagan administration's push to deregulate. "By scaling back their enforcement actions while publicly embracing the generic drug industry as a 'partner' rather than an adversary, the FDA created an 'atmosphere of lawlessness,' says Sydney Wolfe, head of the Public Citizen Health Research Group."[26] Many generic drugs come on the market following the expiration of the brand name patent, as occurred in 1985 when Hoffman-LaRoche's 1959 patent for Valium finally expired. The Food and Drug Administration approved three generic versions of this popular tranquilizer. As a result, the cost difference became significant: In 1989, 100 Valium 5-milligram tablets generally cost $38, while 100 of a generic version, Diazepam, cost only $14. When questioned about the advantages of a brand name drug over a less-expensive alternative product, an authority on drug usage replied, "There is none, unless you enjoy subsidizing television ads at your own expense. The main difference is created by advertising geniuses."[27]

Chapter 5

THE "PATRIOTIC" DEFENSE INDUSTRY

America's problems with defense contractors began with the birth of the nation. During the Revolutionary War, George Washington himself blasted the defense contractors who were supplying his Continental Army with defective arms and bullets. "These murderers of our cause ought to be hunted down as pests of society and the greatest enemies to the happiness of America. I wish to God that the most atrocious of each state was hung...upon a gallows five times as high as the one prepared for Haman." Throughout the Civil War, the country was also plagued by the exploitation and corruption of the arms suppliers; bullets were even filled with sawdust instead of gunpowder. These rip-offs have continued into the twentieth century. During World War I, profiteering, abuse of political power, arrogance, and fraud typified the defense industry, with DuPont and Bethlehem Steel leading the pack. During World War II, a little-known senator from Missouri, Harry Truman, suddenly found himself catapulted into fame, the vice presidency, and ultimately the presidency of the United States, primarily because of his investigations into armsmakers' fraud and excessive profiteering. Congressional hearings conducted by Senator William Proxmire (D-Wis.) during the Vietnam War revealed similar defense industry exploitation.

As sordid as these accounts of past history have been, they are a mere prelude to the defense industry's present-day failure to put patriotism before profits. During the 1980s, the Reagan administration spent over $1 trillion on armaments; investigations have revealed thousands of fraudulent overcharges, billings for non-existent work, double sets of books, kickbacks, illegal gifts to government personnel, and the wide-

spread misuse of funds, including support of the flamboyant lifestyles
of defense industry executives. General Dynamics was suspended from
doing defense work twice in 1985 for numerous allegations of wrongdoing. General Electric pleaded guilty in 1985 to 108 counts of submitting false claims and false statements. Also in 1985, Rockwell
International pleaded guilty to 20 counts of timecard fraud. In 1986,
the Department of Justice indicted two divisions of Litton Industries for
fraudulent charges; the company paid $15 million in fines and three
former employees were sentenced. Martin Marietta pleaded guilty in
1987 to mail fraud and making false statements on a $1-million travel
voucher fraud scheme. TRW, Inc., pleaded guilty in 1987 to 10 counts
of making false statements and reimbursed the government $17 million
in a "global settlement" that allowed it to escape suspension from the
defense business.

Fraud in the defense industry continued unabated through the late
1980s. In 1988, for example, Sunstrand Corporation, a defense contractor with $1.4 billion in annual sales, pleaded guilty to federal criminal
fraud charges and paid a $115 million settlement for overbilling for
airplane parts. This was, to date, the largest settlement of a criminal
defense-fraud procurement case. The company admitted to having concealed millions of dollars of cost overruns by improperly billing those
costs to the government as overhead. Sunstrand admitted to having
devised a scheme to take tax write-offs on bogus losses. It also admitted
to overbilling for millions of dollars for such unallowable expenses as
baby-sitters, saunas, golf, movies, and dog kennels as well as servants for
Sunstrand executives' homes. In addition, the corporation admitted that
it concealed more than $100,000 used to provide wine, liquor, and meals,
as well as tickets to the theater and sporting events, for Defense Department employees and their spouses, "to improve its ability to market
its product to the Defense Department."[1]

A scandal of unprecedented proportions swept the defense industry
in 1988, following two years of secret FBI investigations. The scandal
involved bribery, fraud, and bid-rigging on an immense scale. It implicated at least 14 major defense contractors and was related to 100 defense
contracts worth tens of billions of dollars. The Army reacted immediately
by suspending all contracts with several major defense contractors, including McDonnell Douglas, Litton Industries, Northrop, United Technologies, Teledyne, and Unisys, until a task force drew up a contract
clause allowing the government to recover profits from "illegal or improper activity."

According to the accusations, defense contractors had illegally bought
secret Department of Defense information about plans, budgets, and
contract bids of other corporations from government employees. The
contractors bribed Department of Defense employees using cash gifts

or promises of future employment. The deals were largely made through paid "defense consultants" who acted as conduits for gathering proprietary information from the military services and then passed it on to the defense contractors. Their work resembled that of "agents" who do the dirty work in the bribery of foreign officials by U.S. corporations. According to an FBI warrant, for example, United Technologies obtained secret documents from the Pentagon that detailed General Electric proposals for engines of a new type of Navy aircraft. Unsealed court papers revealed that McDonnell Douglas gained extraordinary access to competitors' bids on the F-18 fighter program and other weapons systems. Charges that defense contractors would engage in such wholesale bribery of Department of Defense employees, at both minor and top-rung levels, shocked even hardened observers of the defense industry. Congress reacted to this scandal by raising the fine for a single fraud case by a defense contractor from $500,000 to $1 million and requiring up to a 10-year prison term for individuals.

Corporate trials were in process as of 1989. Teledyne, one of the nation's large defense contractors, pleaded guilty to conspiracy and agreed to pay more than $4.3 million in penalties. A senior Navy engineer had admitted to taking payoffs for leaking data that helped the firm win a $24 million contract. Teledyne agreed to pay $1.5 million in fines, $2.07 million in civil penalties, and $786,000 in federal investigative costs, and also agreed to sacrifice 13.5 percent of its profit on the contract. Subsequently, two former vice presidents of Teledyne were convicted in connection with the case. They were found guilty of participating in a scheme to hire a defense consultant who, in turn, bribed a Navy official to help Teledyne get a $24-million contract. The officials each drew lenient one-year prison sentences; part of the terms were suspended and the rest was served in half-way houses. The U.S. attorney commented, "This sends a message to corporate America that they cannot wash their hands of this type of activity."[2] A former Unisys vice president pleaded guilty to bribing former Navy research chief, Melvyn Paisley, by helping to arrange the purchase of an Idaho condominium for Mr. Paisley.

These sordid dealings with Defense Department officials are not new. A somewhat similar scandal that involved a number of large corporations in black market activities in secret Pentagon planning documents was disclosed in 1984. As a consequence, Boeing Co., a leading defense contractor and the world's largest aircraft manufacturer, finally pleaded guilty in 1989 to criminal charges and agreed to pay the government more than $5 million for having illegally used classified Pentagon planning documents obtained five years earlier.

Such scandals showed a sharp contrast between the way U.S. taxpayers were being taken and the glowing full-page advertisements defense corporations frequently ran in the *Wall Street Journal* and other news media that bragged of the industry's devotion, efficiency, achievements and success in "making America strong." Congress was shocked by continuing scandalous disclosures. The chairman of the Senate Armed Services Committee, Senator Barry Goldwater (R-Ariz.), complained that "great corporations have unscrupulously been cheating the American public." Senator Charles Grassley (R-Iowa) likened the exploitation of the defense industry to welfare abuse of entitlement programs. "The defense budget has in effect become one of our largest entitlement programs, and it has nursed a new generation of welfare queens: the defense industry."[3] Congressman John D. Dingell (D-Michigan), chairman of the House subcommittee that was then investigating General Dynamics (the nation's second largest defense contractor in 1985) for gross overcharges on Navy nuclear submarine contracts, wrote the following to all House members:

The type of violations found in the General Dynamics case are a way of life throughout the defense industry. Unbelievably, when contractors are challenged on such issues they act offended, as though the behavior were acceptable and the charges against them improper. This is typical of the "catch-me-if-you-can" approach we have so often seen.[4]

THE MILITARY-INDUSTRIAL COMPLEX

During the 1950s, President Dwight D. Eisenhower decried what he considered an unholy alliance between the military and the American arms industry, which he labeled the "military-industrial complex." In his farewell address to the American people in January 1961, he warned: "In the councils of government, we must guard against the acquisition of unwarranted influence, whether sought or unsought, by the military-industrial complex." As a former commander-in-chief of the Allied forces in World War II, he recognized this dangerous coalition of money, power, and politics, and said that the government's excessive expenditures on the military were being caused by the armament industry's pressures on government and Congress. In fact, he feared that the increased power of the military working in conjunction with the armament industry would seriously damage the entire democratic process. Eisenhower cautioned that "the potential for the disastrous rise of misplaced power exists and will persist." In this connection, Norman Cousins has pointed out the dangerous results from letting the military and the defense corporations gain too large a voice in making decisions in matters that concern the life and death of the nation. A military-industrial complex will, he said, result in creating an open channel between the weapon makers and the U.S. Treasury ... in allowing the groups producing the weapons to have a strong voice in deciding what weapons are to be produced and in what quantities ... and in making the national security synonymous with the personal security of those who benefit from military spending.[5]

In 1985, the defense industry employed over 3 million workers; military orders accounted for 30 percent of technological growth in the manufacturing sector, and 20 percent of GNP growth. Military projects accounted for three-fourths of federal research-and-development spending. The diversion of scientists and skilled workers from the commercial sector has contributed significantly to the United States' inability to compete successfully in the international market place.

In 1987 the number one defense contractor, McDonnell Douglas, had prime contracts totaling $8.9 billion, followed by General Dynamics with $7.4 billion, and General Electric with $6.3 billion. The other top defense contractors, in order of dollar amount of contracts, were Lockheed, General Motors, Raytheon, Martin Marietta, United Technologies, Boeing, and Grumman. Potential profits on these contracts run into hundreds of millions of dollars each year. In 1983, major contractors made the following profits from their defense contracts: General Electric, $2.4 billion; General Dynamics, $492.5 million; Boeing, $475 million; and Lockheed, $461.8 million. Notwithstanding such enormous profits, the use of a number of tax loopholes and write-offs enabled 8 of the top 10 Department of Defense contractors typically to pay no corporate income tax for the 1983 tax year.[6] General Dynamics paid no federal income taxes between 1972 and 1985.[7] Senator Dennis DeConcini (D-Ariz.) remarked: "This is incredible. Many of the same corporations that are building systems to defend this country are not paying a cent to contribute to that defense.... Sufficient to say that a minimum corporate income tax is long over-due."[8]

Many of the giant defense contractors are virtual monopolies in the industry; a single corporation may well be the sole, or nearly the sole, producer of certain weapons and weapons parts. General Dynamics, for example, is one of only two firms that build nuclear submarines, and it is the primary producer. During an ABC-network interview in 1985, Secretary of the Navy John Lehman pointed out that it is difficult to expect a defense contractor to cut costs, become more efficient, or obey the law when it knows that it has an arms production stranglehold on the Department of Defense. A good example of this monopolistic stranglehold is the sequence of events that followed the 1985 Department of Justice's criminal investigation of General Dynamics for fraudulent overcharges in its work on a nuclear submarine contract. The government barred General Dynamics from future defense contracts for the second time in a single year. What happened the very next day, however, is typical of what occurs when the government tries to suspend major defense contracts. The Navy announced that it was extending the deadline for bids on four nuclear attack submarines to be used to hunt Soviet subs so that General Dynamics could also submit its bid. The reason for the extension, the Navy said, was that only two companies build nuclear submarines, and a second bid was needed from General Dynamics against the Newport News Shipbuilding and Drydock Company. The assistant secretary of the navy said, "But the problem we're faced with is if we don't extend the deadline, we're facing a sole-source bid. We consider this competition to be very healthy."[9] Then he added a curious twist: "Anyway, they have been suspended because of misconduct on an Army contract."

Large corporations seek lucrative defense and other government contracts because they provide a good chunk of their total revenue and far higher proportionate profits than normal commercial business contracts.[10] Sales to the government in 1984 accounted for more than 70 percent of total sales for General Dynamics, Lockheed, Boeing, McDonnell Douglas, and Northrop. According to a 1986 General Accounting Office study, defense contractors earned 35 percent higher profits than commercial manufacturers during the period from 1970 to 1979, and 120 percent higher profits during the 1980-to-1983 period. The General Accounting Office study found that defense work was even more lucrative when profits were measured as a percentage of corporate assets. For example, General Dynamics' aerospace work yielded a 49-percent return on its assets in 1984, while its ordinary shipbuilding yielded a return of 4.4 percent.

The defense industry's political clout in Congress is so enormous that one can well understand Eisenhower's warning about the unholy alliance between the military-industrial complex and the government. Defense corporations are large political contributors; in fact, the defense industry was the third largest Political Action Committee (PAC) contributor in the 1985 congressional campaign. The underlying purpose of these contributions is clear: *Common Cause* magazine reported that 41 percent of the contributions went to incumbent members of the House and Senate armed services committees and to the appropriations defense subcommittees. Nearly all the leading defense contractors gave substantial honoraria in 1987 to members of Congress serving on House and Senate Armed Services committees. The defense contractors under investigation in the 1988 Pentagon bribery procurement case had poured millions of dollars into the pockets and campaign treasuries of members of Congress. In 1987, 37 of the 101 members who serve on the four military committees reported receiving about $137,000 in speaking fees from defense contractors publicly linked to the Pentagon inquiry.[11]

The defense industry not only carries out military policy—it helps to create it. Washington, D.C.-based defense lobbyists press for huge arms budgets. Some top lobbyists were formerly important members of Congress; others are former Pentagon officials. These lobbyists impress upon members of Congress that defense appropriations produce jobs back in home districts or states and thus add much to the total economy back home. Forty-eight states have defense plants that employ tens of thousands of persons, and members of Congress are expected to look out for the welfare of their constituents. As Norman Cousins concluded: "Defense plants must be kept going lest the folks back home suffer agonizing withdrawal pains. Like street-corner drug pushers, the Pentagon-Congress-Contractor troika makes America acquiescent by threatening to hold back on the country's supply."[12] Defense contractors also try in other ways to increase the defense budget; for example, General Dynamics once gave a $100,000 contribution to the American Security Council Foundation, a defense lobbying group.

As an example, defense corporations made a major effort to influence legislators to support the controversial 1985 MX missile program, a defense project worth billions of dollars in contracts and thousands of jobs in at least half a dozen states. GTE Corporation, one of the prime MX contractors, gave members of the Massachusetts congressional delegation a detailed sheet showing how much money and how many jobs this project would bring to their state. Some members of congress received form letters from defense contractor employees in their districts, asking them to support the missile project. If elected officials remain unmoved by statistics on defense employment in their districts or by letters from defense employees, the defense contractors have further powers of persuasion, chief among them being their PAC contributions. Thirteen major MX contractors contributed a total of $2.1 million to congressional candidates in the 1983–1984 election campaign, up 47 percent over the previous campaign and up 132 percent from the 1979–1980 election. Some of the increases were large: Northrop Corporation, a leading MX contractor, more than doubled its political contributions of $99,294 in 1981–1982 to $235,298 in 1983–1984.

FRAUDULENT COST OVERRUNS

In the 1980s the Department of Defense could have saved at least an estimated $10 to $30 billion in any given year if defense contractors had cut their cost overruns.[13] Many of the overruns are due to fraudulent or deceptive charges. A 1984 General Accounting Office study revealed that corporate defense contractors deliberately underestimated contract costs by an average of as much as 14 percent. Representative Rose Oaker

(D-Ohio) dramatized these cost overruns when she asked the Department of Defense to prepare a list of all projects in 1982 in which the final costs exceeded 25 percent of the original estimates. The computer list that she finally received was a phenomenal 14.5 feet in length, and it listed billions of dollars in cost overruns. Representative Oaker rolled the list out on the House floor and pointed to a $4-billion cost overrun on a single helicopter project. This sum was about equal to the amount the Reagan administration had proposed for cuts in the Medicare program at the time. In speaking of the cost overruns in his corporation that are characteristic of the aerospace industry, a retired middle-management *Fortune* 500 executive stated:

The big thing was cost overruns on government contracts. Costs were often switched or charged to other projects. For example, the cost of research and development was spread over all projects, even though only one particular project was involved. We promised to meet schedules that we never intended to keep. We were more ethical, however, than some in the aerospace industry.[14]

Admiral Hyman Rickover designed the first American nuclear submarine, and later when he supervised its construction, he constantly brought charges of cost overrun fraud against defense contractors. He said that the frauds included billings for unjustified overhead costs and overpricing, totaling billions of dollars. In one of his many public protests about these frauds, Admiral Rickover declared:

Large defense contractors can let costs come out where they will, and count on getting relief from the Department of Defense.... Wasteful subcontracting practices, inadequate cost controls, shop loafing, and production errors mean little to these contractors, because they will make their money whether their product is good or bad; whether the price is fair or higher than it should be; whether delivery is on time or late. Such matters are inconsequential to the management of most large defense contractors because, as with other regulated industries, they are able to conceal the real facts concerning their management ineptitude from the public and from their stockholders, until they stumble finally into the arms of the government for their salvation.[15]

A favorite scheme of defense contractors is to pad labor costs. Sometimes defense contractors also submit false work time cards. In the past few years, the government has charged General Electric and Sperry Corporation, as well as Rockwell International, the builder of the space shuttle, with using this fraudulent device. The government charged that General Electric, for example, had altered time cards without employees' knowledge and, in some cases, filled in blank time cards and then charged the labor costs to other contracts. Rockwell International pleaded guilty to 20 counts of false billings, and they agreed to pay $1.2 million for false time card fraud. Sperry Corporation admitted in 1983 that it had submitted false time cards to the government. The cards showed work on an airborne launch system for Minuteman missiles when it was actually performed on a target processor for the MX missile. The company made the shift because it could no longer bill the cost overruns to the MX program. Sperry paid the government $850,000 in criminal penalties for this fraud. General Electric and Rockwell International also received a business suspension, although, like General Electric, the suspensions generally lasted a few weeks at most.

General Dynamics' record of corporate misbehavior in the defense industry is hard to top. Navy Secretary John Lehman characterized General Dynamics's corporate philosophy as "Catch us if you can," and Representative Ron Wyden (D-Oregon) said the company's dealings could form the basis for a "handbook on how to fleece the taxpayer."[16] Nonetheless, General Dynamics is generally the nation's second largest defense contractor, with an annual business during the 1980s of more than $8 billion. Its output in guns, tanks, jets, missiles, and nuclear submarines alone could well equip the effective fighting force of many countries. General Dynamics has carried out much of its operations effectively, and for this it should be praised. Far too often, however, it has abused its power and the government has had to charge the corporation with excessive cost overruns, fraudulent claims and poor workmanship, and questionable dealings with the government. In 1984, T. Takis Veliotis, a former vice president and member of General Dynamics' board of directors who had fled to Greece to escape prosecution for kickback charges, publicly accused the corporation of having bilked the Navy out of tens of millions of dollars by fraudulent means, including the falsifying of claims on the Trident nuclear submarine program.[17] The most serious charges involved General Dynamics' overcharges in the construction of the Trident submarines.[18] The submarines were supposed to cost $1.4 billion each; the Navy actually paid $2.5 billion each, a cost overrun of more than $1 billion per submarine. Later, a congressional Joint Economics Committee found that General Dynamics had kept two sets of books. It had submitted one series of cost reports and delivery schedules to the Navy, but it had withheld other estimates that would certainly have raised serious concerns on the part of the Navy about the company's contract performance. Senator William Proxmire (D-Wisconsin) contended that General Dynamics had falsely attributed the cost overruns to thousands of engineering changes that the Navy had ordered when the real reason for them was corporate mismanagement and fraud.[19]

By 1985, government problems with General Dynamics, particularly cost overcharges, had become so serious that the Department of Justice began a criminal investigation. The then Secretary of the Navy John Lehman publicly spoke out about them. He said that General Dynamics

had falsely stated the delivery date of the first Trident submarine, that
the workmanship was faulty, that the corporation had claimed unallowable overhead costs, and that it had used classified government documents to prepare its contract proposals. Secretary Lehman charged,
moreover, that for 12 years the General Dynamics Electric Boat Division
had given the Navy "grossly inaccurate" information on its submarine
contracts.[20] In spite of all these complaints, Secretary Lehman refused
to follow the Pentagon inspector general's recommendation that three
top General Dynamics executives be barred from participating in future
defense business.

What then happened to these charges that General Dynamics had lied
about cost overruns and delivery dates? In spite of the serious charges
made, the Department of Justice closed the case in May 1987, on the
incredible grounds that Navy contracting personnel appeared to have
known that the original cost estimates submitted by General Dynamics
were not reliable. According to *Business Week*, this claim was immaterial
because a fraudulent statement would have supported a criminal prosecution under the Federal False Claims Act.[21] Senator Proxmire called
it "another stain on this administration's [Reagan's] poor record of law
enforcement where large corporations are concerned."[22] He even
wanted to take defense industry prosecutions out of the Reagan administration's Justice Department in Washington, D.C., and leave them to
the tougher local U.S. attorneys.

In 1985 there was still another serious charge leveled against General
Dynamics. A federal grand jury charged James M. Beggs, a former
General Dynamics executive vice president and at the time director of
the National Aeronautics and Space Administration (NASA), and three
other General Dynamics officials, with having improperly charged the
Pentagon $7.5 million in cost overruns on a prototype of the Sergeant
York anti-aircraft gun. The Army had awarded General Dynamics a
$40-million contract; the corporation incurred several million dollars of
cost overruns that could not be charged to the contract. Looking for a
way to recoup, top executives at the Pomona Division plant, according
to the criminal indictment, hit on the idea of recovering the losses by
charging them to two other Department of Defense accounts, one for
work on future bids and the other for research on future contracts for
which there could be cost overruns. It was charged that the plant executives obtained approval for the fraudulent deception from Beggs.
Because the company had never informed the Department of Defense
of the false charging, if true, it had essentially lied to the government
about the contract operations. However, in 1987, the Department of
Justice dropped the criminal charges against General Dynamics, Beggs,
and the other officials before the case was scheduled to go to trial on
the grounds that the contract for the Sergeant York prototype was not

a "firm fixed price." This meant that all General Dynamics had had to show was that it had made its "best efforts" to comply with the contract provisions. This decision, coupled with the Justice Department's dismissal of General Dynamics's submarine overcharging case only a few weeks previously, had a chilling effect on efforts to prosecute large defense contractors suspected of fraudulent overcharges. Senator Charles Grassley (R-Iowa) charged that the Justice Department's efforts in the area of defense contractor fraud suffered from a "severe lack of effective enforcement initiatives."[23]

As a footnote and an indication of the moral climate in which some Reagan administration officials viewed such cases, President Reagan praised Beggs at a press conference announcing Beggs' resignation from NASA after he was indicted. In his laudatory remarks about Beggs, Reagan made two extraordinarily mitigating statements: that Beggs had been indicted "for something that is supposed to have happened prior to his government service," and "if he were doing this at all," it was not "something that would have been done for Beggs' (personal) benefit."[24]

Back in the 1950s, Ronald Reagan served as the master of ceremonies on a weekly General Electric television program. He also gave many speeches for General Electric and served the company in a public relations capacity. In fact, some have said that this relationship was crucial in Reagan's conversion from a Roosevelt New Deal Democrat into the ardent supporter of corporate free enterprise that he later became. When Reagan became president, his $1-trillion arms program gave General Electric an opportunity to engage in large-scale defense activities not always conducted with a high moral tone. For example, in 1985 the government indicted this huge corporation, the fourth largest defense contractor in the nation, for having defrauded the United States in connection with labor charges on the Minuteman missile contract, a weapon vital to the country's defense program. This federal grand jury criminal indictment followed a 4-year investigation of General Electric's illegal procedures. The indictment listed 104 counts of false statements and 4 counts of false labor-cost claims between 1980 and 1983. The indictment charged that General Electric had altered some time cards and that it had filled in others without the employees' knowledge. A study by the Defense Contract Audit Agency estimated that General Electric had billed as much as $7.2 million of idle time to the government. In some cases, General Electric had charged labor costs to other contracts to make higher profits. The court fined General Electric the maximum criminal penalty of $1.4 million, and it also required them to repay overcharges of $800,000. In 1989, General Electric agreed to pay $3.5 million to settle out of court four law suits brought by the federal government and GE whistle-blowers alleging fraud in military contract work. One of the federal suits accused General Electric of falsely certifying engine parts as having been tested according to contract requirements at its aircraft engine center in Seattle. Two other suits charged that General Electric had submitted false labor vouchers for work done at its Evendale, Ohio, aircraft engine plant. These suits were brought under the federal False Claims Act that allowed the whistle-blower to collect $750,000, or 22 percent. The False Claims Act includes provisions allowing private citizens to bring civil suits on behalf of the government. They are based on a principle called *qui tam*—Latin shorthand for "he who sues for the king as well as for himself."[25] Also in 1989 federal prosecutors charged that high-level General electric executives and lawyers had provided "misleading and false information to the Pentagon in 1985 to obscure the extent and details of widespread fraudulent billing practices."

In 1989 Rockwell International paid $800,000 to settle civil claims that the company had submitted inaccurate cost data on certain Air Force contracts; the recovery brought to about $1.3 million the total the government had recovered from the defense contractor in settlement of civil claims involving Rockwell contracts for navigational systems for Air Force planes and other mobile units. The Justice Department had charged that Rockwell misrepresented to the Air Force during contract negotiations the actual costs of a subcontract that Rockwell had negotiated with a unit of International Telephone and Telegraph Corporation. Earlier, the company pleaded guilty to criminal contract fraud charges stemming from the matters, and it was fined $5.5 million.

Northrop, the large defense contractor that makes the B-2 Stealth bomber, found itself in deep trouble in mid-1987 when the Air Force and the House Armed Services Committee investigated some $14 million in possible overcharges. The investigation focused on Northrop's possible double charges for duplicate parts, inflated charges for other parts to hide the duplications, falsification of test results on critical MX parts, and its incorrect labor costs billings. In 1989, the Justice Department joined in a civil suit filed under the False Claims Act by a Northrop whistleblower David Peterson, over purported mischarges on MX missile equipment.[26] Peterson had testified before Congress in 1987 that Northrop had set up a series of shell companies to make parts and thus to circumvent a cumbersome procurement system and to speed up the MX system. When duplicate parts arrived through regular channels, Northrop threw away hundreds of boxes of MX parts. Peterson also testified that Northrop improperly tested many of the parts that came through the shell company he headed. Some of the parts were even purchased from Radio Shack stores and put right on the MX guidance system.

Serious law violations also involved TRW, a major defense contractor, in the production of military aircraft engines and parts for the M-1, the Army's most sophisticated tank. The government charged that the company's employees had altered, back-dated, and destroyed production documents, and that top division officials had instructed accounting department employees "to do what was necessary to falsely inflate" labor charges on certain parts.[27] In 1988, TRW pleaded guilty to the charges and agreed to pay $6 million, half in criminal penalties and half as advance payment on a pending government civil action. The U.S. attorney said that the motives of the employees involved in the conspiracy had been to "enrich TRW" and "defraud the United States."[28]

Martin Marietta, one of the larger defense contractors, perpetuated a novel fraud. It worked out a scheme to keep more than $1 million in travel money it was supposed to return to the Department of Defense in connection with contract-related travel. A Martin Marietta subsidiary, created to handle travel, had falsified travel papers to show that more trips had been taken than had actually been the case. In 1987, Martin Marietta pleaded guilty to this charge and paid a fine of $12,000, plus $250,000 for costs incurred by the government.

Although defense cost overruns and fraud have bilked taxpayers of billions of dollars, they have not generally caused as much public and congressional furor as did the outrageous prices the defense corporations charged the government for such commonplace items as tools, parts, and coffee makers. This is the type of defense item to which the ordinary person can relate and that also provides enticing media coverage. Fifteen-cent nuts and bolts cost the taxpayers $25 each, and in one purchase, the Army paid $387 each for washers and $37 for screws, both of which could have been bought for a few cents retail. Grumman Aerospace Corporation charged the Navy $659 for each ashtray, which was reduced to $50 when the higher price was publicly challenged. However, the corporation kept their charges of $404 for a socket wrench and $2,710 for a clamp for which they had charged $102 a year and a half earlier. Lockheed charged taxpayers $646 for an airplane toilet seat, but reduced it to $100 when the story of the higher charge was made public. The government was charged $15,000 for a sofa that cost $700. General Electric billed the Pentagon $9,609 for a tiny wrench worth 12 cents in a hardware store, and $7,417 for a 3-inch length of wire that an electric supply store would probably have given away. Boeing charged the Pentagon $748 each for a pair of pliers that could be purchased at a local hardware store for $7 to $10, but after a government protest they reduced the price to $90. The Air Force was paying $7,600 for a coffee maker similar to one purchased for about $200 by commercial airlines. Because many of these items were purchased in large quantities, the overcharges cost the American public many millions of dollars. Still, they were small when compared with those related to the weapons systems. Unless Department of Defense auditors or congressional committees closely scrutinize the bills, which they appear seldom to do, defense contractors often can get away with overcharges on small items by billing for total rather than itemized costs. In one contract bill, Boeing, for example, submitted a total cost of $557,000 under the umbrella listing of "tools."

Such scandalous defense industry overcharges cannot be dismissed as mere oddities. In his appraisal of the defense industry, Norman Cousins pointed out that

> they were the result of systematic and exorbitant pricing formulas used by major defense contractors, not only for hammers and pliers but for ships, tanks, planes and almost everything else bought by the Pentagon. They were integrated into a system designed for maximum expenditure of public funds and maximum profit to the suppliers.[29]

CHARGING FOR ANYTHING AND EVERYTHING

The door is often wide open for fraudulent costs because little really competitive bidding has taken place in the defense industry. In 1985, for example, the government let out fewer than 6 percent of all defense contract dollars through true, normal competitive bidding, which the law requires in other branches of government. It awarded the remaining 94 percent of the defense contracts on a "negotiated" basis. In this system of bid-letting, procurement officers simply ask one or two large contractors to build a weapons prototype, and then they negotiate the price with the corporations. Supposedly, the bidding is competitive, and the contract goes to the lowest bidder, one usually favored by the Pentagon. After a short while, however, the corporation that receives the contract generally sends in revised estimates that often call for whopping increases over the original bid. The firm will generally have little trouble in obtaining approval for the new schedules and contract prices.

The procurement issue becomes complicated, and loopholes appear over two key issues in calculating overhead costs. The price for an item is not a set amount; instead, the contractor submits its costs and adds a share of its expenses and profit. A plethora of abuses then occurs in defining expenses. For example, an overhead regulation allows defense contractors to charge for memberships and contributions to trade, business, technical, and professional organizations. General Dynamics even charged for a $15,000 contribution to the Reagan-appointed Grace Commission on Government Waste. Defense contractors also stretch the definition of overhead costs to include advertising. Supposedly, they cannot bill the government for advertising except to recruit personnel, but if they include the phrase "equal opportunity employer" in the ad, they have been able to charge the taxpayers for some of their large display ads which usually have a patriotic theme and extoll the corporation's virtues.

A House Armed Services Committee investigation in 1985 of seven top defense contractors revealed nearly $110 million of "questionable" expense vouchers out of $4.2 billion paid during the 1972–1982 billing period. Many major defense corporations were involved in these rip-offs. McDonnell Douglas Corporation, for example, charged taxpayers $62,071 to cover the costs of an "image-refurbishing campaign" following the crash of one of the company's DC-10 aircraft in Chicago in 1979. Boeing charged $2,000 for a dinner at which the company's chief executive officer was honored, $9,305 for a "get-together" at a hotel, and $2,485 for golf outings. Rockwell International billed the government for $1 million in operating losses for its cafeterias and executive dining rooms. Such losses are allowable only if the company can prove it made every effort to break even, but Rockwell consistently charged low prices in the cafeterias and nothing at all for meals in the executive dining room. Sperry Corporation billed $1.7 million for "entertainment" and $665,774 in undocumented costs of the firm's Washington, D.C., office. It also billed for payments of executive memberships in rod and gun clubs, yacht and country clubs, golf courses, and the Metropolitan Opera.

Senior defense corporation executives get very high salaries. For example, in 1987, the chairmen and chief executive officers of Northrop and Lockheed each received over $1 million in salary and bonuses. A General Accounting Office study during the 1980s of 12 aerospace corporations, including General Dynamics, Boeing, Grumman, McDonnell Douglas, and Northrop, found that executive pay (that is, salary plus bonuses) averaged 42 percent above that of comparably sized firms engaged in non-military businesses. The defense industry labor force, on the other hand, earns wages only slightly higher than the national average.

All top corporate executives, whether or not they are in the defense industry, also receive numerous perks, but there is a decided difference in the perks paid by defense corporations—these are charged directly to the taxpayers. An investigation of General Dynamics revealed, for example, that the corporation had charged the government for executive use of their corporate jets for purposes not related to defense contracts. The government challenged about 90 percent of the $22 million charged by General Dynamics for "executive flights." Of particular interest was the bill for $320,000 for 76 flights of the chairman of the board to his Georgia farm for weekend retreats. He justified the expense charge because he did corporate work at the farm and also because flying in a corporate jet enabled him "to avoid possible terrorist threats." The corporation also billed the government directly for executive membership fees in prominent country clubs and other social clubs, for example, a

$17,000 golf initiation fee. Another defense corporation even billed the government for boarding costs for one of the executive's dogs. To add to this list of charges, the government received a bill for a $10,713 loss incurred in the operation of a senior executive's barber shop.

ILLEGAL GIFTS TO GOVERNMENT PERSONNEL

For more than three decades, federal laws and regulations have strictly prohibited defense contractors from giving gifts to government officials associated with defense work. Penalties for violations include forbidding contractors from obtaining future federal contracts and assessing them damages of up to 10 times the gift cost. As an example, ITT, which did $1.3 billion in defense business in 1987, pleaded guilty in late 1988 to spending $15,000 on entertainment of Air Force employees, including golf club fees, baseball tickets, meals, and liquor in exchange for information used to bid on Air Force contracts worth $180 million. A Boston federal judge fined the corporation $200,000. Regulations likewise prohibit military officials from soliciting or accepting gratuities from contractors. It is a well-known fact, however, that corporations have flagrantly violated these laws without the government taking punitive action. One case in 1985 involved Martin Marietta. The Pentagon revealed that over the past 20 years this corporation had been giving expensive replicas of model aircraft both to highly placed Air Force officers who were retiring, as well as to active officers, as mementos of their service. The corporation even charged these gifts, which cost as much as $5,000 each, to a Pentagon contract, a total taxpayer bill of $200,000. When the government brought action against them, Martin Marietta was allowed simply to pay back this amount rather than being assessed 10 times the value of the gifts, which could have been as much as $2 million.

In spite of a federal law prohibiting gift-giving, in the early 1980s General Dynamics gave Admiral Hyman Rickover, founder and head of the Navy's nuclear submarine program, a number of gifts that amounted to $67,628. There has been no indication, however, that Admiral Rickover extended preferential treatment to General Dynamics because of the gifts. In fact, in the late 1970s, he had charged General Dynamics with having submitted false claims of cost overruns on certain nuclear submarine work. Even though the corporation violated the law, Rickover himself, in accepting the gifts, tarnished his own highly honored name after he finally retired from the Navy at age 84. Chairman John Dingell (D-Mich.) of the House Oversight and Investigations Subcommittee was so irate about the matter that he asked the Navy to terminate two contracts with General Dynamics. According to Representative Dingell, General Dynamics' chief financial officer, Gordon MacDonald, had arranged to buy two pieces of valuable jewelry for Admiral Rickover in 1977. The financial officer also directed an employee of the company's Electric Boat division, which did the submarine work, to handle paying for the jewelry and delivering it to Rickover. The employee was told to keep the gifts secret because "it could be very embarrassing to me and to General Dynamics."[30] In the end, the government fined General Dynamics $676,283, or 10 times the value of the gratuities given to the admiral.

Department of Defense regulations prohibit defense industry contractors from entertaining military officers, yet violations of this regulation are a persistent problem. For example, in 1983 the government charged Pratt and Whitney Aircraft, a division of United Technology, with having illegally entertained high-ranking Air Force officers. A retired middle-management executive of a large aerospace firm has described the mechanics of this entertainment in his own corporation:

Most of the aerospace industry is involved in government contracts. There is an attitude of "dog eat dog" in the industry, all competing to get contracts. There is entertainment of the military personnel. The industry did things for officers attached to our plants, such as getting them free tickets, transportation, food and drink for football games, etc. Corporations in the industry sponsored country club memberships, trips, etc., for the military to get contracts. They are all buttered up by the corporation.[31]

DEFECTIVE WEAPONS

The Department of Defense spends vast sums of money on armaments, but often they purchase weapons that only give the American people an illusion of security. In fact, some defense contractors make items incapable of performing the tasks for which the government purchased them. Among the great fiascoes of armaments that have failed to function as claimed have been the $1.8-billion Sergeant York antiaircraft gun; the $11.3-billion Bradley M-2 Fighting Vehicle, which is still a dud; the vulnerable Apache Attack Helicopter, over 4,900 of which were officially shot down in Vietnam; and the M-1 tank. The potential for a military catastrophe must be shared by the defense contractors and the Pentagon planners. Horrendous tales of bad design, poor quality, and defective workmanship of the weapons the defense industry has produced for the military have come to light. A few examples culled from a large number of cases illustrate what has been happening. For years, the armed services have been rejecting shoddy products. There have been serious troubles with almost every major weapons system in the U.S. arsenal: its most sophisticated nuclear warheads (General Electric), its nuclear missile guidance system (Northrop), its nuclear submarines (General Dynamics), its finest missiles (Hughes Aircraft), its best fighter planes (General Dynamics and McDonnell Douglas), and important military weapons supplied to allies (Martin Marietta).

Frequently, defense contractors have been charged with inadequately or improperly testing or inspecting defense weapons or their parts. For example, General Dynamics's Phalanx missile, designed to shoot down incoming missiles directed at Navy ships, has been the subject of serious charges that General Dynamics did not carry out required tests on vital components in order to meet production quotas.

Defective bolts have been a problem in many defense weapons. It was revealed in 1988 that 1,200 M-60 tanks were removed from Army front lines for two months while defective bolts in the gun mounts were replaced. The bolts contained more boron and less carbon than specified in industry standards, thus making them more likely to break or shear. Fairchild's Voi-Sham unit, a major manufacturer of aerospace parts, was suspended in 1989 from bidding on defense contracts while it was under further investigation for falsifying test results on nuts, bolts, and other fasteners sold to leading defense aircraft manufacturers such as Boeing and Lockheed. Investigation had revealed evidence that employees routinely falsified manufacturing reports and test results from 1980 to 1989. FBI agents found also that there was a fictitious "inspector" stamp that was not assigned to any employee and was routinely used to indicate that parts passed inspection even when tests were not employed.

The Navy grounded a fifth of its AGE attack aircraft, which at the time was the only all-weather bomber to operate from carriers, when tests showed that the plane's wings lasted only half as long as the contract had originally specified. In 1987, the Pentagon grounded a substantial portion of its F-18 fleet because too many of them had developed engine fires. The engines were made by General Electric. On the same plane in the same year, McDonnell Douglas began modification of the air frame to correct a problem involving metal fatigue. The nuclear submarine fleet has been plagued with defective and hazardous welding problems. The Navy had to recall more than a third of its first batch of Trident nuclear missiles due to problems with the first-stage engine. The Air Force in 1987 withheld some payments from Morton Thiokol because of "poor workmanship" in some of the rockets it supplied. Nearly 250 U.S. servicemen were killed from 1967 to 1987 aboard Bell helicopters that have crashed largely because of a design flaw.

Northrop faked testing of vital guidance components for the Air Force's cruise missile, the federal government alleged in 1988 in joining a $63 million law suit brought by whistle-blowing ex-employees. The law suit, which the U.S. District Court judge ordered unsealed in 1989, accused Northrop Corporation of having falsified test results on parts for nearly 1,800 of the nuclear-tipped missiles that are launched from bombers and skim the earth toward their targets, and that are critical guidance and flight-control systems parts for the air-launched cruise missile. The units are on B-52 and B-1 bombers stationed both in the United States and overseas. The law suit was filed in 1987 under the False Claims Act, which allows whistle-blowers to share damage awards with the government. It was joined by the Justice Department in February 1989, a move the government makes if it determines that the allegations have merit. In still another case, the government charged that Northrop Corporation failed properly to test the crucial component that guides the MX nuclear missile and the Marines' Harrier jets to their targets. In a 1989 amended indictment, the government charged the corporation with selling 200 improperly tested guidance systems. They also charged Northrop with conspiracy and lying to the government in the testing and sales of the stabilization devices. Northrop vice chairman Frank Lynch admitted to the House Energy and Commerce Committee that there had been management lapses and errors of judgment.

Serious problems with the manufacture and supply of military silicon chips have gravely endangered many parts of the defense capability of the United States. Silicon chips detonate nuclear warheads, serve as electronic eyes of spy satellites, aim guns and missiles, and guide aircraft and ships. As Admiral Frank C. Collins, the executive director of quality for the Pentagon's Defense Logistics Agency, commented in 1982: "I have been at sea and I have used missiles. When you are out in the middle of the Indian Ocean or the Tonkin Gulf, you know: Our bottom line isn't profits or loss, it's life or death."[32]

In spite of their essential nature, major companies that manufacture silicon chips, however, cannot always be relied on to maintain the highest product quality. From 1981 to 1985, five corporations that make semiconductor chips admitted to irregularities ranging from minor infractions to full-scale cheating on the critical heat tests the government requires. The biggest names in the industry have been involved in cheating: Texas Instruments, National Semiconductor, Fairchild, and Signetics.[33]

After carefully examining the defense industry in 1987, Norman Cousins concluded: "The Pentagon's trillion-dollar arms build-up is ostensibly aimed at bolstering the nation's security, but the combination of design and construction flaws, questionable decisions concerning actual needs, and sweetheart deals with contractors could have the effect of sapping America's vitality for generations to come."[34]

THE REVOLVING DOOR

Corporations frequently hire former civilian or military officials of the Department of Defense, a practice that is mutually advantageous both to the employees and the corporations. This "revolving door" helps to explain, in part, the limited government response to defense contractors' excessive abuses, particularly in cost overruns and fraud.[35] A retired Navy engineer has explained how tempting it is when a defense contractor offers him a job that pays as much as $75,000 a year: "If he stands up and makes a fuss about high costs and poor quality, no nice man will come to see him when he retires."[36]

Department of Defense officers have been employed subsequently by a corporation whose plant work they were directly supervising to see how the corporation was meeting cost and performance standards. These high-ranking officers are called Plant Representative Officers or PROs. A *St. Louis Post Dispatch* investigation concluded that if an officer began to write reports that were too critical of plant operations, he soon learned that his chances of landing a job with that defense firm, or any other, upon his retirement was negligible. All of these factors led Senator Carl Levin (D-Mich.) to comment, "We are tolerating a situation that encourages people to negotiate with future employers while working for the government."[37] In 1985, the Office of Government Ethics stated, "Government employees openly discuss what the former employee had done over the past few years for the contractor in order to obtain the new job."[38]

According to the *Washington Spectator*, companies that were doing $10 million or more business in Pentagon contracts in 1983 employed more than 2,100 former government employees who had left government service within the previous three years.[39] In one 3-year period, 3,200 Pentagon officers with the rank of major or above left their jobs to work for defense firms, General Dynamics in particular. Frequently, former Department of Defense personnel go to work on the same projects on which they had been working previously. In fact, in 1986 a fifth of the persons who went to work for defense contractors continued to work on the same projects that they had in the Department of Defense. In 1982, when the General Accounting Office was studying 256 defense contracts, it found potential conflicts of interest in all but one. The General Accounting Office questioned the influence of former top-level officials in securing defense contracts. When Ford Motor Company was selected over General Dynamics to produce the DIVAD, a major air defense gun whose later performance was not good, the General Accounting Office began an investigation because a parade of senior Army officers associated with the program had obtained jobs associated with the production of the Ford gun.

Many cases illustrate the operation of this revolving door policy. A top Department of Defense official had negotiated a settlement with a warship builder for nearly half a million dollars in cost overruns. Shortly afterward, he resigned and took a position as a paid consultant to the same corporation. In this case, it was former Secretary of the Navy Edward Hildago who negotiated such a settlement with General Dynamics.[40] When he left the government, the same corporation paid him $66,000 for his work in trying to sell F-16 fighter sets to Spain. A former General Dynamics executive later said that company officials had "subtly" suggested to Hildago that they would take care of him after he left the company. This is not an unusual case. In 1983, Navy assistant secretary George Sawyer became an executive vice president of General Dynamics at a $210,000 annual salary.[41] General Dynamics's chairman, David Lewis, later told a congressional committee that he had talked with Sawyer about the possibility of a job at least three months before he left the Navy. During that time, Sawyer oversaw billions of dollars in General Dynamics' shipbuilding contracts, and he authorized negotiations with the firm on a new contract. In still another case, an Air Force officer who was responsible for supervising $700 million in defense contracts retired and immediately took a lucrative position with one of the corporations he had been supervising.

When Pentagon officials leave their government positions, it is against the law for them, within the following two years, to represent a corporation in any dealings with the government that relate to matters in which they had had substantial supervisory responsibilities prior to their departure for government service. Those who go to work for a defense corporation are supposed to complete a "revolving door form" informing the government of the facts. Few do. Moreover, Department of Defense contracting officers can go to work for defense contractors with whom they previously worked as long as they work in the "back room." Brigadier General Donald Bowen, for example, prior to his retirement from the Air Force, was head of the Command and Control Technical Center where he supervised a dozen defense contractors.[42] Two weeks after retiring, he became vice president in charge of command-and-control systems for one of the defense corporations, but he did not directly deal with the previous contracts. In another example, an Air Force colonel in charge of managing a competitive contract contest between General Electric and United Technologies that involved $14 billion later took a position with General Electric, to whom the government awarded the contract. His position with General Electric was as quality control supervisor of the same engines that had been involved in the contract negotiation.

On the whole, the government has handled the misdeeds of our giant defense corporations with great leniency. Few criminal indictments have been brought against them, and even fewer corporate executives have been convicted. In cases where there have been criminal indictments, the government has usually either dropped them or it has settled for "peanuts." In 1985, Senator William Proxmire (D-Wis.) reported that an internal Pentagon memorandum had revealed that only 11 of 400 cases of suspected defense contractor fraud uncovered over the prior five years had resulted in criminal prosecutions, none of them involving top executives. In fact, the first case of prosecution of top executives of a large corporation was that of General Dynamics's overcharges on the Sergeant York anti-aircraft gun late in 1985, but the charges were later dropped. Senator Proxmire stated that, "Defense contractor fraud does pay. It is one of the safest games in town. Even if the Pentagon catches you, there is less than a 3 percent chance you (the corporation) will be brought to justice."[43]

Chapter 6

CORPORATE VIOLENCE

Corporations are responsible for the deaths of far more persons than are killed by individuals. Hundreds of thousands of worker and consumer injuries, some of which are deadly serious, are caused by corporate actions. Plant workers may receive injuries in accidents in an unsafe workplace or become ill from a work-related disease; in other cases, consumers of corporate products are hurt directly through unsafe or even dangerous products. In addition, millions of persons may become ill because of industrial air pollution, by improper waste disposal from factories, and through other forms of environmental contamination. Yet the public is far more fearful of street muggers than of polluters and dumpers. People are much less afraid of dying a slow death from air pollution, chemical exposure, or cigarette smoking than of violent injury or death at the hands of a street criminal. One expert asserted that corporate "crimes against health and safety are frightening, shocking and disturbing."[1]

INJURY AND DEATH ON THE JOB

Over a period of two years during the 1970s, journalist Rachel Scott visited a number of *Fortune* 500 plants, including Ford, Chrysler, and Mobil Oil.[2] She described a horrendous situation: Workers were frequently killed and often badly injured in preventable plant accidents due to faulty equipment and inadequate safety procedures. Unnecessary exposure to vinyl chloride and other chemicals such as silica resulted in death and illness to many plant employees. Two well-known writers on business issues commented on her work:

She concluded that corporations have the resources to measure and control industrial hazards. Yet now as throughout American history, companies such as these shrug at the pleas of workers whose health they destroy in order to save money. They hire experts—physicians and researchers—who purposely misdiagnose industrial diseases as the ordinary diseases of life, write biased reports, and divert research from vital questions. They fight against regulations as unnecessary and cry that it will bring ruination.[3]

Corporations often disregard the health of workers in order to save money. For example, Allied Chemical knew, from its own laboratory research, that its chemical pesticide Kepone, which is similar to DDT, could cause serious injuries, including cancer.[4] Still, they produced and marketed the deadly substance, thus poisoning many workers. The affected workers suffered from severe tension, weight loss, tenderness of the liver, brain damage, chest pains, and walking difficulties.

According to the Bureau of Labor Statistics, in 1987 a total of 2,212,600 manufacturing workers were injured on the job. Allowing for inadequate reporting, about 1,000 manufacturing workers were killed on the job. According to a 1989 report of the National Safe Workplace Institute, more workers are killed on the job in the United States than in most other major industrialized countries of the world. In this country, workers are 36 times more likely to be killed than are workers in Sweden, and nine times more likely to be killed than in England. The Institute estimates that these deaths cost the U.S. economy $15 billion each year. The Bureau of Labor Statistics reports that work days lost in the manufacturing industry due to on-the-job injuries in 1987 were 16,293,700. Still, these statistics do not give the full picture, since corporations, like other employers, are solely responsible for reporting job-related injuries and diseases. The evidence suggests that many grossly underreport the cases, largely because a lower number of such incidents makes for a better corporate image; it also reduces corporate insurance costs and discourages visits from government inspectors.[5] In 1986, for example, the Occupational Safety and Health Administration (OSHA) fined Chrysler $910,000 for failure to report many accidents at one of their large plants, and they fined Caterpillar Tractor $776,000 on similar charges. OSHA assessed General Dynamics a fine of $615,000 in 1987 for wilfully underreporting job injuries and illness at its Rhode Island submarine-building yard. As another example, Kohler Company was fined $1,398,000 in 1988 for inadequate record-keeping of employee injuries.

Injuries and deaths due to occupational diseases include silicosis (caused by fine sand and other materials), brown lung (caused by coal and cotton dust), and cancer (of the lung, kidney, liver, and bladder) caused by chemical agents. Studies of the National Institute of Occupational Safety and Health during the early 1980s show that 1.7 million of the 38 million workers in manufacturing industries are exposed to a potential carcinogen each year.[6] The institute estimates that on-the-job exposure to chemicals causes 20 to 40 percent of all cancers. A worker at a large chemical plant described his job-related mercury poisoning: "Tremors, the blurring of vision, dizziness. I couldn't sleep at night. I would dribble at the mouth like a baby and wet my bed. I was irritable to the point I became violent at times."[7]

Fighting all the way, most large corporations in the past generally resisted nearly all government efforts to improve worker health and safety conditions.[8] Even in the 1920s, however, a few large corporations did show a genuine interest in health care and provided disability benefits for their workers.[9] Generally, however, this was not the case. In the Dodge auto plant in 1932, for example, there was no attempt to ventilate the work areas or to remove the pollutants from the air. It was an accepted fact that thousands of metal finishers in the auto industry suffered from lead poisoning; many workers paid with their lives. The government finally enacted the eight-hour workday, largely for health reasons, but it was not until 1933, after a long and often bloody struggle, that the Depression-born National Recovery Act (NRA) guaranteed workers the right to organize unions, which, among other things, could help improve working conditions. By the late 1960s, however, the toll of unsafe working conditions had become so great that something had to be done. According to studies by safety expert David Berman, worker cuts and lacerations, amputations, muscle disorders, respiratory diseases, and dozens of types of cancer were becoming increasingly common.[10]

Finally, in 1968, President Lyndon Johnson proposed a federal occupational safety and health program, the purpose of which was to assure every working man and woman in the nation safe and healthy working conditions, as far as possible. Congress created the Occupational Safety and Health Administration (OSHA) in 1970 under mounting pressure from unions, greater worker dissatisfaction, a tighter labor market, increased environmental consciousness, and the general climate of social unrest in the early 1970s. Under federal law, a state can set up its own enforcement agency as long as it protects workers as well as does OSHA, which pays half the cost of the state programs. By 1989, 21 states had elected to run their own regulatory programs.

Prior to OSHA, according to Berman, large corporations had almost totally ignored the problems of occupational disease, long-term disability, and worker rehabilitation.[11] Between 1972 and 1978, after OSHA's enactment, total injuries and illnesses in workplaces dropped 14 percent, and reported deaths due to on-the-job accidents fell 20 percent. This trend was reversed during the Reagan administration, which was unusually friendly to corporations and sought to cut budgets of federal agencies regulating them. Between 1983 and 1984, the number of workplace deaths, injuries, and illnesses rose 12 percent. President Reagan slashed OSHA's staff from 3,015 in 1980 to 2,355 in 1984. The agency had to close one-third of its field offices and reduce the inspection staff, its foot soldiers, by 25 percent. Between 1980 and 1986, total penalties declined from an annual $24.4 million to $6.7 million. OSHA became extraordinarily slow in issuing needed safety and health standards. However, according to a 1982 *Wall Street Journal*/NBC News poll, over half the American people favored more government regulation of on-the-job safety and health. A sample of retired middle managers of the *Fortune* 500 with long service felt that OSHA was the second most important of all government agencies.[12] These middle managers felt that worker safety is one of the most important responsibilities of any corporation. Should workers feel they are not adequately protected, 80 percent of the middle managers said that they should report the corporate violation directly to the government.

With the appointment of William Brock as Secretary of Labor in 1985, after a storm of criticism of OSHA's ineffectiveness, events finally changed direction. For example, Bath Iron Works was fined $4.2 million in 1987 for worker health and safety violations, the largest fine in OSHA's history. In mid-1987, OSHA cited Chrysler for 811 violations, including 225 alleged wilful violations of rules relating to overexposure to lead and arsenic. The government fined Chrysler $1.6 million for health and safety violations, and reversed the deregulatory trend in which the Reagan administration had slowed enforcement efforts. Critics complained, however, that the blitz of big fines was largely a propaganda gimmick because OSHA generally settled for half the original fine, and it rarely employed criminal prosecutions of the corporation or its top executives. In fact, a 1988 study made by the National Safe Workplace Institute found that of 11 OSHA-imposed fines of over $100,000 since 1986, only 2 of them were paid in full.[13]

IBP, Inc., the nation's largest meat-packer, of which Occidental Petroleum owns 51 percent, agreed in 1988 to pay a fine of $975,000, reduced from $3.1 million, and to launch a three-year program aimed at reducing crippling injuries among its workers. In 1988, IBP was not the only large meat-packer in trouble, as OSHA slapped a $4.33 million fine on John Morrell, the country's fifth largest meat-packer, the largest fine against a single employer in OSHA's history. From May, 1987 to May, 1988, 800 of the 2,000 Morrell workers in their Sioux Falls, South Dakota, plant had sustained serious and sometimes disabling injuries.

These injuries were "cumulative trauma" disorders, which are often crippling injuries caused by repeated hand, wrist, and arm rotation in meat-packing procedures. Of the injured workers, 93 percent received no time off, and 39 percent were denied lighter work during recovery. The 63 workers who underwent surgery received an average of 1.1 days off, as compared to OSHA's recommended standard of 30 to 60 days. In the previous four years, OSHA had fined Morrell six times for a total of $758,910. Pepperidge Farm, a unit of Campbell Soup Company, was also charged in 1988 with a similar type of worker injuries. The Assistant Secretary of Labor said: "Management was clearly aware of the need to address ergonomic [cumulative trauma] hazards at the plant, yet chose to ignore its own experts and employers, while more and more employees suffered crippling injury."[14] The Department of Labor proposed fines of $1.4 million.

To cite other examples of the abuse of worker safety standards, Chrysler agreed to pay $1.6 million in 1987 to settle OSHA charges of worker overexposure to lead and arsenic and other health and safety violations. It cited 225 alleged instances of "wilful violations" in that the company knowingly broke the rules or was aware of a hazardous condition and made no reasonable effort to correct it. A Lockheed Corporation unit was cited by OSHA in 1989 for 440 worker-safety violations, some very serious. The alleged violations included failure to keep proper employee-safety records, mislabeling or failing to label chemical containers, neglecting to post mandatory health warnings, and overexposing workers to asbestos, which is now deemed dangerous.

From these examples it is clear that large segments of American industry still will not deal voluntarily with even serious problems of worker safety. As an example, as late as 1988, the Labor Department had to impose a regulation making employers put warning tags or locks on machinery as it is being cleaned or serviced to prevent the equipment from being inadvertently restarted while someone is working on it. Such a procedure would serve to prevent up to 10 percent of all serious injuries in some major manufacturing industries. This rule came nine years after unions requested the regulation and after more than 1,000 deaths and 600,000 injuries as a result of its absence during that period. One wonders why the corporations shirked their duty and why government regulation was even necessary.

Turning to the chemical industry, an EPA study showed that, between 1980 and 1985, 135 people had been killed and about 1,500 injured in some 7,000 accidents that occurred in chemical production and storage facilities in the United States. As an example, in 1985 the Union Carbide pesticide plant in West Virginia leaked a dangerous toxic chemical that injured 140 people. A six-month inspection of the plant in 1986 revealed what Secretary of Labor William Brock called a "situation characterized by complacency and what we believe to be a willful disregard for health and safety." He added: "We were just surprised to find conscious, overt, willful violations on such a widespread basis." Among an array of problems that inspectors found were employees who had been asked to detect the presence of deadly gas, after alarms had indicated a leak, by sniffing the air without respirators. Secretary Brock said: "We used to use canaries for that."[15] The government charged Union Carbide with 221 safety and health violations, including the use of inadequately designed storage tanks for toxic mixtures, failure to properly monitor the heat and pressure of volatile chemicals, negligence in the repair of a malfunctioning computerized alarm system, operation of an improperly designed control room where an air conditioner brought fumes inside, and failure to provide a sufficient number of respirators to employees. In the control room proper, for example, there were only three respirators for six employees. OSHA proposed a $1.4-million fine against Union Carbide and $90,000 in fines for 335 wilful safety violations at another nearby Union Carbide plant; it was settled in 1987 for a total fine of $408,500. The corporation made the usual statement: They denied violating the law, saying that resolving the case and agreeing to pay the fine was cheaper than continuing to fight the charges.

As another example, in 1987 OSHA charged the giant International Paper Company with 37 violations of wilfully disregarding employees' protection from the effects of exposure to toxic gases such as chlorine and hydrogen sulfide in their Maine paper mill. Among the specific violations were charges that the company had provided their workers with respirators not approved for protection against toxic gases, failure to identify and label pipes carrying hazardous substances, and failure to provide the workers with information on hazardous chemicals in the work area. OSHA recommended a fine of $242,000.

Workers whose daily lives are spent working with dangerous chemicals have a right to know what the materials are, even though corporations have often not told them. Largely due to industry opposition, it was not until 1983 that OSHA began requiring manufacturers to label toxic substances used in the workplace. This requirement affected about 14 million workers. In the first settlement of a major case involving OSHA's rules that require an employer to inform workers of exposure to hazardous chemicals, in 1989 Lockheed agreed to pay $1.5 million in fines. Moreover, Lockheed agreed to correct unsafe or unhealthy working conditions throughout its operations plants. Again, government regulation had been necessary to deal with the occupational injuries and deaths that corporations would not deal with themselves.

Now and then a single worker-safety case gains national attention. Karen Silkwood was one of the first employees in the nuclear industry to challenge plant safety standards publicly. As a laboratory analyst, she had been exposed in the early 1980s to radiation contamination as a result of lax safety precautions at the large Kerr-McGee Oklahoma plutonium plant, which produced fuel rods for use in nuclear power plants. She died in a car accident on her way to a meeting with a reporter to discuss alleged safety violations at the plant. The police say she had fallen asleep while driving. Foul play was hinted at but never proven. An autopsy showed her body had been contaminated by plutonium. Her fight against the giant corporation became the subject of a critically acclaimed movie, as well as two books. A jury awarded her husband and three children $505,000 in actual damages and $10 million in punitive damages in a plutonium contamination suit against the corporation. When the award was later reduced, the U.S. Supreme Court restored the original award.

THE DEADLY ASBESTOS INDUSTRY

Marcos Vela was a slight, courtly man when he was young. Some say that he looked like Rudolph Valentino. Around 1935, he began to work as a machine tender in an asbestos factory of the Johns-Manville Corporation, which at that time was the country's largest manufacturer of asbestos products. In 1959, and again in 1962 and 1965, in routine physical examinations, a company doctor found that he was developing the sometimes fatal disease asbestosis. However, the physician did not inform Vela of his findings, and he did not suggest a change in his work environment. In February 1968, during his fourth routine physical examination for Johns-Manville, Vela complained of a cough and shortness of breath. At that time, his chest X-ray showed a "ground glass appearance"—but still the company doctor told him that everything was fine. In August, he was hospitalized because he was unable to breathe properly.

Vela would never return to work. He said that he had been working in clouds of asbestos dust so thick that he could hardly see across the shop. "When I had to quit, the company did nothing for me. They said, 'Go look for another job.'" Doctors did not expect him to live as long as he did. His lung capacity in 1978 was down to one-fourth normal, and he stopped to take shallow breaths when he spoke. He often had to take as many as 18 kinds of medications each day, and he used a respirator connected to an oxygen tank. Nonetheless, Vela was still wearing a $100 gold watch presented to him in 1960 by Johns-Manville "in appreciation for 25 years of loyal service." For many years, Johns-Manville covered up these dangers, happy to give out gold watches to those who retired but loathe to improve working conditions.[16]

Marcos Vela is now dead, but he was not the only one to die from asbestos-related cancer. Dr. Irving Selikoff of the Mt. Sinai School of

Medicine, the leading authority on the relation between cancer and asbestosis, has estimated that 240,000 of the one million workers who were exposed to or are working with asbestos will die within 30 years due to asbestos-related cancer. In addition, innumerable consumers, as well as other workers and the general public, have been exposed to this dangerous product. By early 1984, more than 25,500 personal law suits were pending against asbestos companies, charging them with inflicting hundreds of millions of damages on the public. School districts, cities, and states are trying to force asbestos companies to fund, remove, or cover up asbestos in schools, offices, hospitals, and other public buildings.

The toll of occupational disease and cancer caused by asbestos is now reaching epidemic proportions; it is estimated that asbestos causes 10,000 deaths annually. The EPA has issued emissions standards for asbestos as a hazardous air pollutant. The Navy has abandoned the use of asbestos in shipbuilding, and countless schools and other public buildings have been renovated to remove asbestos contamination. Today it seems clear that, except under the most restrictive conditions, the human toll from nearly all forms of asbestos use has become too costly for its continued use. According to Grover Wrenn, a chemical management consultant formerly with OSHA, asbestos usage has declined 90 percent since 1975. Although its use is heavily regulated, it is still put in car brakes, cement water pipes, shingles, and other products. The Environmental Protection Agency announced in 1989 that it would ban almost all remaining uses of asbestos by 1997.

The U.S. asbestos industry claimed that it was not aware of the hazardous nature of its product. The record shows, however, that over a long period of time the industry had suppressed and distorted information about the hazards of asbestos to workers and consumers.[17] For example, a British article first revealed asbestos hazards as early as 1906; by 1931, the British had fully documented the occupational hazards of asbestos dust inhalation, which can lead to asbestosis and lung cancer. Parliament enacted legislation that required periodic examinations of workers in asbestos-textile factories, and made asbestosis a compensable disease. Even in the United States, as early as 1917, it was no secret that asbestos could cause disease. By 1955, asbestos was definitely linked to cancer. By 1960, a total of 51 scientific papers had revealed asbestos exposure as a major threat to human life.

In spite of the existence of such damning evidence, in a 1978 asbestos death case, a judge concluded that there had been a "conscious effort by the industry in the 1930s to downplay, or arguably suppress, the dissemination of information to employees and the public for fear of promotion of lawsuits."[18] Up until the late 1960s, Johns-Manville Corporation refused to tell workers of early evidence of asbestosis diagnosed (by X-ray, for example) by the medical staff. One internal memorandum stated that "the workers have not been told of this diagnosis, for it is felt that as long as the man feels well, is happy at home and at work, and his physical condition remains good, nothing should be said." The industry recognized the broader health dangers of the use of asbestos, but it chose to ignore and deny their existence. In testimony before a congressional committee in 1977, Johns-Manville Corporation's medical director was asked if he had ever advised corporate officials to put warning labels on asbestos-containing insulation products. He replied:

The reasons why the caution labels were not implemented immediately was a business decision as far as I could understand.... The corporation is in business to provide jobs for people and make money for stockholders and they have to take into consideration the effects of everything they did, and if the application of a caution label identifying a product as hazardous would cut out sales, there would be serious financial implications.[19]

The asbestos industry disregarded all the evidence presented, including the asbestos-related illness reports from company physicians. The corporations continued to manufacture a dangerous product. Because they did not inform their workers, consumers or the public about the serious dangers of asbestos, they were committing a massive criminal act. They were corporate killers in a real sense.

By 1982, former workers and consumers had filed over 15,000 lawsuits against Johns-Manville Corporation (now Manville Corporation), and the company anticipated another 60,000 to 70,000 suits, with claims totaling more than $1 billion. In fact, so numerous and costly have these suits become that the corporation, the world's largest asbestos manufacturer, filed for bankruptcy in 1984 in order to avoid the financial cost resulting from workers' suits. In 1986, present and former asbestos manufacturers agreed to settle a class action suit, brought by 751 former workers or workers' survivors, for more than $100 million, the largest settlement ever paid to victims of asbestos-related diseases. These corporations included Manville Corporation, Celotex, Owens-Corning, Fiberglass, and Armstrong World Industries.

The courts approved Manville's bankruptcy reorganization plan in 1986. The plan sought to deal with worker claims by compensating them through a $2.5-billion trust fund to be paid over three decades. The money came from various corporate sources, including the annual funneling of $75 million in common stock for 24 years, plus up to 20 percent of its annual net earnings for 26 years, if needed, to cover claims. Indemnification would run around $26,000 per claim, but it could go higher. The entire plan represented a severe financial loss to an American industry, but American workers represent great worth also and must be protected. As a final note, in 1986 two top Manville executives, who had been forced out of Manville when it filed for bankruptcy in order to avoid payments of huge damage claims, received more than $1.8 million in "golden parachute" payments.

Fortunately, Manville's president since 1986, W. Thomas Stephens, recognized the seriousness of the situation and said that Manville must set an example for ethical behavior in the future. "This asbestos case, more than anything, has reflected the views of society about what it expects from a company. Society has sent a very clear message: 'We want producers of products to fully inform us about the risks we take when we consume a product and we have the right to assume it is safe, unless we have been warned.' "[20]

MARKETING UNSAFE PRODUCTS

Government investigations show that numerous corporations and their executives have knowingly concealed the fact that their unsafe products have caused injury and sickness, and even death, to thousands, in addition to endangering millions of others. When Congress became more aware of the extent of death and injury that various products can cause, it created the Consumer Product Safety Commission in 1972. Instrumental were the findings of a presidential commission that had estimated that unsafe consumer products cause 20 million injuries each year, and that 110,000 of those injuries result in permanent disability, and 30,000 in death. The duty of the Consumer Product Safety Commission is to establish safety rules to cover such products as fireproof fabrics, mattresses, carpeting, children's clothing and toys, dangerous medicine bottle caps, refrigerator door latches, baby cribs, and electrical wiring. The commission has estimated, for example, that more than 170,000 children suffer toy-related injuries each year involving toys made of brittle plastic, easy-to-break glass, or metal or plastic with sharp edges, and toys on which children can choke. It is estimated that children suffer more than 40,000 injuries each year from sharp edges on toys alone. Each Christmas, newspapers carry articles with a new list from the Consumer Product Safety Commission of manufactured toys considered dangerous for children, warning parents not to purchase them.

The power lawn mower industry is only one of numerous examples of the need for government intervention when manufacturers continue marketing an unsafe consumer product. Until the commission took action, there were more than 77,000 reported annual injuries to hands and feet (such as bruises or the loss of fingers or toes) that cost consumers an estimated $253 million each year, exclusive of suffering. The Consumer Products Safety Commission finally ordered a crackdown on walk-behind power lawn mowers, many of which carried the industry "seal of approval." For five years, between 1974 and 1979, the power mower industry resisted recommended safety measures, even though the cost to add them would not have exceeded $35 per machine. When the commission issued final safety standards in 1979, the manufacturers delayed making the changes, and they appealed the commission ruling in court.[21] In spite of 35,000 pages of testimony and comments amassed over several years about the danger of power mowers, the Outdoor Power Equipment Institute claimed that there was not enough evidence to warrant the issuance of a safety standard. Finally, a federal court ordered compliance, concluding that "the safety benefits expected from the standards bear a reasonable relationship to its cost." Today, the government requires that power mowers be equipped with protective shields so that feet cannot come in contact with a blade. "Dead man" controls prevent the machine from running except when the user is in contact with the controls.

As another example, about 2,000 medical devices, many of them made by large corporations, are currently used for diagnosis, surgery, or body implantation. Many medical devices, such as pacemakers, artificial joints, oxygen masks, x-ray machines, and assorted surgical equipment, present serious potential hazards to the patient-user. The manufacturers have often failed to report to the FDA malfunctions that could cause injury or death. Until 1984, the FDA had tried to encourage the manufacturers of these devices to report voluntarily any injuries or deaths, but the agency finally concluded that the average report of 200 deaths and injuries annually represented less than a tenth of the actual numbers. In several cases that involved faulty pacemakers and malfunctioning anesthesia equipment, the FDA learned about problems three to six months later. Fed up, the agency in 1984 began to require the manufacturers to report promptly any deaths or serious injuries from the use of these products, but as of 1989 the Public Citizen Health Research Group reported that the FDA was not adequately enforcing the regulation, resulting in numerous injuries and deaths. For example, unreported was a case involving apparent alarm failures on an infant respiration and heart rate monitor that resulted in the deaths of four infants and serious injuries to four others. The group charged that FDA records showed that at least 35 manufacturers had flouted the law requiring them to report any malfunction that results in death or serious injury.[22] Another 33 companies failed to meet the reporting deadline.

As an example, during the 1970s, the Food and Drug Administration charged the Cordis Corporation, the second largest producer of pacemakers, with 148 counts of violating quality-control standards in their pacemaker plant. Many of them were so flagrant that the FDA said the entire quality-control function was dangerously sloppy and that quality

goals were subservient to production goals and profits. The case precipitated the enactment of stronger federal legislation to ensure high-quality
medical devices. The law now specifies that these vital medical products
must be produced and tested under strict safety standards. Despite this,
Cordis pleaded guilty in 1988 to ten counts of shipping pacemakers that
were faulty or mislabeled, and agreed to pay $264,000 in fines and other
costs.[23] The pacemakers had the potential of suddenly losing their ability
to stimulate the heart.

By the time the giant pharmaceutical company Pfizer withdrew its
Bjork-Shiley convexo concave prosthetic heart valve from the market in
November 1986, more than 200 victims, or their survivors, had sued
Pfizer for valve implants that were prone to fracture and failure. More
than 150 deaths had been linked to more than 230 strut fractures of
defective valves that were manufactured by Pfizer's Shiley subsidiary in
Irvine, California. Up to that point, these heart valves had been implanted in 85,000 patients, approximately half of whom were outside
the United States. In August 1988, Dr. Sidney Wolfe, director of Public
Citizen's Health Research Group, said that criminal action should be
brought against this pharmaceutical corporation because of Pfizer's
"reckless disregard for human life and their knowing and willful marketing and promoting of a product that they were aware was defectively
designed, defectively manufactured and continued killing people despite
their claims that they were fixing it by doing these, in retrospect, proven
fruitless quality control adjustments." Wolfe said that there was "a whole
clearinghouse" of smoking gun documents relating to the heart valve.
"We have all these internal memos and documents, the original engineering drawings, memos from employees there, saying there are serious
problems with the valve and so forth, and that is why these companies
are not letting any of these cases go to trial."[24]

Except for good brakes, there is probably no greater safety factor in
an automobile than its tires. Until the government increased tire safety
by requiring the industry to issue tread-life grading rules in 1979, tire
manufacturers could produce what they pleased. As a result, manufacturers marketed millions of unsafe tires; millions of customers had no
way of knowing whether one tire was actually safer than another. The
most infamous tire case involved Firestone Rubber Company's production of defective steel-belted radial "500" tires sold for several years prior
to 1977. These defective tires contributed to hundreds of accidents and
injuries, and caused at least 41 deaths. Firestone officials knew that they
were marketing a dangerous tire, as one internal memorandum had
stated that "we are making an inferior quality radial" subject to belt-
edge separation at high speeds. Firestone finally recalled 10 million of
its tires, and in 1980 the government fined the corporation $500,000
for illegally delaying the recall.

Corporations that knowingly manufacture, advertise and promote hazardous products should be liable for their disregard for human life and safety. Fortunately, many corporations today are making greater efforts to produce safer consumer products. These changes have come about more from government intervention against manufacturers and as a consequence of growing consumer product-liability suits than from any qualms of corporate conscience. According to *Common Cause*, in 1989 victims were filing over 100,000 liability suits annually, most of them product-related. The corporations fear not only the mounting monetary loss resulting from these suits but also the bad publicity.

THE DALKON SHIELD

Americans and people throughout the world rely on the assumed high quality and safety of products made and sold by U.S. transnational corporations. The Dalkon shield is the most notorious instance of a large corporation's manufacture of a dangerous product and of its having concealed the serious harmful effects of its use.[25] A major health-product manufacturer, A. H. Robins, introduced the shield in 1971 as a "modern, superior and safe" intrauterine device (IUD) of thumb-nail-size made of metal or plastic used to prevent conception. Doctors implanted the shield in some 2.2 million American women; the U.S. Agency for International Development (AID) bought 800,000 to 1 million of them for distribution in the Third World. Eventually, Robins sold 4.5 million IUDs in the United States and 79 other countries before the Food and Drug Administration made Robins halt sales in 1974.

A catastrophe of profound proportions followed the implantation of this device. Over 200,000 American women reported having suffered injuries. The Dalkon shield tended to cause life-threatening forms of infection known as pelvic inflammatory disease. The tail string of the shield, made up of tiny strands encased in nylon, hangs out of the uterus in such a way that a woman could check to verify that it is in place. The wicking properties of the string facilitated the movement of bacteria from the outside into the uterus, resulting in infection. In case of a pregnancy, which sometimes did occur, the infection was much worse, possibly impairing or destroying the woman's ability to bear children. Even after the removal of the device, former shield wearers suffered chronic pain and illnesses that sometimes required hospitalization and surgery. Thousands of women throughout the world who had conceived while the shield was still implanted miscarried, developed infections, or gave birth to children with grave congenital defects, including blindness, cerebral palsy, and mental retardation.

Prior to marketing the Dalkon shield, A. H. Robins had not properly tested it for safety, either in animals or humans. It had turned down proposals from outside the company to conduct a series of studies ascertaining the safety of the shield. Within a year after the contraceptive's introduction, the company received reports from doctors of disastrous infections and pregnancies. Had A. H. Robins acted voluntarily then to withdraw the device, many deaths and injuries could have been avoided. In spite of all the evidence that the shield was dangerous, Robins continued to market it.

In 1985, two court-appointed examiners stated that Robins had "engaged in ongoing fraud by knowingly misrepresenting the nature, quality, safety and efficacy of the Dalkon shield. The ongoing fraud had also involved the destruction and withholding of relevant evidence." A. H. Robins hired public relations experts to provide misleading information about the number of women affected; it generally reported only those tests that showed the shield in a favorable light. When lawsuits followed, thousands of company documents relating to the device disappeared. A long line of Robins officials testified in court that they did not know, could not remember, or had not seen reports on the injuries and deaths of American women.

The 14,300 product liability suits filed against the company through mid-1985, with many others filed thereafter, illustrates the widespread extent of damage caused by the shield. By 1987, Robins and its insurer had paid out $378 million in damages, plus $107 million in legal fees; juries had awarded $25 million in punitive damages. This was not the end of this sordid corporate case. Robins had eventually filed for bankruptcy in 1985 because of the large number of liability suits. Subsequently, a federal judge castigated Robins for paying $8 million to creditors and substantial bonuses to top executives contrary to the provisions of the bankruptcy laws. In late 1987, the court ordered Robins to set aside $2.4 billion in a trust fund to be used to compensate women who were hurt by the contraceptive device. Nearly 200,000 women had filed claims of infections, sterility, miscarriages, and the birth of defective children. In 1988, the administrators of the trust fund offered $725 each to women who were willing to settle the claims and "whose injuries are less severe or have very little, if any, proof to support their claims." A stockholder sued Robins and its three chief officers for having made misleading statements about the shield; as a result, Robins agreed to pay $6.9 million to persons who had bought stock between 1971 and 1974 and who still held it. In 1989, federal prosecutors were proceeding with a grand jury investigation of Robins and some of its officers. The U.S. Supreme Court affirmed their right to review company documents about the shield. Referring to Robins as "Company X," the prosecutors had contended before the court that Robins had "engaged in on-going criminal activities for roughly 15 years." Among the possible criminal violations under investigation were conspiracy, mail and wire fraud, obstruction of justice, perjury and racketeering.

Miles W. Lord, chief U.S. district judge for Minnesota in 1983, heard some 400 shield cases. After approving a $4.6 million settlement of seven cases, he ordered Robins president and chief executive officer, the vice president for research and development, and the general counsel to appear before him on February 29, 1984. In his statement to them he said:

"I did not know." "It was not me." "Look elsewhere." Time and again, each of you has used this kind of argument in refusing to acknowledge your responsibility and in pretending to the world that the chief officers and the directors of your gigantic multinational corporation have no responsibility for the company's acts and omissions. Gentlemen, the results of these activities and attitudes on your part have been catastrophic. Today, as you sit here attempting once more to extricate yourselves from the legal consequences of your acts, none of you has faced up to the fact that more than 9,000 women have made claims that they gave up part of their womanhood so that your company might prosper. It is alleged that others gave their lives so you might prosper. And there stand behind them legions more who have been injured but who have not sought relief in the courts of this land. If one poor young man were, by some act of his— without authority or consent—to inflict such damage upon one woman, he would be jailed for a good portion of the rest of his life. And yet your company, without warning to women, invaded their bodies by the millions and caused them injuries by the thousands. And when the time came for these women to make their claims against your company, you attacked their characters. You inquired into their sexual practices and into the identity of their sexual partners. You . . . ruined families and reputations and careers—in order to intimidate those who would raise their voices against you. You introduced issues that had no relationship whatsoever to the fact that you planted in the bodies of these women instruments of death, of mutilation, of disease. Mr. Robins . . . you have taken the bottom line as your guiding beacon and the low road as your route. This is corporate irresponsibility at its meanest.

Robins Corporation was not the only one in serious trouble for having marketed an IUD device. G. D. Searle, a large pharmaceutical company and a division of Monsanto Company, made Copper–7, which became the most widely used IUD on the market; nearly 10 million sold between 1974 and 1986 when it was pulled off the market because of hundreds of damage suits. The device, it was charged, allowed bacteria to migrate to the wearer's uterus, causing pelvic inflammatory disease and sterility. Internal Searle documents released in a 1988 consumer damage case appeared to reveal that Searle did not pass information about potentially hazardous design flaws in the Copper–7 to the U.S. Food and Drug Administration.[26] Company medical officials rushed through early testing of the Copper–7 to meet marketing schedules, ignoring concern from researchers and the acknowledgement from one of its own senior medical officials that the Copper–7 design "leaves much to be desired." Moreover, an FDA task force that reviewed critical Searle animal tests on its products found "serious deficiencies" and questioned the company's integrity in reporting results of the tests to the FDA. A federal grand jury in 1988 awarded a Massachusetts woman nearly $9 million in finding that G. D. Searle intentionally misrepresented the Copper–7 uterine device, leading to the woman's sterility. The jury also decided the company was negligent in its testing of the device.

THE COFFIN NAIL–MAKERS

The tobacco corporations should have more on their consciences, if they have such consciences, than any other consumer product industry. Their products have killed and maimed hundreds of thousands of persons. The past six surgeons general of the United States, as early as 1964 and without exception, have declared that cigarette smoking is the chief single avoidable cause of death in our society and the most important public health issue of our time. In spite of the massive data that support the dangers of cigarette smoking, American corporations still manufacture "coffin nails" with no restrictions except the government-required package label health warning. Government reports estimate that over 395,000 deaths annually are related to cigarette smoking and that cigarette-related diseases cost taxpayers an estimated $3.8 billion in Medicare and Medicaid payments. Deaths caused by the legal drug nicotine in cigarettes are easily many times the number of deaths from illegal drugs.

Each year, the tobacco companies produce 600 billion cigarettes. In 1988, Americans consumed 3,121 cigarettes per person: The peak consumption was 4,345 in 1963. During 1988 Americans consumed a total of 500 billion cigarettes. Some of the largest U.S. corporations are cigarette manufacturers. The two largest of them in 1988 were Phillip Morris and Reynolds, each of which had about one-third of the total market. Marlboro brand, made by Phillip Morris, had one-fourth of all cigarette sales for 1988. Tobacco companies contribute more than $57 billion annually to the nation's gross national product, and the industry employs some 2.1 million workers, representing 2.5 percent of private-sector jobs. Those who would seek to curb or even destroy the tobacco industry must recognize that there would be severe economic repercussions if the industry were to be banned or were to reduce production drastically. Tobacco corporations contribute $15 billion in taxes, a favorite defense by cigarette-makers of their pernicious activities.

Fifty million Americans, about a fourth of the adult population, are hooked on the nicotine in cigarettes, and tobacco corporations encourage this addiction. Nicotine is a drug like any other drug. In May 1988, Surgeon General C. Everett Koop declared nicotine to be not just a habit but an addictive drug, "addicting in the same sense as are drugs such as heroin and cocaine, and this is supported by much evidence." According to the American Cancer Society, nicotine actually reaches the brain of the smoker twice as fast as does mainlined heroin.

Nicotine makes the heart beat faster; as a result, the heart is forced to work harder, needing more oxygen. At the same time, the carbon monoxide from the tobacco smoke reduces the amount of much-needed oxygen reaching the bloodstream and carried to the heart. As much as 30 percent of all coronary heart disease is linked to smoking. Pregnant women who smoke have a higher incidence of miscarriage and fetal death as smoking reduces the amount of oxygen available to the fetus. Diseases related to cigarette smoking include heart and blood-vessel disorders, lung diseases, cancer, digestive system illnesses, and increased infant mortality. Smoking increases the incidence of cancers of the larynx, mouth, throat, esophagus, bladder, pancreas, and kidneys. One-fourth of all cancer deaths are linked to smoking: 83 percent of lung cancer in men, and 43 percent of lung cancer in women. A report of the National Cancer Institute estimates that the risk of developing lung cancer is four to twenty-five times greater for smokers than for non-smokers, depending on the amount and duration of the smoking habit. For the first time in U.S. history, lung cancer is killing more women than breast cancer.

Cigarettes are America's most advertised product. The six largest cigarette makers are spending, as of now, about $2.5 billion each year on product advertising, three times the sum spent in 1976, all to promote the glories of smoking. This is about $9 for every man, woman, and child in the country. Because several hundred million of this total is tax deductible, the taxpayers pick up some of the tab. The advertising companies the cigarette manufacturers engage are masters in the art of persuading people to smoke cigarettes, particularly the brands they advertise. Their ads portray the desirability and acceptance of smoking by associating it with contemporary lifestyles, fashion, and recreation. The ads link smoking with youthful vigor, masculinity, feminine beauty, and social and sexual success. They depict cowboys, women in bathing suits, handsome young couples frolicking on the beach, and rugged wilderness scenes. They picture Philip Morris's Marlboro Man as rugged and handsome, and durable and tall in the saddle, even though many cowboys who have smoked Marlboros have died of lung cancer. The directors of the British television documentary, "Death in the West: The Marlboro Story," interviewed real-life cowboys who had all been heavy smokers but who now were in various stages of dying from cancer or emphysema.

Cigarette-makers like to give their products names that hardly fit a bit of ground-up tobacco wrapped in a piece of paper, names like Pall Mall, Malibu, Viceroy, Salem, Parliament, and Capri. In 1985, the R. J. Reynolds Tobacco Company marketed a new cigarette called Ritz. It carries the YSL logo of the French fashion designer, Yves Saint Laurent, and comes in an elegant box designed to appeal to style-conscious young women. Just what is needed—designer lung cancer.

In the bulk of their advertising, cigarette manufacturers target the young. About 20 percent of juveniles smoke; each year about 2 million teenagers take up the habit. A former model for Winston cigarette ads, David Goerlitz, testified in 1989 before Congressional hearings on a bill to ban cigarette advertising that he was "told very clearly that young people were the market we were after." He appeared in 42 Winston ads between 1981 and 1987, generally in ad sequences that pictured daring mountain rescues. He testified: "What I did for the past seven years is wrong. I glamorized something that kills you."[27] Tobacco companies argue, however, that their advertising is primarily directed at adults and that it seeks only to encourage smokers to switch to their brands. However, this is by no means always the case. Nationally syndicated columnist, Jack Anderson, reported that the R. J. Reynolds plan for marketing Salem cigarettes stated: "Through the association of Salem and its brand styles with emulatable personalities who are compatible with the aspirations and lifestyles of contemporary young adults, this important largest segment will be attracted to the brand."[28] As more middle- and upper-class white Americans have quit smoking, cigarette companies have greatly increased and directed their advertising to black-oriented magazines and newspapers. The cigarette companies also contributed to activities such as fashion shows and sponsor other events that draw large black audiences; in addition, they make generous contributions to black charities and colleges. Blacks have the nation's highest rates of lung cancer and coronary heart disease, the illnesses most linked to smoking, as well as the highest death rates from these diseases. Still, the tobacco industry encourages even more of them to smoke.

The mammoth tobacco industry completely and explicitly rejects the health hazards of smoking as it continues to try to create a positive social climate for smoking.[29] The tobacco industry fought hard to avoid the use of warning labels on cigarette packages. A prominent writer on health issues concluded: "Its [the tobacco industry's] arguments defy belief. Industry witnesses maintain, for example, that science has yet to show cigarettes to be the precise *cause* of cancer or anything else—despite widely accepted epidemiological evidence and more than 30,000 reports in medical literature of smoking links."[30] Even after cigarette manufacturers had agreed in 1972 to comply with the warning labels in advertising, the Federal Trade Commission subsequently had to force the three leading cigarette-makers to make the health-hazard warnings more prominent, fining each company $100,000.

Through advertising and other means, the industry fights hard against restrictions on passive smoking or smoking in public areas. Through the surgeon general, the government has issued a strong warning about the possible health risks to non-smokers who inhale smoke from others' cigarettes. It has been shown that on-the-job cigarette smoking adversely affects company profits, worker productivity, insurance rates, health costs, morale, and the health of the non-smokers.[31] The industry has responded by vigorously denying the health hazards to non-smokers. Their spokespersons ask: "What good is a law that is unenforceable, that creates expenses, inconveniences, and confrontations? That kind of law hurts *all* law. Then, too, when smoking is restricted, all of us lose a bit of freedom, smokers and non-smokers alike."[32]

The United States has banned the advertising of cigarettes on television and radio for nearly 20 years. For more than 32 years, the American Medical Association has banned cigarette advertising in all of its publications, and it has asked Congress for a ban on all cigarette advertising. The Lukens bill, introduced in the United States Congress in 1988, would ban all promotion and advertising of cigarettes in this country. The Canadian government, in 1989, banned all tobacco advertising and promotion. The law not only bans all print and broadcast advertising of tobacco products, it also orders the phase-out of all existing billboards and in-store tobacco advertising, and requires stronger health warnings on tobacco packaging. During the debate on the bill, cabinet member Jake Epp told the Canadian House of Commons: "If tobacco were discovered tomorrow, no government would permit its sale, much less its advertising." At least 14 other countries ban cigarette advertising; Norway and Italy have banned it for 23 years.[33] Even though cigarettes produce big tax revenues, the Soviet Union, East Germany, Poland, and other communist countries ban their advertising and have strong anti-smoking programs.

Anti-smoking sentiments have increased, and as early as 1987 the number of product liability suits that seek compensation for smoke-related deaths or injuries against major tobacco companies had risen to over 125.[34] The major tobacco companies had spent more than $100 million on legal help; they had retained more than 70 prestigious law firms. They also mobilized psychologists, physicians, economists, and medical researchers. The companies' defense is that each individual is responsible for such personal decisions in his or her life as smoking and failure to heed the cigarette warning labels. In presenting an unsuccessful damage suit in Newark in 1988, against the Liggett Group, Philip Morris, and the Lorillard unit of Loews Corporation, Federal Judge H. Lee Sorokin ruled that the jury could consider that the industry of which these defendants are a part entered into a sophisticated conspiracy . . . organized to refute, undermine and neutralize information coming from the scientific and medical community, and at the same time, to mislead the consuming public in an effort to encourage existing smokers to continue and new persons to commence.[35]

Cigarette ads of the 1950s, for example, indicated this. One said the new L&M filter brand of the Liggett Group was "just what the doctor ordered"; another said, "Play safe—Smoke Chesterfields" and another claimed "Nose, throat and accessory organs are not adversely affected by smoking Chesterfields." Other widely used slogans at the time included "Not a Cough in a Carload" (Old Gold), "The Throat Tested Cigarette" (Philip Morris), and "More Doctors Smoke Camels Than Any Other Cigarette" (Camels).

By the late 1980s, the tobacco industry and its spokesperson, the Tobacco Institute, founded in 1958 by leading cigarette manufacturers, was in serious difficulty. Among efforts to change the public's negative attitude toward cigarette companies, seven of them contributed $1.2 million of the total $2.2 million spent to refurbish the historic Treaty Room of the State Department, which was redecorated in a tobacco leaf motif complete with seed pods and blossoms. Tobacco firms also act as angels of the arts in an effort to cleanse a nicotine-stained corporate image. In 1987, for example, Philip Morris's "strategic philanthropy" enriched cultural institutions that ranged from New York's Carnegie Hall to the bicoastal Joffrey Ballet and Washington's National Art Gallery to the tune of $13 million, and in the same year RJR Nabisco, maker of Camels and Winstons, contributed nearly $3 million, primarily to community art organizations.

As cigarette consumption in the United States declines, the cigarette companies have increased their successful promotion of overseas sales. They have launched gigantic advertising campaigns in Europe and, increasingly, in Third World countries. The United States is fast becoming an exporter of death to the far corners of the globe. Almost everywhere overseas, huge advertisements on buses, buildings, and boardwalks display Marlboro and other American cigarettes. Patrick Reynolds, grandson of the tobacco king R. J. Reynolds and a leading anti-smoking advocate, likens American tobacco companies' massive efforts to market cigarettes abroad to a "new Opium Trade."[36] It would appear that there is one set of health standards for smoking being established for American citizens, and another for those of foreign countries, particularly in the Third World.

The tobacco issue, however, is not limited to cigarette smoking. Pipe smoking is frequently linked to cancer of the lips, while "smokeless tobacco" (snuff and chewing tobacco) are linked to cancers of the mouth.

The United States Tobacco Company's promotion of "smokeless tobacco," of which it is the chief manufacturer, contributed to the largest profit margin among the *Fortune* 500 in 1985. The ads of this corporation and those of other tobacco companies have turned 12 million Americans into users, a fourth of them under age 21. In 1986, the FTC had to issue rules that one of three specific conspicuous warnings must be placed on all smokeless tobacco: "This product may cause cancer of the mouth"; "This product may cause gum disease and tooth loss"; and "This product is not a safe alternative to cigarettes."[37]

A warning of things likely to happen in the tobacco and other potentially lethal industries came in a 1985 Maryland Supreme Court decision in a case related to the handgun industry. Although it does not rival the cigarette industry, the U.S. handgun industry is also a great killer of Americans. In 1983, handguns killed over 9,000 Americans. This figure compares with 35 people killed in Japan, 8 in Great Britain, 7 in Sweden, 10 in Australia, and 6 in Canada, all of which prohibit the possession of handguns. Many American groups have lobbied unsuccessfully to outlaw certain handguns and to institute strict gun controls. Like the American Tobacco Institute with cigarettes, the National Rifle Association, through its powerful lobbying efforts, has not only resisted all these efforts but has also sought to weaken the existing laws. It was thus gratifying to have Maryland's Supreme Court, in 1985, rule in a startling decision that manufacturers and retailers of "Saturday Night Specials" can be sued by victims of crime in the state. The court ruled that such product liability is today clear, for the makers and sellers of these guns "know, or should know" that they are virtually useless except for criminal activities.[38]

POLLUTING AIR AND WATER

Many *Fortune* 500 corporations have shown utter contempt for the environment and have continually opposed state and federal efforts to protect it. The federal government finally had to intervene in 1970 with the Clean Air Act which regulates how much and where industries and motor vehicles may release contaminants into the air. Subsequently, a 1974 law enabled the federal government with the Clean Water Act to control water pollution. Nonetheless, since the passage of these two laws, the American public has been the victim of pollution scams run by some of America's most respected corporations. The "Filthy Five" was an annual designation by Washington, D.C.-based Environmental Action Foundation for corporations "having a sorry environmental record and making large campaign contributions to congressional candidates with anti-environmental records." In 1981, the accolade went to Dow Chemical, Standard Oil of Indiana, Occidental Petroleum, Republic Steel, and Weyerhauser. In 1989, the Natural Resources Defense Council named Eastman Kodak, General Electric, Upjohn, and Boeing as operating plants emitting particularly large amounts of dangerous chemical pollutants into the air. The oil companies in particular have had a poor record in air and water pollution. The New York-based Council on Economic Priorities gave Mobil and Texaco poor environmental marks in 1989. A study of *Fortune* 500 law violators found that the oil industry accounted for half of all environmental violations and a third of the more serious ones.[39]

So extensive has the corporate abuse of the environment become that a coalition of environmental groups, religious organizations, and investors (among them the pension funds of California and New York City) that collectively control more than $100 billion in investments, formulated a Code of Conduct in 1989 to be used in judging which corporations are "environmentally responsible."[40] This ten-part code, designated as The Valdez Principles after the Alaskan oil spill of the Exxon Valdez tanker, calls on corporations to address the environmental effects of both production processes and products. It also includes requirements that corporations appoint environmental experts to their boards of directors and that they conduct and publicize an annual audit of their compliance with the environmental code. The code will serve as a basis for shareholder pressures on companies to improve environmental performance, in much the same manner as pressure is exerted on corporate business and investments in South Africa.

For 20 years corporate magnates have been bemoaning the effects of air- and water-pollution controls on business, even though a wealth of evidence has shown that such pollution controls have resulted in better health, lower medical bills, and diminished damage to vegetation, crops, and buildings. In fact, between 1970 and 1985, the enforcement of the federal Clean Air Act resulted in cutting sulfur oxides by 62 percent, hydrocarbons by 26 percent, and carbon monoxide by 31 percent.[41] Only nitrogen oxides increased, but only by 7 percent.

Corporations claim that compliance costs have caused capital shortages, markedly reduced corporate profits, and have also resulted in unemployment. These claims largely lack substantiation. A 1984 EPA policy analysis concluded that although the costs of pollution control programs may be high in absolute terms, their overall effects on prices and gross national product are negligible. In fact, a 1982 study by the Washington, D.C.-based Natural Resources Defense Council found that while $65.2 billion was spent between 1972 and 1979 to comply with the law, the country realized an estimated $97.3 billion in benefits to health and the environment. A considerable net gain in employment has resulted from the implementation of anti-pollution laws, including the manufacture of pollution control equipment. Corporate executives also maintain that anti-pollution laws are partly responsible for the high price of U.S. exports. In response, it is significant that Japan has even stricter anti-pollution measures.

Typical of corporate disregard for the environment was National Steel's failure to protect the local environment, and thus the health of local residents, near their plants.[42] One of National Steel's largest blast furnaces, for example, is only a few hundred yards from a school in one of Detroit's low-income neighborhoods. For years the plant spewed out tons of soot and dangerous pollutants which are closely linked to various diseases. National Steel had done nothing to correct the problem, even though the pollution was illegal, until finally, after a great public outcry, a federal court ordered the company to quit stalling and put adequate controls on the blast furnace by the end of 1982. National Steel continued to stall, asking for a Clean Air "credit" for having paved plant dirt roads to control dust. In 1982, a federal judge hauled National Steel back into court, reprimanded it, fined the company $2.5 million in back pollution penalties, and finally forced it to install pollution controls on the blast furnace.

In yet another case, in 1984 an estimated 30 to 50 gallons of methyl isocyanate (MIC) was carelessly spilled onto the ground at the FMC Corporation pesticide plant at Middleport, New York.[43] The chemical vaporized instantly and was swept by the wind to the nearby elementary school where it was drawn into the building through a ventilation system. Nearly 500 students and teachers were in the building. The estimated concentration of deadly MIC at the school was 100 to 200 times the 8-hour worker-exposure limit. More than 100 children received eye washes, and several needed oxygen. FMC and the town of Middleport were lucky, for had it been a 60-degree day rather than a colder 40-degree day, numerous deaths would have occurred. The state department of environmental conservation imposed a civil fine of $5,000 on the giant corporation.

As another example, corporate disregard for clean air laws caused the Justice Department in 1988 to file an $8.2-million suit against giant E. I. du Pont de Nemours and Co., charging that between 1983 and 1986 the company helped produced gasoline containing excessive levels of dangerous lead at a New Jersey refinery. According to the EPA, the company had injected 2,200 tons of excess lead into gasoline—and eventually released into the air—in the largest violation of the federal law passed in 1979, that is phasing down the use of lead.

The chemical industry is a major polluter. In fact, Rachel Carson's 1962 book, *Silent Spring*, alerted the United States to the hazards of toxic chemicals and other pollutants. She wrote: "The most alarming of all man's assaults upon the environment is the contamination of air, earth, rivers, and sea with dangerous and even lethal chemicals." Carson's book, which was attacked by chemical corporations and which sold 165,000 hardcover and 1.8 million softcover copies, had much to do with the creation of the Environmental Protection Agency in 1970.

By 1988, however, the chemical industry was running scared. Citizens and workers were angry and pressures were being put on the government to do more. As a consequence, the Chemical Manufacturers Association and several large corporations, including Dow Chemical and Monsanto, began increasing their efforts to clean up their production processes. The goal was to calm apprehensions before the imposition of even stricter laws. For the first time, the Chemical Manufacturers Association proposed operating and safety standards that its 170 members would have to meet to retain membership. Monsanto, for example, proceeded to reduce all its hazardous emissions by 90 percent, even though they already met federal standards. Dow realized that their hazardous-waste landfills of the 1970s were increasingly costly because of cleanups and law suits. Their 1986 program for reducing waste was named a model for other companies. Du Pont vowed to stop making chlorofluorocarbons, which are thought to eat away the Earth's protective ozone layer, by the 1990s. Barry Commoner, a chief founder of the environmental movement, commented, "The cutting edge of the unresolved environmental crisis lies with the chemical industry. When [a chemical company] says they are doing their best, my first response is 'How come you didn't do this 30 years ago?' "[44]

DUMPING HAZARDOUS WASTES

Love Canal is probably the most publicized case of environmental pollution in the history of the United States. The site was named after a failed hydroelectrical canal built by an entrepreneur named William Love. Houses later sprang up around the site, and when the city of Niagara Falls needed some land near the canal in 1953 for a school, Hooker Chemical Company (later a subsidiary of Occidental Petroleum) sold it to them for $1, with a proviso that the school absolve the company from any future liability for injuries or property damage caused by the dump's contents. Hooker knew it had buried 43 million pounds of highly toxic industrial wastes in the dump and that the area should really not be used as a site for homes and a school. Within a few years, residents were calling the Hooker dispensary to ask about many problems that were increasingly being noticed. Children's feet became burned by a brown-black liquid that oozed from the canal, neighborhood dogs lost their hair and developed severe skin diseases, nothing would grow in yards, and dark liquids oozed into basements, particularly after heavy rains. Even more frightening, diseases began to occur such as asthma, nephritis, and hepatitis, particularly among the children. There were also reports of an abnormal number of miscarriages, stillbirths, birth defects, loss of hair, and cancer. In 1978, following numerous complaints, New York state health officials investigated the area. They found the air, water, and soil of the entire canal area to be highly contaminated with a wide range of carcinogenic chemicals coming from the Hooker dump. They found particularly high levels in the air of basements. The federal government called for immediate action to clean up Love Canal and compensation for the $7 million the government had already spent. The federal suit required a $45-million bond to ensure a proper cleanup. Had Hooker originally taken proper steps to dispose of the toxic chemicals, the cleanup would have cost about $4 million. However, many lives had been irreparably damaged, and the total legal claims exceeded $2 billion. Primarily because of the Love Canal tragedy, in 1981 Congress set up a $1.6-billion "superfund" to bankroll a nationwide cleanup of old waste dumps and spill sites that posed grave danger to water supplies and human health. The waste disposal law also provided penalties of five-year prison terms and fines ($250,000 fine for an individual, $1 million for a corporation) for knowingly putting people in danger of serious injury. Subsequently, information revealed that Hooker had also dumped approximately 350 million pounds of toxic industrial waste at three other sites near Niagara Falls.

These wastes generally have no use, but some means must be found for their disposal. Typically, in the past, few major corporations were concerned about these matters; they simply got rid of them by the cheapest means possible, with little or no concern for the effects on people or the environment. Such wastes can contaminate the soil and water supplies, destroy animal habitats, and kill fish and other marine life as well as birds and land animals when the vegetation or the water becomes contaminated. They can seriously affect human health; particularly vulnerable are persons who live near hazardous-waste disposal sites. More serious problems yet result when the toxic wastes pollute drinking water supplies.

The wide-ranging problems of dumping hazardous wastes have only been well recognized in fairly recent years.[45] Serious hazardous-waste violations committed by major U.S. corporations have continued into the 1980s, in spite of many new laws. A former head of the Justice Department's environmental crime section was quoted in 1989 as having said, "It is not the midnight dumpers who are being prosecuted; it is some of the best known names of corporate America."[46] As an example, the government charged General Motors in 1984 with failure to comply with EPA water pollution regulations at 10 plants; it had asked General Motors to remove water contaminants such as cyanide, copper, chromium, and zinc discharged as byproducts in making bumpers and other auto parts. The company faced a maximum fine of $1 million per week. As another example of flagrant disregard for problems of hazardous waste, in 1985, under government pressure, Westinghouse agreed to the largest hazardous waste settlement in the history of the EPA: $75 million. Westinghouse was forced to dig up plant wastes that were contaminated with highly toxic PCB. When the government filed the suit in 1983, Westinghouse denied all responsibility, saying, "As far as Westinghouse is aware, the sites have remained dormant and unused for the past 10 years or more with no adverse impact on public health." A 1985 judgment, however, forced Westinghouse to dig up 650,000 cubic yards of contaminated material, build an incinerator, monitor groundwater near the sites for as long as 30 years, and provide pure water to any resident within a few miles whose water had been contaminated by PCB. The EPA administrator said the agreement was "the largest hazardous-waste settlement in the history of the agency"; the government estimated the total cost at $75 million to $100 million.[47] Pennwalt was indicted by the federal government in 1988 for negligence and for covering up the real amount of a 75,000-gallon spill of sodium chlorate into a river. It faced a maximum fine of $1 million. Some other large corporations that have been involved in other waste disposal cases include Shell Oil, Monsanto, United Technologies, Allied Signal, and Pfizer. INFORM, a New York-based environmental organization, reported in 1985 that a survey of 29 chemical plants found little reduction in the volume of hazardous waste; such reduction is the most effective way to minimize future risks of toxic discharges.

In a flagrant case, the giant W. R. Grace Company agreed to pay $8 million, or $1 million per claimant, to the families of child leukemia victims in Woburn, Massachusetts, to settle a civil lawsuit accusing the company of having negligently dumped two cancer-causing agents that had allegedly contaminated the Woburn drinking water and had thereby caused leukemia and other illnesses. In 1987, the government indicted W. R. Grace Company for having made false statements to the EPA in 1982 about certain dangerous chemicals in their possession and of having concealed from the EPA the fact that waste materials, including waste solvents, had been poured on the ground behind their plant on numerous occasions.

The proper disposal of hazardous wastes, particularly nuclear wastes, has come to rank high in concern to American citizens. Nearly four out of five Americans, according to a 1985 *Time* poll, felt that not enough had been done to clean up toxic waste sites; more than two-thirds said they would be willing to pay higher taxes to fund cleanup programs in their areas. Both the government and the public is looking on the proper disposal of hazardous wastes, particularly by major industrial producers, as a serious issue. At issue is the assurance that the makers of these products do not simply dump them; they must handle wastes properly without creating health or environmental problems. Chemical and oil companies produce the bulk of dangerous wastes. Some 66,000 chemicals are used in the United States; the EPA has identified 60,000 of them as potential hazards, and 402 as extremely hazardous. A number of major corporations have expended large sums on better disposal means such as burning. For years, waste incinerators with scrubbing devices have been used by such companies as 3M Corporation, Dow Chemical, and Kodak. Tax credits also provide great incentives for these constructive measures.

Due to public pressure, federal, state and local governments are adopting increasingly strong measures concerning hazardous-waste disposal. Los Angeles County's special Toxic Waste Strike Force, for example, has been particularly strict, and many executives of large firms have been put behind bars. One executive who went to jail for illegal dumping was the president of the local Culligan International Company, a Los Angeles franchise of the nationwide water softener firm. In another case, the company vice president went to jail, and the firm paid a $75,000 fine in addition to $500,000 in cleanup costs. Many Los Angeles violators also risk the shame of being forced to "repent" their dumping by being required to take out full-page newspaper ads telling the public about their illegal activities.

Residents of local areas now have access to a "right to know" law that forces manufacturers of poisonous chemical to disclose the nature of the chemicals and of their disposal in order to safeguard company employees and local residents. Twenty-one states had already established such laws when, in 1987, Congress passed the Community Right to Know Act, a drastic amendment to the federal Hazardous Waste Superfund law. This act requires companies that operate nationally to notify local community residents of toxic substances released into their environment. It also requires that the local public have broad access to company files regarding the type, quantities, and location of chemicals at local plant facilities. The giant corporations appear to have slept all these years until a federal law finally awakened them.

In the end, there must be even greater efforts on the part of the industries that profit from their chemical products to bring the waste problem under control. One drastic solution might be to curtail certain chemical processes and, if necessary, to impose an outright ban on the manufacture of highly dangerous substances until the chemical industry has demonstrated adequate measures to properly dispose of its own industrial wastes.

AGENT ORANGE

Even under conditions of war, some American corporations (not to mention some presidents) appear to lack all sense of social responsibility. If a corporation can make a profit from a chemical weapon so dangerous that it injures our own soldiers, it often will not hesitate to produce it. This happened during the Vietnam War when the army used the chemical "Agent Orange," which contains the deadly compound dioxin, to defoliate large forest areas and thus expose enemy targets. Seven large U.S. corporations, including Dow Chemical, manufactured this herbicide. After application of this defoliant, the jungles became silent; there were no more insects, birds, or animals. The soldiers called it "The Land of the Dead." After the war, widespread reports came from veterans that they suffered damage to their nerves and livers, became sensitive to light, developed cancers and skin problems involving rashes all over their bodies, and also suffered from mental disturbances. Soldiers had been forced to handle the chemical, to march through areas being sprayed with it, and to drink from streams contaminated with it. It is estimated that 40,000 veterans may eventually become ill or die from the effects of Agent Orange, and 3,000 of their children may be deformed.[48]

After the war, more than 16,000 Vietnam veterans brought suit against Dow and the six other large U.S. chemical corporations. The suit was finally resolved by a court settlement of a paltry $180 million in cash benefits to totally disabled veterans and to survivors of deceased veterans. Dow documents made public during the court proceedings revealed that in 1965, when the government was purchasing millions of pounds of Agent Orange, Dow's toxicology director wrote an internal report to the effect that dioxin could be exceptionally toxic to human beings, and there was other evidence that most chemical corporations knew for a long time of other indications of the adverse effects of this chemical.[49] Dow claimed that because it was a government contractor, the government, and not Dow, was to blame for any chemical injuries resulting from the use of Agent Orange in Vietnam. The veterans' attorney called the matter nonsense. "The government contracted to get war materials but under no circumstances did the government contract to have its own men poisoned or killed." Protesting the court settlement, the leader of the veterans' group said: "We wanted to put the chemical companies on the hot seat. We wanted the public to know what they have been doing and that's not going to happen now. Chemical companies are probably going to come out of this smelling like a rose."[50]

A March 1988 *Wall Street Journal*/NBC news poll found that 61 percent of the American people favored more government regulation of the environment, and 50 percent favored more regulation of on-the-job health and safety. If responsible corporate power means a great deal to *Fortune* 500 corporations, as many maintain it does, why did they not beat down the doors during the eight years of the Reagan administration to ask why the administration had gutted the Occupational Safety and Health Administration, wrecked the Environmental Protection Agency, and demonstrated an overall contempt for the health of workers and citizens who were living within the range of toxic wastes and dump sites?

Chapter 7

CORPORATE BRIBERY

No abuse of power has so tarnished the corporate image or shown the need for government legislation as the numerous public revelations of wholesale political and foreign bribery that came to light during the 1970s. These revelations are one of the most sordid chapters in American corporate history. Investigations revealed widespread illegal corporate political contributions and extensive bribery of foreign government officials. When the bribes were large, they significantly distorted the corporation's actual financial picture, thus misleading company stockholders as well as the Securities and Exchange Commission (SEC) and the Internal Revenue Service. When U.S. corporations bribe officials of developing countries, they may help to undermine that country's political stability and in some cases contribute to the spread of anti-American feeling. A particularly serious situation develops when pharmaceutical corporations bribe health officials in other countries to obtain permission to sell dangerous drug products.

BRIBING FOREIGN OFFICIALS

More than 450 large U.S. corporations, mostly *Fortune* 500s, ultimately disclosed to the Securities and Exchange Commission during the late 1970s and early 1980s illegal or questionable payments abroad, totaling more than $1 billion and paid either as direct bribes to foreign government officials or through foreign corporate "sales agents." They included ITT, McDonnell Douglas, Northrop, Grumman, Textron, American Cyanamid, and Xerox Corporation. Thirty-two corporations had each given bribes totaling more than $1 million over the years, and many individual corporations made bribes totaling $10 million or more. Corporations used various illegal methods to bribe, and they manipulated their financial records to conceal or disguise the source of the money or its use. A few large corporations took a stand against foreign bribery. W. Michael Blumenthal, chairman and chief executive officer of Bendix, later said:

I insisted that the company pay not one penny in bribes. I was told we couldn't do that—that we would lose business. Well, we didn't. What did happen was that we attracted the best graduates from Harvard and Stanford who had read about us. It helped morale at Bendix.[1]

Foreign bribes often had far-reaching consequences for U.S. foreign relations, not only in Japan but also in Italy, the Netherlands, and many other countries. As an example, over a period of several years during the 1970s, Lockheed bribed the Japanese prime minister and several other Japanese officials, politicians, and businessmen in order to secure lucrative contracts for the sale of 21 of Lockheed's Tristar jets to Japan's domestic carrier, All Nippon Airways. Prime Minister Kekuei Tanaka received bribes of $1.6 million; the total bribes paid to the Japanese involved in the scheme was $12.6 million. Lockheed's Swiss subsidiary funneled the bribe money through a Swiss bank, and the bribe eventually reached Japan after it had been converted into yen through the services of Deak and Company, a large New York–based international firm that deals in foreign currencies. During this period, Deak provided a courier service from its Hong Kong office for the transfer of the Lockheed bribes from Switzerland or Los Angeles. The conversions to yen were made in Hong Kong. The couriers, who carried specially designed air travel bags in which they could neatly stack millions of yen, then either delivered the yen directly to Lockheed executives in Japan or to a Japanese citizen who maintained a secret bank account in which to deposit the money. Great secrecy surrounded the cash delivery; in some cases, the prime minister's secretary received money in a parked car behind a foreign embassy. In its corporate financial statements, Lockheed listed the money paid out as "prepaid commissions" or "marketing services" in order to avoid prosecution by the Securities and Exchange Commission and the Internal Revenue Service.

After Lockheed's bribes became known, the Japanese government prosecuted their prime minister, three members of the Diet, and 13 Lockheed Japanese directors on charges of bribery, tax evasion, and violations of Japan's foreign exchange laws. In 1983, Prime Minister Tanaka received a 4-year prison sentence and a fine of $3.1 million. A member of the Diet who was convicted of selling bribes received a 2-

year prison sentence, and the court sentenced the head of a huge Japanese financial empire, a friend of the prime minister, to 1 year in prison for having perjured himself in testimony related to the scandal. The chairman of All Nippon Airways was convicted and sentenced to a 3-year prison term. As of 1988, several of the cases were still under final review by the High Court of Japan.

In the United States, the Securities and Exchange Commission filed a complaint against Lockheed charging that it had failed to disclose, as required by law, the payments made to foreign officials, the secret funds used for the payments, and the alteration of financial records to conceal the payments. On the same day, Lockheed agreed "without admitting any wrong" to an injunction forbidding it to engage in any activities of this type in the future. A Senate committee thoroughly investigated the case. After a 3-year investigation, Lockheed pleaded guilty in 1979 to charges that it concealed payoffs to the prime minister and other officials, and was fined $647,000. The Department of Justice then dropped further prosecution of Lockheed or its officials for misconduct. The investigations in this case, however, contributed significantly to the passage in 1977 of the Foreign Corrupt Practices Act specifically outlawing bribery of foreign officials. Lockheed subsequently reported to the Securities and Exchange Commission more than $30 million in improper foreign payments made in various other countries.

In 1975, the chairman and chief executive officer of United Brands jumped to his death from the 44th floor of his New York City office building following the Securities and Exchange Commission disclosure of the $2.5-million bribe that his corporation had paid to high Honduran officials to head off a banana export tax imposed on its subsidiary, United Fruit Company (Chiquita Brand). This poverty-ridden country had imposed a tax amounting to $1 on every 40-pound box of bananas, which would have cost United Brands several million dollars annually. There was no such tax in several other countries where competing U.S. corporations operated. The bribes were successful, as the company won a tax reduction that saved United Brands $7.5 million in the first year alone. United Brands concealed the bribes they paid the Honduran officials through payments made by the Paris branch of the Chase Manhattan Bank. In the case of a bribe of $1.25 million United Brands made to former Honduran President Oswald Lopez Arellan, they made payment through a numbered Swiss bank account.

The widely publicized death of the United Brands board chairman resulted in a large-scale Securities and Exchange Commission investigation of multinational firms' overseas concealment of foreign bribes and questionable payments that violate both SEC and Internal Revenue Service laws requiring full financial disclosure of all corporate transactions to the government. The disclosures were also important factors in the passage of the Foreign Corrupt Practices Act of 1977 which imposed severe penalties on any corporation or top executive that bribed foreign government officials. Most of the data that follow are from the files of the Securities and Exchange Commission.

Surveys have shown that many U.S. corporations often find it easier to make profits in their overseas operations than at home, and many large U.S. corporations have shifted appreciable amounts of their assets and sales efforts abroad. Exxon, for example, operates in more than 100 countries. What may be of benefit to a corporation in its dealings abroad may actually be damaging to the political and national interests of the United States and to those of the foreign countries themselves. In order to achieve their objectives, the corporations may bribe top foreign officials or political parties. They give bribes to secure foreign business; to beat out a competitor, either foreign or domestic; to avoid harassment of the corporation by foreign officials; to reduce corporate taxes in the foreign country; to obtain favorable action in connection with corporate business; or to reduce the risks of unfavorable action by some foreign political party.[2]

According to data of the Securities and Exchange Commission, pharmaceutical corporations had the worst record of foreign bribery of any U.S. transnationals. Of the 20 U.S. drug companies with the largest worldwide sales, 19 disclosed substantial questionable payments. These corporations included Merck, Warner-Lambert, Pfizer, Upjohn, Squibb, and Bristol-Myers. Warner-Lambert disclosed bribe payments of $2.6 million made in 14 countries. In 1976, the giant Upjohn filed a financial report with the Securities and Exchange Commission that revealed questionable company payments totaling $4.2 million in 29 countries between 1971 and 1976. Certain pharmaceutical companies had made large amounts of illegal payments. Of the 32 corporations that had given more than $1 million in improper payments, the 7 pharmaceutical corporations represented the largest number from any industry.

Pharmaceutical companies gave bribes to secure sales and favorable actions on drug product regulations, prices, and taxes, and to influence officials at all levels of government—cabinet ministers, health officers, factory inspectors, customs officials, drug registration and pricing staffs, and tax assessors. For example, reports indicated that a fairly common practice had been to bribe officials in the Italian Ministry of Health to secure approval for new pharmaceutical products.[3] Bribes made to sell drugs in the developing world can have particularly serious consequences for human life. A bribe may persuade a health official to allow the marketing of a dangerous drug, or a customs official may be offered money to allow a banned drug product to be brought into the country. An inspector may take a bribe to overlook unsanitary conditions in a drug manufacturing plant to enable it to pass inspection. A generous bribe to a Third World health official may encourage him or her to have the government purchase a quantity of a company's drugs far in excess of need and so beyond the product's safe shelf life, a particular hazard that can result in deaths and injuries in a tropical climate.

One-third of the companies in the oil industry used bribery to achieve their corporate objectives, according to records of the Securities and Exchange Commission. The companies gave bribes in efforts to secure tax deferrals, to obtain refinery licenses, or to get permission to import materials. For example, Exxon reported total bribes amounting to $78 million. Between 1963 and 1972, an Exxon Italian affiliate secretly contributed $27 million to Italian political parties. In other documents filed with the Securities and Exchange Commission, Exxon disclosed similar payments made to government officials and political parties in Thailand, Indonesia, Australia, and Japan.

Revelations of the extent of the corporation's foreign bribery shocked a 1982 review committee of ITT's board of directors. The committee's review disclosed millions of dollars of previously unrevealed payments, some made even after passage of the Foreign Corrupt Practices Act in 1977. For example, the investigation raised the amount of foreign payments for the years 1971 to 1975 from a reported $8.7 million to $13.9 million. The committee found that ITT's long-time chief executive officer, Harold Geneen, had countenanced foreign bribery from 1971 to 1980 amounting to $20 million of illegal and questionable payments throughout the world. Government officials in Austria, Turkey, Iran, Indonesia, the Philippines, Algeria, and Mexico were among the recipients of these bribes. ITT concealed its questionable behavior by all types of devious practices. For example, an ITT subsidiary in one country would funnel bribes to a subsidiary in another country, and this subsidiary then made the payment on behalf of the first subsidiary. In 1979, ITT had agreed to a federal court order barring future violations of SEC regulations in settling charges of payoffs in foreign countries.

Not only did ITT violate U.S. laws when it failed to report its bribes, it often violated the host country's laws as well. The Securities and Exchange Commission accused ITT of having been involved in questionable transactions made by the officers of an Italian ITT subsidiary that were said to total more than $6 million. Some ITT units had also used an ITT-owned Liechtenstein company simply to evade Italian currency control and income tax laws, and possibly laws of other countries as well. In a well-publicized case, an Austrian court convicted ITT in 1981 of having made more than $1 million in "questionable payments" (bribes) from 1974 to 1979 in connection with its contract to build the 2,000-bed Vienna General Hospital. The company laundered the bribe money through Liechtenstein. The Austrian government convicted ITT's Austrian managing director, the Austrian board chairman, and two other executives. The well-known West German corporation Siemens was also convicted of participating in the bribery conspiracy.

Bribery of foreign officials did not end with the passage of the Foreign Corrupt Practices Act in 1977. The Department of Justice reported to Congress in 1981 that it was conducting 54 ongoing investigations of alleged bribery on the part of U.S. corporations since 1977. In 1984, the Department of Justice investigated the Bechtel Group for bid-rigging and for alleged illegal payments in South Korea. In 1986, the Securities and Exchange Commission accused Ashland Oil and its chief executive officer of paying bribes of $29 million to top foreign officials in order to acquire crude oil to compensate for the shortages that followed the 1979 Iran crisis.[4] Goodyear International Corporation pleaded guilty in 1989 to having paid nearly $1 million in bribes to Kuwaiti officials to obtain tire orders.

A House subcommittee and a federal grand jury in 1988 were looking into Northrop's Korean dealings to determine if its sales of the F-20 fighter jet violated the Foreign Corrupt Practices Act. The *Wall Street Journal* in a lead article of June 8, 1988, reported that the investigation involved $7.8 million in questionable payments made by Northrop between 1984 and 1986 to companies controlled by a well-connected politician and Northrop's lobbyist with ties to two South Korean presidents. Of particular interest was Northrop's 1984 deposit of $6.25 million in a Hong Kong bank that the company claims was for a nebulous hotel venture. After the situation was revealed, several Northrop officials connected to the Korean business resigned, and others were transferred. Northrop's executive committee and outside directors in 1984 formally reprimanded the chairman for his "management style" in attempting to sell the jet fighters to the Korean government. The former chief financial officer and the executive vice-president for programs, who was in charge of marketing the fighter plane in South Korea, subsequently retired.

SHOULD U.S. CORPORATIONS BE PERMITTED TO BRIBE ABROAD?

Many individuals in the American corporate world ardently defend foreign bribery. They argue that if it is customary in foreign countries to give bribes, then it is also necessary for U.S. corporations to give bribes when an essential contract is at stake. As they see it, bribes translate into greater business, higher profits, and more jobs for American workers. They maintain that fortunes of big corporations and hundreds of millions of dollars in contracts depend on the strong desire of foreign officials to skim off some of the money that passes through their hands. Some people in corporate businesses also maintain that the prohibition of bribery has led to a decrease in U.S. exports, as their hands are tied when they have to compete with countries that have no anti-bribery laws.

Until 1977, it was not illegal for corporations to bribe foreign officials. Corporations violated the law, however, only if they had concealed the payments, which they generally did in their financial reports to the Securities and Exchange Commission or the Internal Revenue Service. The Foreign Corrupt Practices Act provided for the imposition of fines of up to $1 million on a corporation, and for jail terms of up to five years for corporate officers who bribed foreign officials. This act had the overwhelming support of both houses of Congress and the public as well, and it passed the Senate by a unanimous vote of 86 to 0. However, the Reagan administration made a concerted attempt, in strong support of corporate interests, to emasculate the Foreign Corrupt Practices Act on grounds that U.S. corporations were suffering losses because they could not compete fairly, and also because the criminal penalty was too severe. Following extensive hearings, in 1988 Congress essentially retained the original legislation, but with some changes that weakened it and made convictions more difficult. The more important amendments provided that the government would have to show that the corporation "knew" or had "reason to know" that their foreign sales agent would use the payments made to him or her to make bribes. Gifts of a "reasonable" value and based on "local custom" to foreign officials are no longer illegal. Nonetheless, the amended law raised criminal fines against a corporation from $1 million to $2 million, increased individual fines from $10,000 to $100,000, and provided a new civil fine of $10,000. Maximum potential imprisonment for an individual remained at 5 years.

In 1981, the General Accounting Office surveyed 250 U.S. firms on the effects of the Foreign Corrupt Practices Act. It found that any serious loss of business had affected less than 1 percent of the surveyed firms. A 1984 study at the University of Southern California concluded that there had been no severe negative effects on U.S. exports, either in terms of total trade with each country or in the sales of individual product categories. In fact, in the three years following the law's passage, U.S. trade with "bribe-prone" countries actually had outpaced trade with "nonbribe-prone" countries.

It is also important to note that U.S. corporations compete against each other. A Justice Department report to Congress on 35 bribery cases it was investigating in 1982 indicated that more than 40 percent of the bribes had been made to secure a contract for which only U.S. corporations were competing.[5] In fact, in only three instances did U.S. corporations make bribes for contracts where there was only foreign competition. Bribes made to gain advantage over other U.S. competitors constitute a violation of U.S. anti-trust laws.

Foreign bribes paid by U.S. corporations provide ample ammunition to political extremists in most countries. For example, large-scale U.S. corporate bribery practiced in Iran under Shah Reza Pahlavi contributed substantially to the extreme anti-American sentiments in that country and the subsequent taking of U.S. embassy hostages in 1979. The shah of Iran was a technology buff who was in a great hurry to modernize his country, and, with Iran's increasing oil money, almost any piece of equipment could be sold there given the right set of agents paying the right bribes to the right people. Under the shah, U.S. exports to Iran totaled billions of dollars; in 1978 alone, non-military exports were $3.4 billion and armaments $2 billion. Rockwell International, for example, paid a bribe of $260,000 to General Khatemi, commander of the Iranian air force, for obtaining his assistance in pushing sales of their aircraft. Grumman paid $2.9 million to various Iranian officials to obtain an order for 80 Grumman F-1R Tomcat fighter planes.

Bribes made by American corporations to Iranian generals and others in high positions—even to the shah himself—became well known in Iran. The shah was overthrown because corruption had become rampant; he had rushed the country into a Western secular industrial age without regard for the strong religious values in Islamic Iran; the royal family and their friends were living in great luxury, and the shah had fallen prey to Western influences, particularly the United States. The large bribes given by American corporations, however, contributed in no small way to the shah's overthrow as they fueled growing political dissent, particularly among the young, and helped fire the wrath of religious fundamentalists led by the Ayatollah Khomeni. The failure on the part of the United States to show more corporate restraint in foreign bribery in Iran and to encourage other industrial countries to show similar restraint carried a fearsome price tag. All these factors contributed to the extreme hatred of the United States that continues today in Iran, a hatred that Iran has exported to Middle Eastern countries. What the U.S. transnationals have sown for their own profit, they have often reaped to the detriment of the American people.

In the long run, an international agreement is needed to curb the use of bribes by transnational corporations. The Draft International Agreement on Illicit Payments drawn up by the UN's Economic and Social Council makes it a crime, under the laws of subscribing countries, for corporations, or their officials, to offer or to accept such payments in international business. It would also require corporations to keep records of their overseas business transactions that would be open to review by designated government agencies. Moving in this direction, in the 1988 Omnibus Trade Act, Congress directed the president to seek an agreement with member governments of the Organization for Economic Cooperation and Development (OECD) to ban the use of bribery by corporations in international dealings.

BRIBING POLITICIANS

More than 300 major corporations illegally contributed millions of dollars to the 1972 re-election campaign of Richard Nixon. They gave these bribes either to obtain favors or because they feared retaliation for failing to contribute. Subsequently, the government brought criminal charges against many of them and their executives. The cases that follow are from the files of the Securities and Exchange Commission and the Senate Watergate hearings. These illegal political contributions struck at the very heart of the democratic process.

Corporate political contributions and political payoffs by business interests for special favors have long been part of the domestic scene in the United States. They had become so frequent and so large by the early 1970s that in 1972 Congress enacted a law prohibiting corporations from making direct contributions to candidates seeking election to federal office. Within a short time of the passage of the law, however, large numbers of corporations illegally contributed large sums of money to the Nixon re-election campaign. Even though the courts did convict many corporations, as well as executives, for making such contributions, it was obvious that there should have been far more prosecutions. Leon Jaworski, the special Watergate prosecutor, said afterward that most corporate officials had clearly known that it was illegal to contribute corporate money to candidates running for federal office. He also stated that those who did not make such contributions were, seemingly, motivated primarily by their fears of being caught rather than because of moral principles.[6]

A few corporate officials later complained that the Nixon re-election campaign committee had "extorted" contributions from them, a rather weak defense of their actions inasmuch as none had made a public statement prior to the Watergate hearings of having been forced to make contributions. Moreover, corporations have always sought to gain a corporate advantage or to defend corporate interests through their political contributions. Gulf Oil's vice president for public relations, for example, told the Senate Watergate committee (although until then he had said nothing) that on one occasion Maurice Stans, the then secretary of commerce who headed President Nixon's re-election campaign, had called him to ask for a $100,000 contribution. He had then obtained this sum in 1,000 $100 bills from a company bank account in Geneva, Switzerland. A courier then personally delivered the money to Stans, who thanked him and dumped the envelope containing the cash in a drawer without looking at it.

Oil corporations were major sources of contributions. They made contributions, presumably, to protect their interests in pricing, drilling, and regulations, and to secure favorable action in other legislation. Congressman Les Aspin (D-Wis.) and his staff compiled a report in 1974 showing that oil company officials, principal stockholders, and the five Rockefeller brothers (who owned 1 percent of Exxon stock) had contributed $5.2 million. The leading contributor was Gulf Oil, giving a total of $1.1 million. The breakdown of the large oil companies' illegal contributions, showing the totals and the sum they gave secretly, was:

Company	Total Political Contribution	Secret Contribution
Gulf Oil	$1,176,500	$1,132,000
Getty Oil	179,292	77,500
Standard Oil of California	166,000	102,000
Sun Oil	157,798	60,000
Phillips Petroleum	137,000	100,000
Exxon	127,747	100,672
Ashland Oil	103,500	100,000

The Securities and Exchange Commission charged that Gulf Oil had falsified its financial reports to conceal $10 million in political payments, including those for the Nixon campaign, which were made from 1960 to 1974. When the Senate committee investigating the illegal contributions questioned the chairman of the board about this sum, he said that this was a relatively small amount of money: "I think the company did some $60 to $70 billion worth of business in that 15-year period and $10 million is not really a large sum of money, it does not stand out." Under pressure from the Securities and Exchange Commission, a special committee subsequently appointed by Gulf's board of directors found that the domestic payments to hundreds of U.S. politicians were "shot through with illegality," as they were "generally clandestine and in disregard of federal as well as a number of state statutes."

Gulf and one of its top executives pleaded guilty in 1973 to contributing to both the 1972 Nixon campaign and also, presumably to play it safe, to two other presidential candidates. Gulf illegally laundered $100,000 of the contribution through a Bahamian subsidiary. It was also revealed that for years Gulf Oil had given Senate Minority Leader Hugh Scott (R-Pa.) $5,000 both in the spring and in the fall of each year. A Gulf lobbyist said that Scott had received these amounts for 13 years, beginning in 1960, but he claimed that they were intended for Senator Scott's personal use, not as a "political contribution."[7]

In order to remain within the letter of the law, a number of major corporations simply "encouraged" their officers to make contributions from their own personal funds, while in reality they were made for the corporation. Corporate officers were reimbursed by phony "bonuses" or "expense accounts," or they furnished their corporate officer funds by various indirect means, thus avoiding the restrictions on direct corporate contributions. For example, Hoerner Waldorf Corporation, the nation's fourth largest producer of paper packaging such as grocery bags and folding cartons, made illegal political contributions through its officers. The corporation later admitted to the Securities and Exchange Commission that it expected its officers to make contributions: "The method consisted of an employee keeping track of his contribution on personal notes or records, and the slow, systematic recovery of the contributed amount by submission of periodic overstated expense accounts. When the contribution had been recouped, records of the transaction were destroyed."[8]

BRIBING TO GET BUSINESS AT HOME

The purpose of commercial bribery is to gain advantages over competitors. Many states have commercial bribery laws that prohibit suppliers from giving anything of value to a buyer or to any other purchasing agent without the knowledge or consent of the latter's employer. These hidden transactions constitute fraud under the IRS code. The Federal Trade Commission calls them unfair competition, the Sherman Anti-Trust Act defines them as restraint of trade and, when not disclosed, violations of the SEC regulations because they conceal true corporate income and expenses from the stockholder or the stock purchaser.

Commercial bribes may be for small amounts, or they may be payments of millions of dollars. For example, Gerald Lee, chairman of the board of Frigitemp Corporation, pleaded guilty in federal court in 1983 to conspiring to pay kickbacks amounting to $2.7 million to a General Dynamics executive vice president and his aide to win a subcontract for the construction of natural gas tankers.

Even though it is illegal, business bribery is so common that it has become almost a part of the American way of life.[9] A March 16, 1976, *New York Times* survey of people in business, lawyers, investigators, and accountants revealed rampant bribery in the corporate world. There are two major forms of corporate bribery. First, the corporation itself may bribe outright, or, second, it may simply countenance bribes made by its employees in order to beat out its competitor's products and thus improve its own corporate profit objectives. Of course, individual employees may engage in bribery to sell products simply to get ahead in the corporation; the interest here, however, is only on bribery that the corporation itself encourages or condones. Large corporations that bribe at home often bribe abroad as well. Two experts on foreign payoffs put it this way: "The corporations that have been cited for international payoffs are engaged in similar activities among private companies who make large purchases or among U.S. agencies who make decisions for billions of dollars in public purchases."[10]

Domestic bribes have involved many large U.S. corporations, including Bethlehem Steel, General Electric, Sears Roebuck, Grumman, International Harvester, and Zenith Radio. For example, a federal judge fined the giant Bethlehem Steel Corporation $325,000 in 1980 for paying hundreds of thousands of dollars in bribes during the 1970s to obtain ship repair business at Bethlehem shipyards.[11] A Justice Department official said that "the crime in this case is peculiarly corporate." Although the charges covered only four years, the assistant U.S. attorney said the bribery amounted to a "corporate tradition" that may have extended back 20 years. General Electric, along with two former top executives, was convicted in 1981 of paying a $1.25-million bribe to an operations manager of Puerto Rico's Water Resources Authority to obtain a $93-million power plant construction contract. The corporation was fined $36,000; one executive received a one- to four-month sentence, and the other received a two-month sentence. The government charged Sears Roebuck in 1983 with failure to disclose $1.1 million in rebates and credits the corporation had arranged with its Japanese suppliers of television sets over a 9-year period. In this way, Sears had misrepresented the net price the company actually paid for the sets.

Commercial bribery occurs in nearly all industries, but it is more common in highly competitive industries such as the beer industry. For example, the government indicted the Joseph Schlitz Brewing Company in 1978 on 3 felony and 732 misdemeanor counts for kickbacks that violated federal tax and liquor control laws, and an additional misdemeanor count for violation of conspiracy laws. According to a later internal Schlitz audit, the illegal payments came to more than $3 million. The company agreed to a court order barring further violations and later pleaded no contest to 2 misdemeanors, paying total civil and criminal fines of $761,000. Schlitz's chairman and chief executive officer argued that this was a classic example of arbitrary selective prosecution, because the marketing practices of which the company was accused had been widespread throughout the industry for a number of years.[12] Although the company was the only brewery to face criminal charges, other national brewing companies were also assessed civil penalties for kickback violations. Anheuser-Busch admitted "voluntarily" to kickback payments totaling $2.7 million; it paid a penalty of $750,000.

Extensive kickback practices also occur in the liquor industry. Seagram admitted to the Securities and Exchange Commission in 1977 that it had engaged in extensive illegal discounting and rebating, which was known to all senior officers of the firm. Also in 1977, a subsidiary of Foremost-McKesson, a major liquor distributor, admitted it had made kickback payments of $6.5 million over a 5-year period. They extended discounts primarily through the delivery of additional free merchandise or in cash rebates that were incorrectly recorded on Foremost's books as, among other things, employee's business expenses, credit extensions, advertising payments, travel vouchers, and breakage claims.

CORPORATE CUNNING

The efforts that large corporations make to conceal their foreign bribes, illegal political payments, and commercial bribes are so elaborate and cunning that they clearly reveal the intent of their illegal actions. In his autobiography, Lee Iacocca said that Henry Ford, chairman of the Ford Motor Company, where Iacocca was then a top executive, had authorized payment of a million-dollar "commission" to an Indonesian general for a $29 million contract to build 15 satellite ground stations in Indonesia. He added that "as soon as the press got wind of the attempted bribe, a full-scale cover-up went into effect within the company. It was at least as impressive as anything that went on during Watergate. There was an internal purging of files. There were even special meetings to coordinate excuses on why we did it."[13]

Many corporations devised highly secretive and ingenious techniques to hide foreign bribes on their books and in their financial reports. They used camouflaged means to conceal their bribes far more often than they gave straight cash payments. Lockheed gave a "commission" of $1.1 million to Prince Bernhard, the royal Netherlands consort, to secure his influence in a large multinational aircraft sale. It channeled the bribe payment through a Swiss lawyer and then deposited installments into a numbered Swiss bank account taken out in the name of the husband of the prince's late mother. In other bribery cases, corporate books have listed bribes as payment for travel expenses, provisions of unsecured loans that they never collected, salaries paid to relatives listed on payrolls as consultants, and provisions of scholarships and educational expenses for the children of foreign officials.

Corporations also made indirect clandestine payments through such intermediaries as foreign subsidiaries, dummy corporations, and sales agents. By this means, corporations could claim no knowledge as to whom they had paid bribes; only with great difficulty could the payments be linked to them. As a typical example, Northrop Corporation set up a dummy corporation in Switzerland for the purpose of paying, over a period of several years, $30 million in questionable and illegal commissions to bribe government officials in the Netherlands, Iran, France,

West Germany, Saudi Arabia, Brazil, Malaysia, and Taiwan. The most common method of channeling foreign payments has been through a so-called foreign "sales agent" located in that country. The agent generally received a fee on a percentage basis of the total contract; from this payment, the agent then paid bribes to government officials. Corporations retained these agents to do their firm's "dirty work," as they did not directly hire them as regular employees.

Most of the illegal political contributions made to the Nixon re-election campaign involved the shady type of deceptive practices that characterize foreign bribery. They included false bookkeeping entries, payments made through phony subsidiaries, and the laundering of money abroad in much the same manner as organized crime syndicates launder money from their illegal drug and other businesses, or in the complex illegal transfers of funds to Swiss banks and other places as was later disclosed in the Iran-Contra scandal.

Ashland Oil, for example, made large illegal political contributions, including $100,000 to the Nixon re-election committee. As a result, the Internal Revenue Service and the Securities and Exchange Commission criminally indicted the corporation. Ashland told the SEC that characteristically it made the payments in cash from a fund maintained by three top officials at corporate headquarters. They obtained the money through various overseas sources and then falsely recorded it in the firm's books. Banks in England, Switzerland, Nigeria, and Libya were the primary sources of the foreign money in a complicated arrangement that involved intricate record keeping. Corporate records often indicated that these political contributions were "oil exploration charges."

Commercial bribes or kickbacks to employees of other concerns take many forms: Commissions are paid for alleged services, illegal rebates and discounts are made, or outright gifts of money or gratuities are given. A common sales practice is to give kickbacks or rebates in the form of money. Corporations do not keep records of the illegal discounts and rebates; instead, they generally conceal kickbacks from government agencies through false invoices, bills of lading, and accounting entries. They may make payments by deposits in secret bank accounts or through phony consulting firms set up solely for this purpose. Often the full scope of the bribery can be determined only after a thorough audit of the accounts of all parties involved.

Domestic bribes paid to influence purchases may take less direct forms. They include paid vacations, the use of corporate recreational facilities, expensive dinners, theater tickets, provisions for call girls, and expensive gifts, particularly at Christmas, that may include cases of liquor, costly art objects, and other forms of "remembrances" that go far beyond a Christmas card. For example, a former senior vice president and sales agent for Boeing said his company often arranged fishing and yachting expeditions for its customers. On one occasion, they hired John Wayne's yacht, the *Wild Goose,* to "entertain" customers. He added, "I don't think we've done any more than the average American business."[14]

Chapter 8

THE RAPE OF THE THIRD WORLD

It was an unseasonably cold night in central India. In the shanty towns of Bhopal, thousands of families were asleep. A scattering of people were waiting for early morning trains nearby. At the local Union Carbide plant, a maintenance worker spotted a problem. A storage tank holding 42 tons of liquid methyl isocyanate (MIC), a deadly chemical used to make pesticides, was showing a dangerously high pressure reading. Soon, a noxious white gas started seeping from the tank and spreading with the northwesterly winds. People awoke to burning, suffocating sensations—"like breathing fire" as one victim described it. As the cloud spread, people began to run helter-skelter to retch, vomit, and defecate uncontrollably. Many collapsed and died. Dogs, cows, and buffaloes lay on the ground, shuddering in their death throes. As the gas seeped through crevices and windows, it turned hovels into gas chambers.

The following morning, the bodies of human beings and animals littered the ground; Bhopal was a city of corpses. Hundreds of people, blinded by poisonous fumes, groped their way through the streets in search of medical attention. Across the city, hospitals and mortuaries became filled to overflowing. Muslims were buried four and five deep in a single grave, while Hindu funeral pyres burned around the clock.

The chairman of Union Carbide, Warren M. Anderson, flew almost immediately to Bhopal, where state authorities promptly arrested him and just as promptly released him under pressure from government of India authorities. Some officials said that Anderson's arrest was necessary to protect him from the wrath of the victims. Within days, swarms of lawyers from the United States descended on Bhopal to sign up victims

for damage suits against Union Carbide. The Indian government also
moved in to file a suit against the corporation. The attorney general of
Connecticut, where Union Carbide is based, said that it could be the
"largest and most lucrative damage case in the history of the world."

The Bhopal disaster was the world's worst industrial accident; even
the Chernobyl nuclear reactor disaster in the Soviet Union could not
compare with it in terms of deaths and injuries. According to official
Indian government figures, more than 2,800 people died (by 1989 this
figure had risen to 3,415) and 200,000 were injured, 40,000 of them
seriously. A separate study by an American investigator put the death
toll at more than 8,000, as hundreds of bodies were cremated by Hindus
and buried by Muslims without notifying authorities.[1] Suddenly, the
world had learned that chemicals that kill insects also kill human beings,
and on a grand scale. Few of Bhopal's residents knew the exact nature
of the pesticides being produced at the factory; they also knew little
about the dangers of the methyl isocyanate that had caused the disaster.
When the massive leak occurred during that fateful night, few of the
residents knew what had happened. Carbide officials took two hours
that night to warn the nearby residents, although many of them lived
in the shacks that surrounded the plant.

For the Bhopal survivors, recovery has been agonizing, and illnesses
insidious. By 1986, two years after the tragedy, the government had
received 500,000 injury claims, equivalent to approximately 60 percent
of the city's population. Many Bhopal residents still suffered from shortness of breath, depression, and eye irritation. One eye specialist reported
that there had been a "gross change" in the eyesight of the city's residents
since the leak, and each day thousands of victims were flocking to hospitals, clinics, and rehabilitation centers. The Indian Council of Medical
Research estimated that one in five of those exposed to the gas will suffer
long-term lung, brain, liver, and kidney damage. By 1986, Bhopal had
four times the national average in India of still births.

Union Carbide is the third largest chemical producer in the United
States, and one of its 50 largest industrial corporations. It operates 700
facilities, including affiliates, in 35 countries around the world. The
transnational's sales in 1988 totalled more than $8 billion, of which
approximately a third came from the company's international operations. The Bhopal plant was started in 1969 and grew to a $25-million
manufacturing facility sprawling over 80 acres. Although the Bhopal
plant was known as Union Carbide of India, Union Carbide headquarters in the United States had authority to exercise financial and technical
controls over the plant. As the parent company, Union Carbide owned
just over half (50.9 percent) of the plant.

Not long after the Bhopal disaster and under pressure from a U.S.
federal judge, Union Carbide agreed to pay $5 million to show "good

faith." Later Union Carbide changed its prior concern for the victims and started to play hard ball. Originally, when Chairman Anderson flew to India, he said that he was moved by humanitarian motives to do whatever the corporation could to alleviate the consequences of the dreadful disaster. The corporation would give money to build hospitals, orphanages, and vocational schools, and it did contribute $1 million for this purpose. Then, a year later, Union Carbide began blaming the media for the public overreaction and was claiming that the suffering had been exaggerated.

In 1986, Union Carbide offered a $350-million settlement of all injury and damage claims brought by Bhopal survivors and the Indian government, but the Indian government rejected the offer as highly inadequate. The haggling over payments became disgraceful. At issue were huge legal fees and attorneys' desires to have suits tried in the United States rather than in India, where liability payments are much lower. A U.S. federal judge finally decided in 1986 that the damage suits should be brought in India, and this was what happened.

Late in 1986, the Indian government filed a suit in Bhopal district court on behalf of the victims, asking $3.1 billion in damages from Union Carbide. In addition, the Indian government asked for punitive damages in an amount sufficient to deter Union Carbide and other multinational corporations from "willful, malicious and wanton disregard of the rights and safety" of Indians. The suit charged that the corporation had "the means to know and guard against hazards likely to be caused . . . and to provide ways of avoiding potential hazards." It pointed out that a Union Carbide engineer was directly responsible for the final design and construction of the plant. India also charged Union Carbide with inadequate safety measures, faulty alarm systems, lack of cooling facilities, storage of excessive quantities of toxic materials, and poor maintenance. In its defense, Union Carbide claimed that the disaster had been due not to sloppy corporate practices in the Third World but to worker sabotage. The company had a hard time selling its sabotage theory.

The Bhopal residents marked the first anniversary of the disaster with a massive demonstration and the burning of hundreds of effigies of Union Carbide's chairman. They shouted, "Down with Killer Carbide," and flew black flags over most of the homes in the slums, where they conducted wakes and marched in protest. In late 1988, four years after the disaster, the people were increasingly bitter, the legal wrangling continued and a settlement still had not been reached. Consequently, an Indian High Court Judge ordered $190 million interim payments to the victims. To add to the confusion, India filed criminal homicide charges against nine Union Carbide top officers, including its former chairman, Warren Anderson, holding them responsible for the disaster. People in Bhopal were waiting to receive the grant that the government had promised each victim. However, a 40-year-old car mechanic had a different point of view: "I don't want any money," he said. He just wanted his breath back. The tragedy was finally resolved in February 1989 when the Indian government, which had unilaterally assumed the exclusive right to litigate on behalf of tens of thousands of Bhopal victims, settled with Union Carbide out of court for $470 million. It will take many months, if not years, for compensation to reach the victims.

Often corporations do not install the same plant safety devices in Third World countries or operate under the same safety standards that they would in the United States. As an example, until 1980 the India plant of Union Carbide had imported the deadly methyl isocyanate (MIC) from the United States; in order to increase profits, it then began to produce it at the Bhopal plant. In a highly dangerous manufacturing process, they used the methyl isocyanate to produce Sevin Carbaryl, a highly effective pesticide. In 1982, prior to the disaster, a team of American experts on plant safety had made an internal report of the Bhopal plant. Their report pointed out certain safety concerns, including deficiencies in instrumentation and safety valves, lax maintenance procedures, and a high turnover of both operational and maintenance staffs.[2] The report warned that the plant presented "serious potentials for sizeable releases of toxic materials." There had also been other warnings of problems at the plant. In January 1982, a phosgene leak had seriously injured 28 workers, and in October of that year, methyl isocyanate had escaped from a broken valve. Several workers were injured in this accident, and nearby residents experienced eye and breathing problems. Two similar incidents were reported in 1983.

At the time of the disaster, the plant was storing a large quantity of MIC. Even though a refrigeration unit had been installed to keep the storage tank at a temperature low enough to prevent runaway chemical reactions, the unit had not been working properly for more than five months.[3] The storage tank temperature was lower than company regulations allowed. Since the refrigeration unit was out of commission, it was vital that instruments measuring temperature and pressure in the storage tank be in good operating order. They were not. The emergency scrubber used to neutralize the gas in the event of a leak had been out of use for six weeks. Finally, the flare tower, designed as the final line of defense to burn off excess MIC, had been closed down ten days before the leak because the line to the tower had corroded. If this were not enough to cause a catastrophe, the workers who operated the faulty equipment were inadequately trained for the job.

As the Bhopal tragedy exemplified, the health and safety of workers throughout the world is threatened when multinationals shift hazardous work processes abroad in an effort to avoid strict U.S. worker protection laws. One plant safety expert posed this question about transnationals:

"Why risk $100 million of liability when you can make it [the product] any way you please somewhere else?" Commenting on the differential safety standards, a leading Indian newspaper, *The Statesman*, asked, "Were the safety measures in Bhopal identical to those in force in the United States plant and equally stringent in their application?" In Third World countries, safety standards are generally quite low and government plant inspections poor, due either to understaffing or underfunding. U.S. transnationals frequently set up manufacturing operations in the very foreign countries where there is little regard for worker safety. The sulfur dioxide limit in Indian chemical plants is six times the limit allowed in U.S. chemical plants, and four times the chemical limit permissible in U.S. battery manufacturing plants. The ammonia limit is seven times greater in India than in U.S. fertilizer plants. In an Indian-owned plant producing DDT, a chemical pesticide banned in the United States, one study found that one-third of the workers were ill from its effects.

In the 1980s, Mexico had only about 230 safety inspectors for a work force of more than 20 million; Indonesia had about 300 labor inspectors for its 110,000 companies; and India had a federal environmental protection staff of only some 150. In comparison to those small staffs, and allowing for population and industrial differences, the Environmental Protection Agency alone had a much larger inspection staff of approximately 4,400.

There was widespread fallout worldwide in the aftermath of the Bhopal catastrophe. It raised serious questions elsewhere about a possible double standard in U.S. versus overseas plant operations. People asked about the comparisons between the Indian plant's safety measures and those of plants in the United States. Were the standards equally enforced? The tragedy alerted both transnational corporations and Third World governments to the greater need for effective safety requirements. With weaker regulations and enforcement in Third World countries, the possibilities for other disasters are worrisome. Other transnationals were most alarmed by the possibility that Union Carbide would be found legally liable for the event and would be financially crippled as a result. This might produce a wholesale shrinkage of multinational manufacturing investment in Third World countries.

Although Bhopal was a high-profile disaster, other plant accidents have exacted high human tolls as well. A Liberian iron ore mine under the partial management of U.S. Steel, for example, was the site of a 1982 disaster in which a rain-swollen tailings dam burst and swamped the mining camp directly below it, killing 200 persons. In 1981, tests showed that one-third of the plant workers in Pennwalt's Nicaraguan plant were suffering from mercury poisoning.[4] This plant had been poisoning Lake Managua for many years. Under the Somoza regime, which was highly favorable to U.S. corporate interests, it had been able to dump between two and four tons of mercury into the lake every year for 12 years, killing fish and polluting the adjacent area. One report indicated that toxic mercury in the air of the plant was 12 times higher than the safety level recommended by the U.S. National Institute of Occupational Safety and Health. In an Indonesian battery manufacturing plant of Union Carbide Corporation, tests showed that more than half the work force was suffering from kidney diseases attributable to mercury poisoning and contamination, according to the company physician.[5]

Some corporations may manufacture products in their plants that are considered so dangerous to worker safety that they are virtually banned in the United States. As an example, arsenic trioxide is the "white" arsenic used in herbicides; it causes a high rate of cancer among workers. Regulatory agencies in the United States have strengthened standards governing workers' exposure to it; at present, the sole producer of such arsenic in the United States is Asarco's plant in Tacoma, Washington. Arsenic production has been largely shifted to less regulated havens in the developing world; in 1980 Asarco owned a 34-percent interest in Mexico's largest mining company, which produces over 5,500 tons of arsenic trioxide annually, 75 percent of which is exported to the United States.[6] This highly dangerous product is manufactured in Mexico without the strict worker-safety restraints imposed on U.S. production.

Third World countries now produce much asbestos and asbestos products. In the United States, the manufacture of asbestos products has declined markedly because of the great concern about public safety and the strict worker-safety programs the government has imposed on asbestos production. An important factor in relocation to Third World countries is the increasing demand there for asbestos products. Following the asbestos furor in this country, Manville Corporation established an asbestos production policy that states: "We will continue to equip our plants with the best available technology to assure the highest degree of personal safety." However, the standards of safety for U.S. production are far higher than those for its Third World plants. For example, Manville has a 10-percent interest in, and receives royalties from, a large Indian-owned asbestos plant that produces thousands of tons of asbestos water pipe and sheeting materials that are sold in India, Southeast Asia, and Africa. Manville corporate officials work closely with the plant, yet, when Bob Wyrick, an American journalist, visited there in 1980, the Indian workers had no shower facilities and had to wear their own clothes.[7] Even though the company supplied its regular workers with filter masks, it did not protect entirely against asbestos exposure, and the company issued temporary workers only a bandanna for their faces. In contrast, workers in the Manville plant in the United States receive clean uniforms each day, and they must shower before they change to their street clothes when leaving the plant. There were other significant differences: Plant temperatures may exceed 100 degrees in India, and the plant was pouring liquid asbestos waste into nearby canals used for irrigation and drinking water until they ran "red, blue, purple, green and white with asbestos and other chemicals." Around the Indian factory, workers build their huts from asbestos trash thrown out of the factory such as broken pipes and flawed sheets with asbestos fibers exposed, and children play in asbestos-littered trash. An Indian health official who visited the Manville plant described the area where asbestos sheets are cut to size: "You become white with asbestos. The air is full of it like a cloud."[8] The Manville Corporation knew all about the dangerous situation at the Indian plant since receiving a 1977 report from one of its own personnel. However, in the early 1980s, the American journalist concluded: "No determined corporate effort to eliminate the obvious dangers was made until the threat of adverse publicity loomed large."

PRESCRIPTIONS FOR DEATH

Although it is illegal in the United States to sell a wide range of specific pharmaceuticals, pesticides, and medical devices, every year large quantities of such American-manufactured products are sold to Third World countries. The federal government, for example, has banned, with one exception for its use, the sale in the United States of Upjohn's controversial Depo-Provera, a synthetic hormone that tests have shown to be highly effective as a contraceptive as it stops the menstrual cycle for as long as three months when injected into a woman's arm or buttocks. It is now being used as a contraceptive by about 5 million women in 82 countries, mostly in the Third World. The overseas sale of the drug provides 1 percent of Upjohn's total sales.

Upjohn tried for many years to obtain approval of Depo-Provera in the United States as a "safe" contraceptive, but the Food and Drug Administration approval has been given for its use only as a palliative for certain cancers.[9] The last Food and Drug Administration rejection for its use as a contraceptive, in late 1984, was based on the lack of conclusive evidence of its long-term safety. A number of medical studies have linked Depo-Provera to a wide range of health disorders, including cancers of the breast and uterus. U.S. law states that drug products not approved by the FDA for sale in the United States cannot be sold abroad in any country whose government has not approved its sale there. Most Third World countries, however, do not have an approval process; it is simply registered with customs. This contraceptive is now produced by Upjohn's Belgian subsidiary and then shipped throughout the Third

World. This is all perfectly legal because the Belgian government has approved the Depo-Provera's sale in Belgium.

As in the case of the Upjohn drug Depo-Provera, many American corporations widely promote and sell a number of drugs or other products in the Third World that have either been banned or that have never been approved for marketing in the United States.[10] Although laws prohibit drug companies from exporting drugs that are banned in the United States, companies have gotten around this prohibition by shipping the ingredients out of the country, assembling the compounds overseas, and then selling the product in Europe and Third World countries.

Drug companies also often fail to advise both doctors and patients in the developing world about necessary restrictions on their use and the possibly dangerous side effects that certain drugs can produce. If a drug is not properly prescribed, labeled, and used, what might have alleviated pain will cause disability, and what might have saved life may bring death. A definitive study of the misuse of drugs concluded that "in the Third World, because of the nonexistence or nonenforcement of laws and regulations and perhaps the social irresponsibility of the companies, claims of product efficacy are exaggerated to an almost ludicrous degree, and hazards, some of them life-threatening, are minimized or not even mentioned."[11]

Dangerous side effects from the use of certain drugs may include damage to the circulatory system, blindness, crippling, and even death. In this respect, there is a great difference between what U.S. drug companies tell physicians and patients in developed versus undeveloped countries. Where regulations are loose, as in most Third World countries, there is a temptation to make greater profits by remaining silent or by misleading patients and physicians, and possible lethal side effects of important and widely used drugs are often either totally ignored or minimized.

Studies made in 18 Third World countries in Africa, Asia, and Latin America in the early 1980s found wide differences in drug use indications and warning labels in those countries and in the labeled information provided in the United States and Great Britain.[12] For example, when Parke Davis distributed its powerful drug chloromycetin, used in the treatment of infections that include typhoid fever in the United States and Great Britain, it labeled specific instructions for use and precise warnings of associated dangers. In the Philippines, however, the company promoted the same drug with wider use indications and fewer warnings; Indonesian labels contained far more indications for use with no warnings at all. Companies promoted specific drugs derived from tetracycline in Third World countries, but labels seldom told users that these drugs could cause injury and death if they were given to patients with impaired kidney or liver function, pregnant women in the last half of their pregnancies, or children under the age of eight. Of 35 tetracycline drugs sold in Indonesia, 19 were distributed with no warnings; in Malaysia no warnings were mentioned in 10 out of 16 tetracycline drugs distributed. Since 1969, the use of Albamycin, an antibiotic related to tetracycline and manufactured by Upjohn, has been severely restricted to use only under certain conditions in the United States due to its dangerous side effects, yet the drug was widely sold for a large variety of illnesses in Brazil, Kenya, Costa Rica, and 27 other countries. As another example,

Consider the adverse reactions listed by the Searle Company for their oral contraceptive, Ovulen. In the United States, Searle lists "nausea, loss of hair, nervousness, jaundice, high blood pressure, weight change, and headaches" as side effects. The farther south the product is sold, however, the safer it seems to become. In Mexico, only two side effects, nausea and weight change, are named, and in Brazil and Argentina, Searle would have physicians believe that Ovulen has no harmful side effects at all.[13]

Drug companies maintain that Third World physicians can always obtain proper drug use information from the company representatives if they ask for it. To this suggestion, a Sri Lankan physician replied, "Of course the company representative or detail man will tell you about the dangers if you ask him. At least I think he will." After a study of pharmaceutical usage in developing countries, three experts have concluded:

In most developing countries, the detail men are often considered to be only salesmen. They have been repeatedly charged with exaggerating the claims and glossing over the dangers of their products, bulwarking their arguments by passing out copies of articles reprinted from journals that are actually owned or controlled by the drug company, and using rumors, innuendos or outright lies to run down competitive products. They have induced physicians or purchasing agents, occasionally by offering bribes, kickbacks or other inducements, to purchase drugs in enormous quantities, with the result that some of these drugs will spoil on the storage shelves long before they can be dispensed.[14]

The pharmaceutical industry achieved a long-sought objective in 1986 when the U.S. Senate, with the support of the Reagan administration, approved a bill to allow the export of drugs not yet sufficiently tested for approval for sale in the United States to 21 other countries, primarily in the Third World. The pharmaceutical industry had claimed it was losing out to foreign competitors for whom no such approval was necessary. Actually, the bill opened up the people of the Third World for greater use as experimental guinea pigs, where they have long been used, for example, in testing the effectiveness of contraceptive drugs.

Senator Howard Metzenbaum (D-Ohio) decried this legislation, charging that the bill grew out of the "greed of the pharmaceutical industry."[15] He added that "the day will come when some pharmaceuticals . . . made in this country will be used by some other nation of the world and hundreds and perhaps thousands of children or senior citizens or people generally will pay with their lives or long-lasting injury." Congressman Henry Waxman (D-Calif.) said that the legislation would allow the United States to become an exporter of unsafe drugs. "It's an immoral foreign policy that hurts our country." In signing the bill, President Reagan said that it would "increase the competitiveness of the American pharmaceutical industry abroad." Left unsaid was the stark reality that the Third World could also be a corporate drug safety testing laboratory for Americans.

EXPORTING BANNED PESTICIDES

Drugs are not the only prescription for death; corporations also export pesticides banned in the United States. In 1982 the Oxford Committee on Famine Relief (Oxfam) estimated that each year in the Third World there are 375,000 pesticide poisonings with a resulting 10,000 deaths.[16] A major reason for this is that many chemical corporations export these banned pesticides to developing countries where they then cause injuries and death. American manufacturers may export even the most dangerous pesticides as long as they are marked "For export only." In order to satisfy the growing market for their products, U.S. chemical companies ship overseas at least 150 million pounds a year of pesticides that are totally prohibited, severely restricted, or never registered for use in this country. This amounts to at least 25 percent of U.S. pesticide exports. Included in the American corporations that have been reported in such sales are American Cyanamid, Union Carbide, Monsanto, Dow, Chevron, DuPont, Velsicol, Hercules, FMC, and Hooker.[17] The advertisements of American chemical corporations that appear in Third World agricultural journals extol the virtues of these banned pesticides. Two writers who won awards for having exposed the dumping of pesticides on developing countries neatly phrased the issue: "For chemical executives, exporting hazardous pesticides is not dumping. If one country bans your product, move to where sales are still legal."[18]

As another method of exporting banned pesticides, many chemical companies simply ship the separate chemical ingredients to a Third World country where they manufacture the product in what they call their formulation plants. They then either sell these products locally or export them to other developing countries. In Malaysia, for example, Dow and Shell alone manufacture one-fourth of all liquid pesticides. In addition, the U.S. transnationals often operate their pesticide-producing plants with far lower worker safety standards than they employ in their U.S. plants. Thus Third World people suffer the double risk of producing these highly hazardous components and then using them in the fields.

The group of leading pesticides that the U.S. government has banned in this country have been termed the Dirty Dozen. Some of the Dirty Dozen include DDT, paraquat, aldrin, and dioxin. Another is parathion, a pesticide that may well be responsible for half the world's pesticide-related deaths. A number of American corporations, such as American Cyanamid and Monsanto, export this product which is so toxic that a teaspoonful spilled on the skin can be fatal. These pesticides are all effective in killing insects, but they can also cause cancer, severe bladder and lung diseases, nerve damage, and male sterility in humans. Dust-cropping planes in Third World countries are likely to spray pesticides indiscriminantly on fields, field hands, and homes. The chemicals infiltrate the soil and subsequently affect those who consume the food grown there or the meat from cattle that have grazed there.

Actually, the use of banned pesticides does little to alleviate poverty and hunger in these countries; such pesticides are not generally used for domestic food production involving small farmers. Some 70 percent of the pesticides are used to increase large-scale export crops such as cotton, coffee, tomatoes, bananas, rubber, pineapple, and a variety of other cash crops grown primarily by transnational corporations or wealthy landowners in these developing countries.[19]

A factor of considerable significance in pesticide-related deaths and injuries is the failure of pesticide producers to include warnings in Third World countries about the possible dangers of using the compounds. Seldom do they state that the pesticides should be used only with a respirator and rubber gloves, nor are workers told that they should bathe after using them. The warnings in themselves, however, may be futile, as two experts on the use of pesticides in the Third World have pointed out.

In countries where most people cannot read, what use are warning labels on pesticide packages? In countries that outlaw unions that could protect farm workers, what chance do peasants have against the crop duster's rain of poison? In countries with neither enough scientists to investigate pesticide dangers, nor enough trained government officials to enforce regulations, should foreign pesticide makers be given a free hand to push products so dangerous they are banned at home?[20]

The mushrooming use of pesticides in the Third World is a daily threat to millions of inhabitants there, and it is also a growing threat to consumers in the United States. Banned pesticides have created a veritable "Circle of Poison" as agricultural products poisoned with banned U.S. pesticides are imported into this country for consumption. According to a 1978 report of the Food and Drug Administration, approximately 10 percent of the food imported by the United States contains varying amounts of illegal pesticides. Other FDA studies at the time showed that over 15 percent of beans and 13 percent of peppers imported from Mexico violated Food and Drug Administration pesticide standards, and nearly half of imported green coffee beans contained traces of illegal pesticides banned in the United States.[21] Large amounts of beef imported from Central America have also been contaminated by pesticides. Thus, when an American eats a hamburger or drinks a cup of coffee in a fast-food restaurant, there is always the possibility that he or she may be poisoned because of a U.S. corporation's unethical behavior in exporting a banned pesticide overseas. The conclusion is clear: In a world of growing food dependence, the United States cannot export its banned chemicals and simply forget about them.

DEATH BY INFANT FORMULA

In the Third World, the use of infant formula often has caused illness and death of babies. In the late nineteenth century, Henri Nestle and the Swiss company he founded developed infant formula as a substitute for breast milk, ostensibly to save the life of an infant who could not be breast-fed. However, the number of infants who cannot be breast-fed has always been small. The vigorous efforts that multinational corporations such as Swiss Nestle and U.S. corporations such as Bristol Myers, Abbott, and American Home Products have made to encourage Third World mothers to use infant feeding formulas rather than to breast-feed their infants has had disastrous consequences. With declining birth rates in industrialized nations like the United States, the sale of infant formula has also declined. On the other hand, Third World markets offer unlimited growth opportunities as birth rates there continue to be high. Advertisements proclaiming the advantages of infant formula have influenced many mothers overseas to change from the traditional breast-feeding to the use of "modern" infant bottle-feeding.

Because the formula must be mixed with water, poverty-stricken mothers of infants in Africa, Asia, and Latin America unwittingly expose their babies to water-borne diseases to which they have not yet developed an immunity. Lacking pure water and often being unaware of the risks they run, mothers use any available water, most of which is contaminated. Being poor, these mothers may also dilute the formula below the recommended standards, causing infants to suffer or die from malnutrition. UNICEF has estimated that with emphasis on the proper use of infant formula and increased breast-feeding, one million infant lives could be saved in Third World countries.

During the early 1980s, the World Health Organization (WHO) and UNICEF drew up a code of conduct for transnationals that sell infant formula in Third World countries. This was in partial response to a worldwide boycott of Nestle products over the export of infant formula in the early 1980s led by the Institutional Chain of the Infant Formula Action Coalition (INFACT), which finally brought Nestle Corporation to its knees and had a major effect on the marketing of infant formula by other corporations. The WHO and UNICEF codes contained provisions that all labels should warn users about the product's improper use. The code also limited free promotional supplies and prohibited direct consumer advertising, gifts to doctors, and hospital promotional distributions.

In 1988, American Home Products/Wyeth was the target of the group Action for Corporate Accountability over their marketing practices which endangered infant health. In many developing countries the corporation encouraged new mothers to forgo breast-feeding by distributing free infant formula through hospitals. Wyeth's booklet for mothers in Taiwan featured a full-page picture of a white mother bottle-feeding a fat baby, presumably with Wyeth's infant formula. Bristol-Myers has distributed literature containing code violations to mothers in the Dominican Republic, Mexico, Taiwan, and other Third World countries.

A new development occurred on October 4, 1987, the fourth anniversary of the end of the Nestle boycott, when Action for Corporate Accountability announced a new boycott of Nestle Corporation and also American Home Products. It was charged that these corporations continued to violate WHO and UNICEF marketing regulations for infant formula in the Third World. The "donation" of infant formula supplies to hospitals and maternity wards is not charitable, according to Dr. Rajanand, a Bombay professor of pediatrics: "The purpose of the industry in bringing the formula to hospitals is to induce sales. This is their one and only purpose."[22]

EXPLOITATION OF THE LAND

Increasingly more land in the underdeveloped countries is being used for greater quantities of export food products that proportionately fewer people in their home countries can afford. Africa now supplies Europe not only with traditional products like palm, peanut, and copra oils but also fresh fruits, vegetables, and even beef. Mexico and countries of Latin America ship many of these products, as well as winter luxury foods such as strawberries, asparagus, and flowers to the United States.

Vital tropical forests are being cut down to make land available for growing these exportable products.

Agribusiness is large-scale corporate agricultural production and processing; a corporation may control all the production, processing, storage, and marketing of an agricultural commodity. In developing countries, agribusinesses, including large plantation and lumbering operations, are largely concentrated in rubber, bananas, pineapple, sugar, palm and other oils, coconuts (copra), tea, cattle, lumber, and various luxury items such as cut flowers and fresh fruits. American corporations have long dominated banana agribusinesses in Central America (for example, United Fruit Company) and rubber in Liberia (Firestone). U.S. conglomerate Gulf and Western dominates sugar production and processing in the Dominican Republic where it controls 8 percent of all cultivated land.

The evidence suggests that Third World agribusinesses, with their huge plantations and ranch lands, frequently help to destroy the local food crop production and employment patterns in the host country. They do little to satisfy local demand for increased food supplies. Nearly all agribusiness products are exported to the industrialized Western nations that pay far more for products than can the local market buyers. Costa Rica, for example, has increased its beef exports to North America by 92 percent in recent years, and this increase has been accompanied by a 26 percent decline in local meat consumption. In Colombia, a hectare of land used to raise carnations for export brings a million pesos a year, while wheat or corn raised there would bring only 12,500 pesos. Consequently, Colombia, like most other Latin American countries, must use its scarce foreign exchange to import wheat. Giant agribusinesses like General Foods, Ralston Purina, Quaker Oats, Swift, and Armour also process and export great quantities of high-protein products like fish meal that could well be used in the host country for human consumption but is used instead to feed America's 35 million dogs and 30 million cats. One expert on world hunger, Susan George, has put it this way: "Any rich mongrel or pampered puss is a better customer for agribusiness than a poor human being. Little has changed since William Hazlitt, replying to Parson Malthus in 1807, stated that the dogs and horses of the rich eat up the food of the children of the poor."[23]

Corporate agribusinesses cloak their activities in the false claims that they are benefiting the ordinary people of the host country. They claim that the people who work for them and the poor as a whole are better off economically. This is often clearly incorrect, as an International Union of Foodworkers' report for the 1974 World Food Conference stated: "There are great numbers of agribusiness workers whose low salaries, substandard housing, poor health and squalid working conditions are such that hunger, malnutrition and under-nourishment for them and for their families are commonplace." Clergy and Laity Concerned, a prominent social activist group, charged in 1977 that Del Monte "has benefited greatly from martial law in the Philippines. [Ferdinand] Marcos has exempted much of the agricultural land owned by foreign corporations from his 'land reform' program and has banned strikes by workers on agribusiness plantations.... Del Monte's operations in the Philippines [are] evidence that hunger and poverty are the darker side of corporate profits." Gulf and Western workers in the Dominican Republic, for example, used to receive extremely low wages; only if they work for the corporation at least 48 years do they become eligible for pensions, which are only worth about $6 a month.

Conversion of forest to grazing and crop land is by far the leading cause of tropical deforestation. Agribusiness connected with providing the industrialized world with beef, rubber and palm oil, and lumber derived from operations like those of Weyerhauser has greatly contributed to the destruction of the tropical rain forests and their giant centuries-old trees. By 1980, almost 40 percent of the world's tropical forests had been destroyed.[24] According to FAO estimates, for 1981–1985, every year over 27 million acres of the developing world's tropical rain forests were destroyed.[25] Some scientists predict the almost total destruction of these giant forests within the next 50 years or so.

Demand for inexpensive beef for fast-food outlets has been one of the primary factors contributing to the destruction of these rain forests. A little over two decades ago, the United States imported only 2,000 tons of beef a year. By 1980, however, beef imports had risen to over 100,000 tons. Meat from grain-fed American beef cattle is far more costly than the tougher, leaner beef that comes from Central and South America. There cattle feed on grass that, in many cases, has replaced the rain forest. This cheaper beef is a plentiful source for the hamburgers, hot dogs, tacos and frozen TV dinners that have helped make the fast-food industry the most rapidly growing segment in the giant U.S. food business. McDonald's, however, advertises that its hamburgers are made from "100 percent pure American beef." Because of these heavy demands, beef production in many developing countries has doubled; over the past 20 years, beef exports from Costa Rica, Guatemala, and Honduras have tripled. Environmentalists Paul and Anne Ehrlich have commented on this situation:

The rainforests are being sacrificed to keep up the flow of meat destined almost exclusively to be hamburgers served by fast-food chains. Beef can be produced at very low cost in poor countries because of the availability of cheap labor and cheap land ("useless" rainforest). Grass-fed beef can be raised in Latin America at a quarter the price at which it can be raised in Colorado. Although imports from Latin America only amount to 1 or 2 percent of U.S. beef consumption, they cut a nickel or so off the price of a hamburger. Ironically, though, while more than a quarter of all Central American forests have been destroyed in the past twenty years to produce beef for the United States, per-capita consumption of beef in Central American nations has dropped steadily.[26]

When once these rain forests are destroyed to provide cattle-raising and other agribusiness lands, a century or more may be required for them to regenerate. The tropical rainforests play an essential role as filters for the Earth's atmosphere. Without them, excessive soil erosion also results, producing increased river silt and flooding. The destruction of the rain forests, furthermore, endangers half the world's 10 million species of plants and animals, which have long made these forests their home. Too much deforestation might even change the world's climate, potentially causing a "greenhouse effect." After the rain forest is gone, all that may be left will be plantations of pasture land for fast-food beef and fast-growing softwood trees which are ground up to make toilet paper.

EXPLOITATION OF THE PEOPLE

Pope John Paul II's third encyclical of 1981 took aim at the transnationals that have built up vast "empires" throughout the world today. The pope claimed that large corporations are contributing to the ever-widening disproportion between the incomes of the rich and poor nations. As the developed countries put the highest possible prices on their products and at the same time try to fix the lowest possible prices for raw materials or semi-manufactured goods, they create a wide gap between the rich and poor countries' national incomes. The pope cautioned that "workers' rights must come ahead of profits" in the poor countries.

U.S. transnational corporations have been in the process of moving many of their manufacturing facilities to the newly developing countries since the time of the Korean War. Third World countries have encouraged these moves in the belief that the introduction of the plants add to industrial growth, increase their people's employment opportunities and, at the same time, decrease their dependence on imports from the developed countries. The U.S. multinationals have different motives, however: cheaper wages, lower employee benefits, less stringent health and safety standards, and a more open labor market. Corporations have been enticed into plant relocations in Third World countries that offer them the right to import raw materials, plant components, and equipment duty-free, and give them tax holidays of up to 20 years. Corporations that do not want to relocate their plants directly can often work out attractive subcontracting arrangements in the Third World.

Most of the work done in Third World countries is labor intensive. For example, Southeast Asia's semiconductor factories of U.S. giants like National Semiconductor, Texas Instruments, and Motorola are part of a "global assembly line" that stretches half way around the world. In much of this labor-intensive work, silicon wafers which are made in New Jersey are shipped to Southeast Asian countries where they are cut into tiny chips, then bonded by the workers to circuit boards. With their Third World operations, Levi Straus, Blue Bell, and other conglomerates, including subsidiaries of General Mills and Gulf and Western, have cornered a fifth of the U.S. clothing market. Rockport shoes are made in Taiwan, Perry Ellis "American Series" slacks are made in Mauritius, Bell telephones come from Singapore and Taiwan, and Spalding's "Official NBA" basketballs are manufactured in Korea.

Much Third World production involves "outward processing." Workers in U.S. plants design and cut the goods, which are then shipped to Mexico and Central American countries for processing. From there they are re-imported for final finishing and packaging in the United States. In this roundabout manner, corporations save import duties on the finished garments, paying duty only on the value added. This process has seriously hurt American workers' jobs. In planning their moves, the multinationals often carefully choose those countries in which labor unions are nonexistent or weak, or countries that are so dominated by a right-wing or military government that they can safely pay low wages and operate with minimal worker safety regulations. The AFL-CIO News stated in 1988 that: "Aided by favorable tariff breaks, hundreds of American firms have migrated to Mexico.... In the past decade alone, American firms have invested $2 billion on assembly plants just across the border, shipping products back into this country at such a pace that they account for nearly 20 percent of Mexico's $3.5 billion annual trade surplus with the United States." At 900 of these "maquiladoras," some 300,000 women and girls work for wages of 30 to 75 cents an hour.

Even though American multinationals claim that they are contributing to the development of these poor countries, their primary goal is to obtain cheap labor. The average worker in the United States in 1988 received $13.90 an hour; in South Korea, it was only $2.45; and in Taiwan, $2.71. The average hourly wage paid in the semiconductor industry in the United States in 1982 was $5.92; in Hong Kong it was $1.15; in Singapore, $.79; in Malaysia and the Philippines, $.48; and in Indonesia, $.19. Fringe benefits are correspondingly low, and there is little or no protection for them from trade unions, which are often banned or their right to strike limited. For example, Philippine President Ferdinand Marcos, in 1982, outlawed all strikes in the U.S.-dominated semiconductor industry. Over and over, reports have circulated that as soon as a worker protest begins over pay or working conditions in South

Korea, Indonesia, Thailand, or Taiwan, for example, carloads of police and government officials descend on the plant to put down the demonstration.

Those who work for American corporations operating in Third World countries often have to tolerate appalling working conditions. They may work 12-hour days, and although toxic fumes and dangerous liquids may be present, workers, unlike those in the United States, are usually not required to wear protective clothing, gloves, or face masks. Women working in the intensive semiconductor plants bend over microscopes all day, and if they develop severe eye ailments, as they commonly do, and thus become unable to work, they have no alternatives except to retire or face dismissal.[27] There is usually no workers' compensation. The health of textile and garment workers, who are primarily women, is often endangered by U.S. multinational overseas garment and textile affiliates. Two experts on this problem have stated:

The firms, generally local subcontractors to large U.S. (and European) chains such as Sears and J.C. Penney, show little concern for the health of their employees. Some of the worst conditions have been documented in South Korea. ... Workers are packed into poorly-lit rooms where summer temperatures rise above 100 degrees Fahrenheit. Textile dust and lint, which can cause brown-lung disease, fill the air. The dampness that is so useful in preserving thread causes rheumatism and arthritis among the workers.[28]

Union Carbide makes Eveready batteries in Indonesia. The employee working conditions that an American journalist found in Union Carbide's Indonesian plant in 1981 would never be tolerated in the United States.[29] The company had failed, for example, to warn workers about the dangers of carbon black, which is used in battery manufacturing. It contains mercury and contaminates the environment in and around the plant. As late as 1981, both male and female employees in the highly dangerous chemical mixing room generally worked 16 hours a day.

Most American multinationals that move abroad to reduce labor costs prefer to hire women for detailed assembly-line work. They work for even less money than men and it is easier to exploit them. In Haiti, for example, where nearly all the baseballs sold in the United States are made, thousands of women perform the final operation for four major U.S. companies in producing a baseball whose parts are sent in from the United States. U.S. Rawlings Sporting Goods Company, the chief manufacturer of baseballs in Haiti, also has a monopoly on all balls used by the National and American baseball leagues.[30] Rawlings pays its workers, most of whom are female, about $2.75 a day for producing 30 to 40 baseballs—about 7 to 9 cents a ball. In the United States, Rawlings sells the baseballs for about $4, almost 50 times what it pays the Haitians to make them.

Multinationals prefer hiring women workers not only because they cost less but because they find them generally more docile than men. Women are more easy to press into boring, repetitive assembly-line work for the low wages the multinationals offer. Women are far less likely to present problems than young males. Even when they do try to press for higher pay or better working conditions, Third World governments often support the multinational's opposition to their demands. One astute observer pointed out that East Asian governments "have taken measures to make their country's women more attractive as potential employees by ensuring that they will not resist demands made on them by foreign firms."[31] The governments sometimes use repressive means to keep women workers in line. During one 5-month labor dispute in Control Data's Korean plant in 1982, the unionized, all-female assembly-line workers were preparing to leave their Seoul plant when the guards shut and locked the gate.[32] Security guards and male supervisory personnel severely beat some of them, causing some pregnant women to miscarry. In another case, when women workers in a a U.S. Guatemalan jeans and jacket factory drew up a list of complaints about low piecework wages and lack of overtime pay, the plant manager reported to local authorities that he was being harassed by "communists." When the women reported for work the following day, they found the factory surrounded by a heavily armed contingent of military police.[33] The so-called communist organizers were identified and fired. Similar episodes have occurred in the Philippines, the Dominican Republic, South Korea, and elsewhere in the Third World.

U.S. transnational corporations often operate on the assumption that the poorer and more malnourished the people, the more likely they are to spend a disproportionate amount of their income on a luxury item. If a profit is to be made through creating a demand, corporations do not stop to consider at whose expense they will make their profit. In many parts of the world, for example, poor rural families will sell a few eggs and a chicken to buy Coke soft drinks, even though their children lack protein; and poor city people may buy American processed baby foods when they could have prepared their own at little cost.

Partly because of decreasing domestic sales, the United States has also become a major partner in the increased promotion, sale, and consumption of death-dealing cigarettes in the very parts of the world where malnutrition and hunger are most prevalent. The cigarette manufacturers have been highly successful. By the early 1980s, according to the World Health Organization, the total consumption of cigarettes in the Third World was already increasing by an average of more than 3 percent a year. According to the World Health Organization, this is primarily due to the aggressive advertising campaigns conducted by "unscrupulous tobacco industries." Of the approximately

600 billion U.S. cigarettes made in 1988, 100 billion went overseas, and half of these to the Far East. As Surgeon General Koop pointed out, "I don't think we as citizens can continue to tolerate exporting disease, disability and death." Moreover, the United States cannot hope to get worldwide cooperation in its fight against drugs, according to Representative Chester Atkins (D-Mass.), "when we have a drug our own government says is addictive, and is killing us, and we are spreading that drug overseas." Representative Mel Levine (D-Calif.) said: "The message we are sending is that Asian lungs are more expendable than American lungs."

Even though American cigarettes cost far more in these developing countries than the local brands, the aggressive advertising campaigns for American brands have greatly boosted their sales. U.S. tobacco companies have responded to awakening concern in developed countries over the link between smoking, cancer, and heart disease by launching an all-out sales assault on potential Third World and Asiatic consumers. Generally many youths there prefer to smoke American brands because the advertisements link them to modernity and prestige. In almost all these countries, the infamous Marlboro cowboy lures youths into feeling they are part of the American West: "Come to Where the Flavor is . . . Marlboro Country." Marlboro is now the world's largest selling cigarette, particularly among the young, with sales that total more than $3.8 million worldwide. According to a 1983 report, the tar and nicotine content of U.S. cigarettes sold in the Third World is often twice the level of identical brands sold in the United States.[35] Throughout the Third World, labels of health hazards on cigarette packages are the exception rather than the rule.

The issue of exporting American cigarettes to Asiatic countries came to a head in 1989. On grounds of "unfair trade discrimination," the U.S. Cigarette Export Association persuaded the government to intimidate Japan, Korea, and Taiwan with threatened economic sanctions when each of these countries had sought to keep out American cigarettes. In 1989, however, Thailand put up a stiffer resistance and enlisted U.S. anti-smoking groups such as the American Heart Association, the American Cancer Society, and others to help out with congressional testimony. Although Thailand has a state-run cigarette monopoly, the Thais feared that the clever advertising of U.S. cigarette companies would induce more of their people to smoke. In addition to forcing Thailand to admit the cigarettes, the cigarette association demanded the right to advertise on Thai TV, which bans all such advertising on health grounds.

As a consequence of callous corporate behavior by American tobacco corporations, four U.S. congressmen joined together in 1989 to introduce a bill to (1) forbid American companies to advertise overseas in ways that are prohibited here; (2) prevent our country from threatening trade sanctions against countries that are unwilling to allow the promotion of cigarettes; and (3) force cigarettes sold abroad to carry the same warning labels they carry here.

EXPLOITATION OF THE COUNTRY

Mexican President Jose Portillo, in an address before the United Nations General Assembly in 1983, said that transnational corporations exhibit a "pattern of domination" over many developing countries that endangers the country's sovereignty over their economic progress, and their very existence as a national state. Through corrupt and often illegal practices, the transnationals interfere to support regimes that maintain conditions favorable to their own activities, or they may endeavor to strengthen their ties to whichever potential ally in the country might provide conditions most suitable to their needs.

In many cases, U.S. transnationals have exhibited an almost total disregard for the political well-being of the people of the Third World. American transnationals have done extensive business with such nefarious regimes as that of Iran's Shah Riza Pahlavi and with Central American dictators like Nicaragua's Anastasio Somoza. In Chile, ITT helped to topple the democratically elected president, Salvador Allende. ITT presumably then got the man it wanted, Augusto Pinochet, a long-ruling, right-wing military dictator who helped the company get what it wanted. U.S. multinationals have long played a major role in the financial as well as the policy control of Central America. Two multinational corporations, Standard Brands and United Fruit, have largely dominated the economy of Honduras, one of the poorest countries in Latin America, where bananas make up the bulk of export earnings. The multinationals have demonstrated their power most effectively when they have feared their profits being reduced or when they have suspected that their business interests might be nationalized. For example, during the early 1950s under the regime of the newly elected democratic Guatemalan president Jacobo Arbenz, the government raised property taxes, encouraged unions, and initiated a land reform program. These changes seriously concerned the large land-holding United Fruit Company, and it unjustly accused the government of being part of an international communist conspiracy. In fact, the communists actually played only a minor role in the Arbenz coalition government.[36] United Fruit, because of its desire to protect its power and assets, pressured Washington to take drastic action in Guatemala. With the threat of U.S. military intervention and the help of the Central Intelligence Agency (CIA), in an operation code-named "Operation Success," the Arbenz coalition government fell. For many years following the coup, Guatemala suffered from right-wing military dictatorships dedicated to backing the wealthy landowners and the United Fruit Company. Only in 1986 was Guatemala once again able to install a democratic government. Long ago, the famed Marine Corps General Smedley Butler explained this policy of government intervention in the Third World to protect corporate interests.

I spent 33 years . . . being a high-class muscleman for big business, for Wall Street and the bankers. . . . I helped purify Nicaragua for the international house of Brown Brothers in 1909–1912. I helped make Mexico and especially Tampico safe for American oil interests in 1916. I brought light to the Dominican Republic for American sugar interests in 1916. I helped make Haiti and Cuba a decent place for the National City Bank boys to collect revenue in. I helped in the rape of half a dozen Central American republics for the benefit of Wall Street.[37]

For most of the blacks (who make up the bulk of South Africa's population), their share of the country is like that in the developing world; for the whites it is not. For many years the highly visible presence of U.S. corporations and their subsidiaries in South Africa has drawn tremendous opposition from anti-apartheid activists. At its peak, U.S. corporations accounted for more than 20 percent of all direct foreign investment in South Africa. U.S. petroleum corporations controlled about 40 percent of all petroleum sales. In 1982, U.S. corporate investments in South Africa totaled $14.6 billion, about 70 percent of them coming from 10 large corporations, including Ford, General Motors, General Electric, U.S. Steel, Goodyear, Caltex, and Mobil Oil.

Nearly all U.S. corporations operating in South Africa eventually signed and generally practiced the American-derived Sullivan Principles which require them not to discriminate in the workplace. However, their continuing presence there gave a corporate blessing from the United States to an unjust system. In the United States, mounting pressures for American corporate divestment in South Africa came from liberal groups, churches, investors, and others. As a result, the U.S. Congress in 1986 passed a law, overriding a veto by President Reagan, that prohibited further private investments in South Africa and banned the import of certain materials. Many U.S. corporations had already pulled out of the country, but as of 1989 a number of large U.S. corporations were still operating there. Among the largest remaining companies were Goodyear Tire and Rubber, International Paper, Johnson and Johnson, United Technologies, and Caltex Petroleum. Also, according to *Fortune*, corporations still operating there but planning to leave were Mobil, RJR Nabisco, Control Data, NCR, and Hewlett-Packard.[38] As corporations pull out of South Africa, however, they leave a foot in the door: some of their operations generally continue under South African ownership. Other corporations have actually improved their profit margins by selling through low-overhead distributors and through licensing agreements. South Africans can still buy CBS records, Levi jeans, and U.S. automobiles, even though the corporations behind these products no longer operate in their country. The real pressures that precipitated the withdrawal of U.S. corporations from South Africa came from social action groups and the Congress. Corporate moral scruples about apartheid were never involved. Instead, the people and the government of the United States had to intervene.

Chapter 9

WHAT CAN BE DONE

Many of our corporate giants reap substantial profits from a callous disregard of their highly proclaimed interest in the consumer, the public, and the environment. Likewise, many flaunt the laws of the very government of the United States that has provided them the freedom under which capitalism can operate. What, then, can be done to change this disrespect for ethical standards and to prevent the abuse of our citizens by the "rotten apples" in the corporate barrel? Self-regulation, it appears, has been only modestly successful in curbing abuses; corporate and industry codes of ethics lack enforcement teeth. Moreover, it is rare that a top corporate executive condemns unethical corporate practices or even gross violations of law in the corporate world. Stronger and more effective enforcement of government regulations may well be the best, and perhaps the only, recourse left to protect our citizens and, fundamentally, our capitalist system.

LIMITATIONS OF SELF-REGULATION

Self-regulation of corporations, not government, is one answer, and the one preferred by many corporations and their executives. James Inman, a leading authority on government regulation, has stressed the need for corporations to put their own houses in order. "The inculcation of ethical principles forms the very basis of all crime prevention and control, whether ordinary, white-collar or corporate crime. The development of stronger business ethics must come first from the individual business firms and second from the ethical codes recognized and supported by the business community."[1] In a similar vein, Professor John Braithwaite, who studies corporate abuses, has advocated "enforced self-regulation," which he prefers to an exclusive reliance on punitive measures.[2] This approach, he feels, helps to overcome corporate resistance to government regulation through the government compelling each company to write a set of rules tailored to the unique set of contingencies facing that particular firm. A government regulatory agency would then either approve these rules or send them back for revision should they be insufficiently stringent. Many other scholars, however, believe that as long as profits remain the "bottom line" for corporations, any question of self-regulation is likely to remain largely a platitude. Enforced self-regulation, for example, might well result in the coaptation of the regulatory process by business, with corporations writing the rules in such a way that they would actually help them to circumvent the very purpose of the regulation.

The chief form of self-regulation is corporate and industrial codes of ethics. A special February 1988 report of the prestigious Business Roundtable, which is made up of a large number of chief executives of the top 100 largest industrial corporations, stated that ethics should be not only a priority in corporate business but a "prime business asset." The report went on to point out that "one manifestation has been the widespread development of codes of ethics or conduct and statements of values in business organizations." However, in the same year, a detailed examination of 202 corporate codes of ethics, most of them *Fortune* 500 companies, did not present an overly encouraging picture of this form of corporate self-regulation.[3] The codes make much of employee actions against the corporation. Beyond that, however, the codes chiefly cover broad corporate relations with the U.S. government, particularly political contributions, foreign government bribery, and the integrity of financial records. They seldom cover specific ethical positions on a significant number of important basic issues, and rarely do they mention specific federal regulatory agencies or specific laws. Only one-third of them even discuss antitrust violations: No code mentioned the Consumer Products Safety Commission. Although policy provisions vary in corporate codes of ethics, over 90 percent of them do not discuss product safety, 78 percent do not mention product quality, 76 percent fail to mention relations with the consumer, and 87 percent ignore environmental issues.

Unless corporate ethical codes contain adequate enforcement provisions, they become meaningless public-relations "gimmicks." A corporation must demonstrate a basic commitment to firm discipline and punishment of code transgressions. The 202 corporate codes of ethics examined in 1988 revealed that although 80 percent of them did contain enforcement or compliance procedures, only 25 percent outlined them in detail. Rarely were there specific penalties. Almost none made reference to reprimand, demotion, or fine, and only a third of them referred to the possibility of an employee being fired.

The failure by corporations to enforce their own codes of ethics probably accounts for the research finding that the relationship between codes of ethics and corporate violations is minimal. In fact, the startling conclusion was that federal agencies actually cite those corporations that do have codes of ethics more than they cite the corporations that do not emphasize ethical standards. The most likely explanation is that although emphasis is placed on individual employees to be ethical, at the same time, they fail to deal with the ways in which the corporation itself creates a general atmosphere that engenders unethical and illegal conduct. The survey concluded that codes of ethics are not real evidence of self-regulation or of corporate social responsibility. To be really effective, for example, a code should impell corporate managers not to put undue pressure on their subordinates to achieve particular economic goals of the corporation. Actually, the size of a corporation and the type of industry in which it operates, the study revealed, had a far greater impact on the extent of law violations than did a code of ethics. Some specialists in this area have suggested that ethical codes will mean little until corporations see some financial rewards for improved ethical behavior.[4] This might be accomplished, in part, if the government, or some other important group, publicly recognized corporations whose ethical standards are high. Unethical corporations might then lose out in the marketplace to their competitors with good and highly publicized ethical track records.

Many businessmen believe that a comprehensive, industry-wide code would help individual corporations to define more clearly the limits of acceptable or ethical conduct and reduce cut-throat practices where competition is intense. Such an industry code would, for example, spell out in some detail acceptable relations with consumers, suppliers, competitors, and the government. Still, the problems of enforcing the codes would remain. A sample of retired *Fortune* 500 middle managers were pessimistic of the success of such self-regulation. In their collective opinion, "the unethical behavior of certain top management personnel within an industry, plus the greed and unethical practices of some corporations, have made government regulations necessary."[5] Moreover, they could visualize no way in which an individual industry could effectively enforce its rules.

Top corporate executives very seldom condemn corporate and industry practices. Interviews with a number of the highest corporate executives indicated that they do not believe that they are responsible for speaking out about the unethical practices in the corporate world, as each executive has enough work to do with his own corporation.[6]

Most of them rationalize their own silence. One said, "It is not the role of corporate executives to condemn other corporations that violate the law." In testimony before a Congressional committee in the 1980s, Admiral Rickover expressed a different opinion: "Businessmen should vigorously advocate respect for law, because law is the foundation of our society, including business." Irving Kristol, a leading conservative writer on business affairs, has written in a similar vein: "Corporate executives almost never criticize other corporate executives, even when the latter are caught in *flagrante delicto*. No one seems to be 'read out' of the corporate community, which inevitably leads the outsider to wonder whether this community has any standards of self-government at all."[7] A 1983 article in the business section of the *New York Times* pointed out:

The business community's quasi-official leaders have remained dispassionate about the crimes. The last time the Business Roundtable, a group of some of the most prestigious businessmen in the country, made a major pronouncement on the subject of corporate ethics was a decade ago.... It has yet to consider, let alone take action on, the current cycle of mushrooming corporate crime.[8]

The faculty at business schools could do more to instill a commitment to high ethical standards among their students, many of whom presumably will come to occupy high positions in the corporate world. Business schools could help students understand the types of ethical quandaries that will confront them in the business world and give them the capability to think more clearly about the responsibilities and obligations that individuals owe to each other in the corporate business world. Unfortunately, however, not much is being done; a 1986 survey by the Ethics Resource Center revealed that only 21 percent of the business schools give a separate course on business ethics. Fortunately, a number of business schools appear to be moving in a more positive direction. Harvard, Stanford, Columbia, Pennsylvania, and Dartmouth are integrating ethics instruction into their curricula. The Harvard Business School announced in 1988 that it would require all entering MBA students to take a three-week course in business ethics that would cover such issues as the moral responsibilities of corporations and consider some of the ethical pressures that corporations and their employees face. In 1989 Stanford announced the endowment of a chair in their business school to deal specifically with issues of ethics and corporate responsibility as keys to the quality of business performance.

One means of stimulating greater corporate self-regulation is for corporations to encourage employees to report corporate law violators.[9] Many top management executives tend to regard employees who express concerns about illegal or unethical corporate activity as trouble-makers. Actually, if such employees could freely communicate their concerns, it would help prevent employees going outside the corporation to secure governmental action that could endanger the corporation's reputation because of unfavorable publicity. Columnist Jack Anderson has pointed out that the whistle-blower is "our principal protection against the designs of public and corporate wrongdoers. He dares to expose a lie or an embarrassment or a scandal that the people in power have conspired to conceal. His likely reward is counterattack; he risks retaliation and ruin."[10] On many occasions, corporate employees have discovered that their own basic ethical standards are completely out of line with what they see happening in the workplace. They can respond to their own questions about these events either by accepting them and saying nothing, or they can blow the whistle. They face a dilemma as they realize they may pay a penalty for telling, as corporations have ways of punishing whistle-blowers. The most common retaliatory measures are transfer, demotion, or dismissal. One of the best known cases of whistle-blowing was Robert Witjyzak's exposure of Rockwell International's shifting of over $1.5 million in costs from other programs to the space shuttle.[11] As a consequence, Witjyzak claimed that Rockwell removed him from his desk job, forced him to do manual labor, then eventually fired him.

If employees could be assured that the law would protect their jobs, it is probably safe to say that more employees would speak out about illegal practices. In this way, whistle-blowing could become a more effective means of control. Even among a sample of corporate middle management, three out of four felt that the government should protect corporate whistle-blowers from dismissal.[12] One out of four middle managers was of the opinion, however, that even if the law protected them from dismissal, the employees might subsequently be in an uncomfortable position with regard to salaries and promotions. As one said, "Life in the corporation would be miserable—you might even be counting paper clips."

In 1989 only a handful of states—California, Michigan, New York, Connecticut and Maine—required that whistle-blowers be protected from corporate recriminations. In addition, a growing number of state court decisions are curbing a corporation's right to fire or otherwise to discipline employees who report illegal activities. For example, a Kentucky jury in 1988 ordered Ashland Oil to pay $69 million to two employees fired for refusing to pay bribes to foreign officials. Each year the Massachusetts Cavallo Foundation gives monetary awards to selected whistle-blowers. In 1988, the foundation awarded $3,000 to a quality inspector of Bath Iron Works for having disclosed that uninspected steel was being used in the construction of Ticonderoga-class Navy cruisers. A federal law is now needed to provide even better protection to corporate whistle-blowers who wish to report law violations to federal agencies. In 1989, Congress approved a law that would provide greater job safeguards for federal employee whistle-blowers who expose government fraud and waste. The vote in the Senate was 97–0. President Reagan had killed a previous bill, but President George Bush signed this one.

STRONGER ENFORCEMENT

Two important factors play a significant role in a corporation's compliance with or its violation of the law: the corporation's own cultural or ethical climate, and the conduct of its top executives. A special *New York Times* business section of June 9, 1985 reported: "Too many companies are ignoring the issue of corporate morality, and thus fostering corporate cultures devoid of ethical values." Each corporation builds its own cultural history over the years; it becomes permeated with the firm's own particular attitudes about ethical standards and law obedience. In this development, a critical factor appears to be the ethical standards of the top management; their emphasis on developing and maintaining a good corporate reputation; the degree of concern for employees, consumers, and the environment; the firm's customary competitive practices; and its attitudes toward continued corporate expansion and power, even at the sacrifice of social responsibility.

Just as a general pattern of respect for law obedience permeates this corporate cultural history, law-breaking can also become a pattern regardless of the economic environment and with or without pressures for profits. Simply put, some corporations take pride in protecting their reputations more than do others. In an interview, one *Fortune* 500 board chairman said that ethical and law violations must be "congenial to the climate of the corporation," while another said, "Some corporations, like those in politics, tolerate corruption."[13] A middle-management executive of a *Fortune* 500 corporation expressed the same view. "A corporation's history often starts from the original founders and their ethical standards prevail from the beginning; corporate reputation means a lot to some, similar to that of a Japanese corporation." Another said, "Often corporations develop a way of doing business unethically and it takes a lot at the top to change it."[14]

A corporation may "socialize" its members to accept a climate of unethical behavior that is conducive to criminality. A former Securities and Exchange Commission enforcement chief said, "Our largest corporations have trained some of our brightest young people to be dishonest." Gilbert Geis, in his appraisal of the infamous large-scale conspiracy to illegally fix prices of generators by the largest U.S. electrical corporations, a conspiracy that bilked consumers of hundreds of millions of dollars, concluded that illegal activity had simply become an "established way of life" for many of these corporations.[15] One executive said, "if I didn't do it, I felt someone else would. I would be removed and someone else would do it." In another large-scale illegal price conspiracy in the folding carton industry, a corporate executive testified that "each was introduced to price-fixing practices by his superiors as he came to the point in his career when he had price-fixing responsibilities."[16] Lockheed's report to the Securities and Exchange Commission on its extensive overseas bribery of foreign officials during the 1970s stated: "Employees learned not to question standard operational procedures and practices.... Employees who questioned foreign marketing practices damaged their claims for career advancement."[17]

All this leads to the conclusion that the imposition of stiffer penalties on corporate violators should, hopefully, bring about constructive changes in the ethical practices of certain corporations and serve as a deterrence to others. As an example, when the courts convicted and punished Gulf Oil for having been involved in millions of dollars of illegal campaign contributions in the Nixon era, a senior vice president commented:

This traumatic experience forced many of us at Gulf to sit back and reflect on the basic purposes of our business and to assess whether the practices in question or any other forms of corner-cutting can properly serve the ends for which our corporation was chartered. I think we now realize, to a far greater degree than before, that by not doing our business well—by not doing it in full accord with the law and ethical standards—we can get hurt and hurt badly.

Larger and more effective government enforcement staffs are essential. The detection, investigation, and prosecution of corporate crime offenses are generally extremely complicated and time-consuming. Mark Green and John Berry, two experts in the area of corporate wrongdoing, have concluded that "a vigorous, dedicated law enforcement official who wants to prosecute corporate wrongdoing ... must scale high walls surrounding a fortress in order to apprehend, convict, and punish a suspect sheltered there."[18] Government agencies must also deal with the immense resources that large corporations can muster for their defense, particularly their highly paid and experienced legal staffs. Lack of resources is also the major factor affecting state prosecution. A California survey of state prosecuting attorneys found that the prosecution of corporate crime is most inhibited by lack of staff, budget strain, and the length of time required to prosecute a corporate crime.[19]

Even before the Reagan administration decimated enforcement funds of agencies handling corporate misbehavior, the grand combined total of enforcement budgets of the Securities and Exchange Commission, the Consumer Product Safety Commission, and the National Highway

Safety Transportation Administration was less than $20 million; under the Reagan administration, budgetary restrictions became much worse. The reduction in government regulation and enforcement operations eventually affected virtually every American, and sometimes in a major way. It seriously altered the crashworthiness of new autos, the safety of consumer products, the risks of contracting cancer in the workplace, and the quality of America's environment. Between 1980 and 1983, for example, the total staffs of federal agencies responsible for health and safety and anti-trust protection declined 19 percent; hardest hit were the enforcement staffs. The work of the Food and Drug Administration was severely handicapped by a reduction from 8,100 to 7,400 employees. During the Reagan years, OSHA's staff was cut 20 percent and the number of plant inspectors dropped 30 percent. Commenting on the EPA at the end of eight years of the Reagan administration, Senator Frank Lautenberg (D-N.J.) said the EPA "instead of acting as a watch dog is acting as a lap dog."[20] An American Bar Association task force reported in 1985 that the Securities and Exchange Commission enforcement staff was too small "for the commission to effectively discharge its statutory responsibilities." According to the president of the state security regulators, "The Securities and Exchange Commission is horribly overmatched by the bad guys in the marketplace."[21]

As an example of what happened to one agency under the Reagan administration, in 1983 the Consumer Product Safety Commission suffered a cut of 25 percent from its 1982 budget. In that year, the total staff of the commission, including administration rule-makers and enforcement officials, totaled only 889, which was thus reduced to 636. This reduction forced the agency to close 13 regional offices. Mandatory reports from businesses that might flag dangerous products dropped by 50 percent, inspections of manufacturing plants fell 46 percent, and regional officers recalled 66 percent fewer products.

The adequate enforcement of corporate regulations goes beyond budgets and staff; it involves policy as well. The Reagan administration, for example, simply adopted the policy of relaxing the enforcement of existing government rules and regulations.[22] The Federal Trade Commission, for example, weakened its vigorous efforts under the Carter administration to protect consumers from deceptive, false or misleading food and drug advertising and other consumer protection activities.[23] During the Reagan years, the Federal Trade Commission generally adopted a hands-off, free market approach. It reduced antitrust and consumer protection work forces by 35 percent. FTC enforcement actions in consumer protection cases declined 48 percent between 1981 and 1982. The commission also reduced enforcement of antitrust laws: In 1979, under the Carter administration, it brought 86 actions, whereas in 1982 there were only 29.

STIFFER CORPORATE PENALTIES

Few of the penalties meted out to law-breaking corporations today are severe. One study of all penalties imposed on 477 *Fortune* 500 corporations during a two-year period for law violations showed that nearly half of them were simply governmental warnings or product recalls.[24] Slightly more than 40 percent of the penalties imposed even in serious or moderately serious cases were simply warnings not to repeat the violation. The overwhelming number of cases of corporate illegal behavior do not involve the use of the criminal penalty but rather the civil injunction, wherein the court enjoins the corporation from further law violations, or by a consent decree, which is a compromise settlement of the violations. Consent decrees usually contain the phrase that the corporation "neither admits or denies" the allegations. Understandably, corporate defendants relish this clause, as it precludes the use of the decree as an admission of guilt in subsequent court proceedings, whether civil or criminal.

In many cases, this clause is worth millions of dollars to corporations; without it private plaintiffs could use the decree as evidence of law violations in private damage actions.... Once the consent is signed, the public perception is that the corporate defendant is not a lawbreaker, not a criminal, not a crook. The defendant is merely 'enjoined.' "[25]

Where employed, a corporate monetary payment or fine, whether administrative, civil or criminal, is extremely small if measured in terms of the often billions in corporate assets and sales. Fines rarely equal the profits made in an illegal transaction; some corporations even look upon them as a cost of doing business. Corporate fines may be likened to license fees to break the law. A study of the financial penalties (administrative, civil and criminal) imposed on the *Fortune* 500 companies revealed that 91.6 percent were for $50,000 or less; 3.7 percent were between $50,000 and $1 million; and only 1 percent were more than $1 million.[26] Criminal fines imposed on the 19 very large corporations convicted in the major price-fixing conspiracy in the folding carton industry ranged from only $25,000 to $45,000. Chevron once paid a $1 million fine for having extensively violated offshore anti-pollution laws, but even this large fine represented about .03 percent of Chevron's gross income.

These minor penalties are a reflection of the clout that corporations carry in Washington. First of all, they exercise their influence in the enactment of legislation affecting corporations; they see to it that the laws provide largely minor penalties and often no criminal penalty for their infringement. They also play a political role in seeing that enforcement policies are lenient. Senator William Proxmire (D-Wis.) commented that "the Reagan administration has a double standard for law enforcement; one for its friends and fellow corporate board members and one for less privileged criminals with whom it deals far more harshly."[27] Large corporations fight cases with such a barrage of highly paid and competent lawyers that the government often chooses a minor penalty in order to avoid a time-consuming trial. Finally, government enforcement officials seldom look upon corporate offenses in the same manner in which they view ordinary crimes like individual fraud and embezzlement.

From this overview of minor penalties that the government imposes on large corporations, it is clear that statutory penalties should be increased, if for no other reason than to deter others. One logical step in maximizing the deterrent effect of fines might be to peg the monetary penalty to the corporation's financial size. Another would set minimum corporate criminal fines at $100,000, with $1 million or even more as a maximum. Another suggestion would be to fine the corporation a sum equal to the illegal profits made through the violation. The U.S. Sentencing Commission in 1988 proposed a different set of criteria, namely that criminal fines for corporations and other business fines be set in relation to the harm that criminal conduct causes victims and society. Included in the fine would be enforcement costs incurred in the investigation, prosecution and punishment of the offender. The antitrust laws of the European Economic Community provide fines that may total 10 percent of the offending company's previous year's financial return. In the case of multinationals, the fine is based on the corporation's worldwide profits.

As a substitution for a monetary fine, provisions could be made to require the guilty firm to implement a socially useful project that could utilize its special skills. This particular approach would be appropriate for environmental or pharmaceutical offenses. A drug company, for example, might set up a medical relief program in a Third World country, then supply it with urgently needed drugs that would not be sufficiently profitable to them under normal circumstances.[28]

The fact that the United States has an exclusively criminal legal system for individuals and largely an administrative or civil legal system for corporations tends to undermine the effectiveness of the criminal justice system in dealing with corporate violators. A criminal prosecution of a corporation can be far more effective than an administrative or civil action because it more seriously "labels" and stigmatizes the corporation. Where provided in the law, criminal cases are filed, but not as frequently as they should be, against corporations. The courts cannot, of course, imprison a criminally convicted corporation; the best they can do is levy a fine. Lord Chancellor Edward Thurlow (1731–1806) put it this way:

"Did you ever expect a corporation to have a conscience when it has no soul to be damned and nobody to be kicked?" Analyzing the matter further on another occasion, he said, "Corporations have neither bodies to be punished, nor souls to be condemned; they therefore do as they like."

When grave corporate illegalities resulted in particularly violent events, prosecutors have in a limited number of cases indicted the offending corporation on the more serious charges of criminal homicide or manslaughter. In the notorious case of Ford's defective Pinto and the resultant deaths, the government brought a charge of criminal homicide against the corporation, but after a long and bitter trial, the jury acquitted Ford. In 1985, Eli Lilly pleaded guilty to criminal misdemeanor charges for failing to advise the government of the fatal side effects linked to their anti-arthritic drug Oraflex. However, the majority of the limited homicide indictments of corporations and their executives have been the result of deaths in the workplace. The government prosecuted Warner-Lambert, the pharmaceutical concern, and several of its officials on charges of second-degree manslaughter and criminally negligent homicide following a 1976 plant explosion that killed six workers. The Justice Department charged General Dynamics with involuntary manslaughter and the criminal violation of state occupational standards in the death of a worker who was exposed to fluorocarbon solvent vapors.

Congress could also enact legislation to prohibit a corporation with a previous conviction for violating a federal law from receiving a federal contract. This would be a particularly appropriate means of controlling illegal behavior in the defense industry, even though the enforcement of such legislation would be difficult where only a few defense contractors manufacture an essential product.

CONVICT AND IMPRISON TOP CORPORATE EXECUTIVES

Top management can either directly involve the corporation in illegal activities or it can create a "climate" favorable to law-breaking. An expert on the notorious Equity Funding case, in which company fraud resulted in a $2 billion loss, concluded that the men who run the company set the corporate moral tone and that their own corruption can then quickly corrupt everything else.[29] In a survey of retired *Fortune* 500 middle-management executives, nine out of 10 stated that top management sets the ethical tone for compliance with government laws and regulations.[30] Three-fourths believed that top management knew about any significant improper conduct, either before it occurred or soon thereafter. As one middle-management executive put it:

Ethics comes and goes in a corporation according to who is in top management. I worked under four corporation presidents and each differed. The first was honest, the next one was a "wheeler-dealer," the third was somewhat better, and the last one was bad. According to their ethical views, varying ethical pressure was put on middle management all the way down.

Top executives who are primarily interested in quick corporate profits, as well as their own compensation, are more likely to lead the corporation into unethical and illegal practices. They are willing and able to carry out illegal behavior, should it seem to be required, in order to enable them to get ahead in the corporate world or to enable the corporation to attain its goals, to prosper or to survive. A long-time corporate middle-management executive has aptly described such top management: "Those corporations that are unethical are managed by persons who are highly competitive, wanting to improve the corporation's profit margins and thinking they will not get caught. Such persons are trying to improve their own personal positions and that of their corporations." A description such as this, although an extreme case, well fits Orin Atkins, chairman and chief executive officer of Ashland Oil from 1965 through 1981. In a front page December 13, 1988, *Wall Street Journal* article about him, various people described the former CEO as a "brilliant revolutionary," a "sly fox," a "buccaneer," a man whose attitude is "let the machine guns rip," and as a person who relished taking risks. He took the company from annual sales of only $329 million to become the 60th largest U.S. industrial concern with annual sales of $9.5 billion. During Atkins' reign as CEO, the government accused Ashland of fixing gasoline prices, rigging bids on construction projects, bribing foreign officials, and making illegal political contributions.[31]

Although corporate executives may well be responsible for the violations of law committed by their company, the law rarely holds them personally accountable for the corporate actions they direct. A study of over 1,500 actions taken against *Fortune* 500 corporations over a two-year period revealed that the courts convicted a corporate executive of failure to carry out his legal responsibility in only 1.5 percent of the total actions.[32] Nonetheless, criminal conviction may have a pronounced effect. After the courts found Rockwell International guilty in 1985 of defrauding the government, the federal judge imposed a $1 million fine on the corporation. Believing, however, that only a jail sentence is effective for corporate executives, rather than even a hefty fine, the judge added: "This is the most effective sentence I can impose under the circumstances. A corporate fine going into the U.S. Treasury does little good." One of the prominent executives convicted in the heavy electrical industry price-fixing case remembered:

The stigma of conviction had a strong impact on me and it has not died away with the termination of my sentence and probation. . . . The consequences of the publicity on me and my family in our social business relationships was beyond anything I had expected. I'm determined never to be exposed to such a risk again through any of my own actions.

A General Electric vice president concluded from his experience that the taint of a prison sentence had the effect of making him "start looking at the moral values a little bit."[33]

In August 1989, an extraordinary action took place. The chairman and chief executive officer of the Philadelphia-based Pennwalt Corporation, Edwin E. Tuttle, personally appeared before a Tacoma judge to enter the corporation's guilty plea to having polluted a waterway in 1985. On two previous occasions, the Tacoma federal judge, Jack Turner, had refused to accept guilty pleas from attorneys and lower-ranking executives, demanding that the "top man" appear before him. Environmentalists and legal experts said that this could set a precedent for punishing corporate negligence. The charges against Pennwalt grew out of the spill of at least 75,000 gallons of bleach into a waterway opening onto Puget Sound. The bleach, sodium dichromate, contained hexavalent chromium, a cancer-causing agent. In May, Pennwalt had agreed to pay a $1.1 million fine and to plead guilty to five misdemeanor counts. The judge told Tuttle that he wanted to send a message that companies and the people who run them must be accountable when they damage the environment.[34]

Corporate executives fear imprisonment even more than they fear a criminal conviction. Senator William Proxmire (D-Wis.) has concluded that "there is nothing that would help our defense procurement system more than a successful prosecution of one of the giant defense firms. It would only take a jail term for one or two chairmen of the board and I guarantee that many of these overcharging abuses would come to a stop."[35] Top management conspirators in the electrical industry price-fixing scandal even refused to permit their families to visit them during the time they were in prison under sentences of slightly less than a month, because of a sense of shame, guilt and injured pride. A federal judge likewise has reflected on the deterrent effects of imprisonment: "My experience at the bar was that one jail sentence was worth 100 consent decrees and that fines are meaningless."[36]

Convicted executives seldom receive prison sentences; however, if they do, the sentences are generally nowhere near the maximum the law provides as, for example, three years in price-fixing convictions. When corporate violators do go to prison, it is generally only for a few days or months; the sentences are completely out of line with the usual 10–, 15–, 20–, or even 50–year sentences meted out to ordinary offenders who commit thefts, steal autos, burglarize houses, commit robberies, or embezzle money. Even though 21 top corporate executives admitted having given illegal political contributions from corporate funds following the Watergate disclosures of widespread illegalities, only 2 of these executives served jail terms, which were for only a few months; others paid fines, usually ranging from $1,000 to $2,000.

Typical were the ridiculously low sentences the courts imposed in the folding-carton price-fixing conspiracy that involved the flagrant "stealing" from consumers of hundreds of millions of dollars over a long period of time. The folding carton industry is large, as their products are used to package thousands of different consumer items, such as cereal, crackers, drugs, cosmetics, beer and soft drinks. According to the government, the corporate defendants in this case were not engaged in short-term price-fixing violations because of sudden market pressures; it was their way of doing business over 14 years. The participants carried out price-fixing throughout the country; they demonstrated a knowing, blatant disregard for antitrust laws. The thousands upon thousands of illegal price exchanges with competitors and the dozens of secret meetings with competitors all had the single purpose of eliminating price competition in their annual $1.7 billion industry. A federal court convicted 23 of them, including the three largest: Container Corporation of America, American Can Company and Federal Paper Board, along with 47 of their executives. Fifteen of the executives originally received jail sentences ranging from 5 days to 2 months; the rest received only fines and probation. All those sentenced to prison finally ended up serving only 15 days or less. Nearly all of those who received prison sentences also received fines of from $3,000 to $25,000, and 10 were placed on probation after the imprisonment. In addition, the courts ordered 7 of them to do community service.

The very fact that the courts gave them prison sentences at all, however small, shocked all the defendants. Each submitted legal briefs citing a variety of reasons why he should not have to serve even a sentence of 5 days. One plea claimed that "jail is not in the best interests of, and will not serve, the defendant, who is an elderly businessman with more than 40 years of corporate service."[37] They claimed that a prison sentence would be traumatic physically and emotionally; they had sick or dependent relatives; their lives had been without previous blemish; they had always been public-spirited citizens; and that the stigma of conviction itself was sufficient punishment. All of these pleas worked, to some extent, for none received a final prison sentence of more than 15 days. H. Harper Brown, chairman of giant Container Corporation of America, originally received a 60-day jail sentence, but the judge reduced it to 15 days, during which time he was released to work during the day and jailed at night and on days off. George V. Bayley, Sr., senior vice president of Tenneco's Packaging Corporation of America, had his jail sentence reduced from 30 to 7 days. Even the five executives originally sentenced to 5 days had their sentences reduced to 1 or 2 days.

In lieu of imprisonment, a common penalty for corporate big guns has been the imposition of several hours of community service work each week. For example, an Arizona federal judge sentenced four prominent dairy officials involved in milk price-fixing, one the general manager of Carnation Company, to do "public penance," for example, by working for the Salvation Army, a food bank, and a charity-operated dining room. Rarely does an ordinary offender have the opportunity to do such "public-spirited" work. Sometimes the corporate offender is sentenced to give speeches about their law violations and the ensuing consequences for them to business groups. For example, a San Francisco federal judge in 1974 ordered a group of convicted price-fixers to deliver 12 speeches each as a substitute for serving time in prison. Mark Richards, a long-time head of the criminal division of the Department of Justice, expressed concern about this dual justice by posing the question: "Why should a ghetto kid who steals a car be put away but a businessman who steals $6 million gets to work in a soup kitchen on weekends?" Moreover, an authority on corporate crime has concluded that "there is little evidence that these community service orders have any deterrent effect, either against the individual convicted criminal or generally against those observing the sanctioning process. Judges imposing these sentences further undermine the nation's system of justice. Second, if community service orders are going to be used to displace prison sentences, they should be used to displace prison sentences across the board, for street as well as for corporate criminals. The current system of jail for street thugs and speeches for corporate thugs creates an inequality of justice that undermines respect for the law."[38] The court levied an unusual number of hours, however, on the chairman of the board of giant Frue-hauf Corporation when it fined both him and the corporation for conspiring to evade $12.3 million in corporate excise taxes. The court sentenced him to work 25 hours each week for 5 months, plus 10 hours a week for an additional year, in an agricultural school that he had founded.

Seldom can the prosecution persuade a judge to order a convicted corporate executive sent to prison, primarily because, almost without exception, he has no criminal record. The courts regard these executives as first offenders, even though they may have fixed prices for 15 years. They are generally well-to-do, white, well-dressed, and articulate community leaders of high social status whose backgrounds are often similar to that of the judge. A reporter described the executives of the several major electrical corporations who were on trial for price-fixing heavy electrical equipment as "middle-class men in Ivy League suits, typical businessmen in appearance, men who would never be taken for lawbreakers."[39] Judges hesitate to impose prison sentences on them, as they do not fit the stereotype of a common criminal offender who generally appears before them. A further factor is the highly skilled defense counsels who handle their cases. After these lawyers have bitterly fought a criminal conviction for their client, they muster every possible argument to assure he does not go to prison.

The year 1985 was a landmark and a likely precedent in the imposition of more severe sentences for corporate executives. That year, chairman Paul Thayer of giant LTV Corporation received a four-year prison sentence for insider trading, probably the longest term ever given a top executive of a major corporation. Also in 1985, a Chicago judge gave the longest sentences ever imposed on corporate executives, although the corporation involved was not a major one. In that case, the courts convicted three top executives of Film Recovery Systems in Chicago of causing the death of a worker from cyanide fumes in their plant. The state's attorney said that parts of the plant were a "huge gas chamber." The judge sentenced the three executives to 25 years in prison and imposed a $10,000 fine. The presiding judge said, "This is not a case of taking a gun and shooting someone. It is more like leaving a time bomb in an airport and then running away."

Despite their legal difficulties, a majority of convicted corporate executives are able to remain with their companies in some capacity. Although a minority are fired or have their position or salary reduced, few are dismissed. This situation is markedly different from that of an ordinary offender or even those convicted of white-collar crimes. One study of 27 corporate executives who were indicted or convicted for corporate crimes found that 10 retained their original position, 6 assumed new positions within the same firm, and 11 resigned.[40] One year after 21 executives of different corporations received fines or prison sentences for making illegal political contributions in 1973 and 1974, 12 of them still held their pre-conviction corporate positions, 5 had resigned or retired, 2 were serving as consultants to the firm, and 2 had been discharged.[41] Another check on what happened to 28 top executives convicted of illegal activity during the period of 1973 to 1978 revealed that 16 of them had either stayed on the job, remained as members of the board of directors, or had been rehired after serving their sentences. As examples, after being criminally convicted of giving illegal political contributions, the chairman of Ashland Oil still made $314,000 annually as chairman. As another example, Fruehauf's board of directors dismissed neither the former chairman nor the former president when they were convicted of conspiracy to evade the federal excise tax. After finishing their period of community service, during which time they received corporate fringe benefits, both returned to their former positions. The then president and chairman of Northrop Corporation in 1974 pleaded guilty to obstructive conduct and was fined $5,000 in connection with aiding and abetting an illegal political contribution. Although replaced as Northrop's president, he remained as the company's $1 million-a-year chairman. The president of Container Corporation of America, after pleading no contest to charges of price-fixing, received a 60-day prison sentence, which was reduced to fifteen days. He remained a member of the board and became vice chairman a year later. Corporate solicitude in the extreme involved a chairman and chief executive officer of Technical Tape Corporation who continued to collect his paycheck, including bonuses, of $325,000 while he was serving a one-year prison sentence following conviction on 11 criminal counts of securities law violations. Regardless of the outcome, most corporate executives retain their retirement benefits.

The federal government might well enact laws to prevent an executive from regaining control over the resources and power associated with his corporate position for a specified period of time. Such a period of "retirement" for these executives might deter others. As the criminologist Gilbert Geis has aptly commented about the issue, "Why put the fox immediately back in the chicken coop?"[42] A more drastic action would be to bar an executive from holding any office in other corporations as well if his management decisions had led to a conviction for a crime. A special Securities and Exchange Commission panel in 1987 did urge the commission to seek statutory authority to suspend temporarily or to bar permanently corporate officers and directors from official posts in a publicly held corporation if they are involved in fraudulent financial reporting.

PUBLICIZE CORPORATE MISBEHAVIOR

More than they fear the law itself, since its impact is generally weak, corporations fear wide adverse publicity that tarnishes their corporate images and their reputations. A 1975 Opinion Research Corporation survey of 531 top and middle managers found that 92 percent of the respondents believed that legislation itself would not stop corporate bribery of foreign officials, but that adverse publicity about corporations who engage in the bribery might be effective. A *Harvard Business Review* reader survey in 1977 also found that corporate executives believe any improvement in ethical business standards is primarily the result of public disclosures of corporate transgressions.[43] These views indicate that corporations highly value the importance of their reputations and fear any damage to them. Companies also hope that their prestige may attract better applicants for executive and professional positions, that investors will purchase their stock, that banks may be more willing to extend credit, and that government officials may be more inclined to give the company a better hearing for its concerns.

Media publicity can significantly affect corporations that have gotten into trouble. In 17 case studies of corporations that had gotten into serious and highly publicized ethical or legal trouble, media publicity related to wrongdoing tended to snowball into other unrelated issues such as reducing corporate earnings and decreasing executive morale.[44] Many corporations found publicity quite damaging to the good reputations they tried to build up over many years. A corporation that comes under a congressional inquiry can be subjected to considerable adverse media publicity. When congressional hearings revealed, for example, that General Motors had snooped into the private life of Ralph Nader during the 1960s by hiring private detectives to harass and intimidate him, it made headline news. The chairman of the board, James Roche, eventually made a public apology before the committee for his corporation's actions. As a further example, many corporations received adverse publicity from congressional investigating committees as a result of their illegal contributions to the Nixon political campaign and for their bribery of foreign officials. On several occasions, congressional hearings have exposed the transgressions of the pharmaceutical industry and the corruption of the defense industry.

Consumer action groups, such as those Ralph Nader promotes, also publicize cases where corporations have turned out faulty products or otherwise engaged in unethical or illegal activities. The auto and pharmaceutical industries are favorite targets. A growing international consumer movement has made it possible to increase adverse publicity as an informal means of controlling transnational corporations that dump dangerous chemicals and other banned products, including pharmaceuticals, on the Third World. Other concerned groups have directed attention to corporate exploitation and destruction of Third World rain forests.

In addition to notifying the public of harmful corporate activities, newspaper investigative reporting has sometimes led to indictments and other court actions against the offending corporations. Best known among these journalistic reports are the exposure of the dangers of Love Canal, the coverage of the Ford Pinto auto case, the E. F. Hutton check-kiting scandal, and the stories of the infant deaths that resulted from the use of infant formulas in Third World countries. The *New York Times* in 1977 did a 6-month investigation of the Gulf and Western Corporation; their three articles described the top officials' false testimony, destruction of important evidence, complex stock dealings that concealed profits and losses, and the illegal use of corporate funds to cover million-dollar personal loans.

Studies reveal, however, that relatively few violations by *Fortune* 500 corporations and subsequent enforcement actions receive much general media publicity. Rarely does the public have an opportunity to view a television news story about transgressions of large corporations; seldom do corporate crimes make the evening news. Even the Public Broadcasting System (PBS) tends to shy away from such a hot subject as it becomes increasingly dependent upon corporate contributions. When corporate crime stories do appear in print, they are frequently relegated to the business or financial sections. A survey of the news coverage of 12 leading cases of corporate crime revealed that less than a third to a half of leading newspapers and news magazines carried stories of the cases, and they were usually brief news items on back pages, particularly in the business section. The corporate cases were downplayed, understated or omitted. A survey of the general newspaper coverage of the price-fixing conspiracy case in the giant folding carton industry concluded that "newspapers protect corporate reputations by failing to provide frequent, prominent, and criminally oriented coverage of common corporate crimes such as price-fixing."[45] Only half of the 29 newspapers that the survey covered publicized the corporate pleas and the sentences the court handed down; only four named all 23 corporations (the rest named only a few); and only one newspaper used the word "crime" in its account of the case. None of the newspapers surveyed covered the sentencing of the corporations on the front page, and only 7 percent covered the sentences given the corporate executives. In actuality, only the *Wall Street Journal* and some trade journals regularly report much illegal corporate behavior, primarily because they are financial publications; such news is of special interest and may have significant financial repercussions. The *Wall Street Journal*, in a single year, carried approximately 160 such articles (the *Journal* publishes five issues a week) dealing with legal sanctions instituted or imposed against 582 large corporations.[46]

The limited general press coverage of corporate illegalities makes the compulsory use of publicity a necessary sanction in many corporate crime cases. This type of sanction would require that a corporation buy media coverage to advertise its own guilt. The public's subsequent awareness of the offense is even better assured if the courts force corporate defendants to publish certain information about their offenses. In addition to the punitive ad's detailed account of the violation, the corporation may also have to enumerate the measures it is taking to correct it. An advocate of this approach has stated:

Surely corporate heads would turn and listen more attentively to law enforcement agents if, for example, Hooker Chemical Company were required to buy television ads to tell the nation about its pollution activities, or if the Ford Motor Company were required to run television ads informing the nation about how it marketed the unsafe Pinto, or if Grunenthal were required to tell the world about how it marketed thalidomide and how thalidomide affected its consumers. To use adverse publicity sanctions, not just in remedial orders but as punitive and educational measures, is one of the more effective and efficient ways of shaming corporate America out of its antisocial behavior and bringing it back within the bounds of legal commerce.[47]

The use of formal publicity as a sanction has a long history. As early as 1822, English magistrates could order the publication of the names of persons who adulterated bread. During World War II, the government ordered service stations that had violated gasoline price and rationing regulations to display public notices of their business suspension for a certain period of time for "violation of wartime regulations." The Federal Trade Commission, as well as the Food and Drug Administration and other agencies, have also used some obligatory corrective advertising. On occasion, such ads have forced the manufacturers of STP Oil Treatment, Listerine, and a number of other products to run a series of nationwide advertisements in important news magazines to admit that some previously made claims for their products were false. The Food and Drug Administration has likewise required drug companies found guilty in some major cases of false or deceptive advertising to send physicians corrective letters retracting their incorrect claims.

Some efforts have been made to enact federal and state legislation to formally publicize corporate misbehavior. The U.S. National Commission on Reform of Criminal Laws in 1970 proposed federal legislation that would publicize sanctions on convicted corporate offenders. "When an organization is convicted of an offense, the court may, in addition to or in lieu of imposing other sanctions . . . require the organization to give appropriate publicity to the conviction . . . by advertising in designated areas or by designated media." The Washington-based Center for Study of Responsive Law also has proposed that states adopt a uniform Corporate Decency Act. It contains the provision that "any corporate entity that violates any provision of the Act may be required to publicize the details of its offenses in full-page advertisements in the largest state newspaper and largest newspaper in the local community." The Los Angeles County Toxic Waste Strike Force has become well known for its use of punitive advertising as a sanction in illegal toxic waste disposal cases. For example, a half-page ad purchased by the American Caster Corporation in the *Los Angeles Times* stated: "Warning. The illegal disposal of toxic waste will result in jail. We should know. We got caught! . . . We are paying the price. Today, while you read this ad, our president and vice president are serving time in jail and we were forced to place this ad."

INCREASED CONSUMER ROLE

Greater publicity about corporate offenses can increase consumer pressures that might more effectively control unethical and illegal corporate behavior through boycotts. For example, the withdrawal of consumer patronage has an effective impact where it is organized, as in the case of the consumer boycotts in the 1980s against Gallo, J. P. Stevens, and Farrah corporations, primarily for their anti-union activities.

An increase in consumer use of product liability laws can also help to control corporate misbehavior. Most states have laws that enable victims to sue corporations in attempts to recover compensatory and punitive damages for product injuries they have sustained. Product liability suits on behalf of several named plaintiffs, representing an entire class action of victims, offer even more effectual deterrence. Such a class action suit allows thousands of individuals to pool their legal resources against the far greater corporate resources. The U.S. Supreme Court, in a 7–0 decision in 1989, ruled that states may even permit individuals or groups of individuals who suffer indirect financial losses, as a result of state antitrust price-fixing violations, to sue the violators. Fifteen states have such laws.

REQUIRE A FEDERAL CORPORATE CHARTER

All corporations, regardless of size, operate under a charter that subjects them to diverse measures of control. At present, corporations obtain these charters to do business through individual states, even though these state charters permit them to do business both at the national and international levels. Many states benefit from this chartering system; it has become an important business as fees of incorporation and taxes bring in substantial revenues. Since state governments lack both the initiative and the resources to examine critically the vast scope of a chartered large corporation's operations throughout the United States and around the world, a far better system would be a federal corporate charter.

Delaware is a good example of the present state chartering fiasco: It has even been referred to as the Las Vegas of Corporate Cheating. It charters 56 percent of the top *Fortune* 500 corporations, including half the 100 largest companies and 45 percent of all corporations listed on the New York Stock Exchange. No state, particularly a small one like Delaware, could possibly supervise the worldwide operations of a giant like General Motors: Similarly, New Jersey could never hope to control Exxon, which is chartered there. Since 1899, Delaware has been particularly attractive to large corporations as a chartering vehicle, in much the same manner that Liberia and Panama attract the business of chartering for large shipping companies. Delaware has highly permissive laws of incorporation; they reduce restrictions on the power and management of the corporation to a minimum. Management power is paramount, not shareholders' rights. Corporations in Delaware are free to conduct business in almost any way they choose, as long as the state does not explicitly forbid the behavior. Corporate directors and stockholders need not even hold their meetings there. The state also lacks adequate charter enforcement provisions and the will to use them. Indeed, it is likely that should a chartering state begin to exercise much control over a corporation chartered there, the company would simply incorporate in another state.

Federal charters would cover only large corporations in interstate commerce; small corporations would continue to operate under state charters. A federal charter would provide safeguards such as financial reporting regulations and stockholder rights in much the same manner in which the federal government now regulates banks, insurance companies, and public utilities.[48] It could require full disclosure of a corporation's national and international operations, and would enable federal agencies to oversee corporations more effectively and thus be in a better position to prevent illegal activities. Federal charters, rather than state ones, would make the enforcement agent, namely, the federal government, more of a match for the large corporations under its control. In cases of corporate law violations, specific penalties could include obligatory management reorganization, the suspension of top executives, or even the revocation of the charter. The last penalty, however, might be too severe in the case of large corporations whose products and work force are economically essential to the nation.

Federal charters could bring about important changes in corporate management itself, changes that might well help to prevent unethical and illegal practices. They could, for example, require the election of certain specified "public members" to the boards of directors of the largest *Fortune* 500 companies. It would be their duty to represent the interests of the general public and the consumer, as well as those of the corporation and its stockholders. The SEC could nominate persons to become public members, to serve full-time and receive salaries from corporate funds. These public members would be in a position to make proposals that could improve corporate responsibility.

Although this proposal may appear to be quite unusual, it is somewhat comparable to the increasingly common practice in the United States and elsewhere of naming union members to the board of directors to represent labor interests. Chrysler added a prominent union official to its board of directors as early as 1980. As of 1989, more than 15 large publicly held American corporations had worker representatives on their boards. The Federal German Republic now requires all large corporations to have substantial labor representation on their boards. For some time, Sweden has had worker-directors in all companies that employ at least 100 persons.

Critics claim that a federal charter would make it more difficult and costly to conduct business. Others maintain that we need a renewed emphasis on corporate social responsibility, not new laws. Still others fear that federal chartering will eventually lead to the public ownership or a federal takeover of business. These criticisms fail to recognize fully that for a long period of time, all corporations have had to operate under a charter; federal chartering would simply recognize the present problems that the immense size and power of many corporations have created as their national and international operations have become more complex. Certainly, it has become evident that there is a great need to provide some chartering uniformity in the regulations under which these giants now operate.

Many people are unaware that federal chartering is neither new nor is it revolutionary: It has a long history. Twice during the Constitutional Convention of 1787, James Madison unsuccessfully proposed that the Constitution expressly empower Congress to grant charters to corporations in cases where the public good might require them and where a single state authority might not be competent. The proposal never came to a formal vote. Over 100 years later, as the public became concerned about the economic and political power of the huge corporate "trusts," legislative proposals for federal chartering were introduced and strongly supported. Between 1903 and 1914, presidents Roosevelt, Taft, and Wilson voiced support for a federal incorporation or licensing act in their annual messages to Congress; the *Wall Street Journal* and the National Association of Manufacturers supported this federal licensing bill in 1908; President Taft had his attorney general draft a federal corporate licensing bill that he proposed to Congress in 1911; and both William Jennings Bryan and Mark Hanna favored it. During this period, 20 different bills were introduced into one or both houses of Congress, but opposition from the powerful corporate world defeated them all.

CONTROL CORPORATE SIZE

Large corporations are becoming ever larger in a process now termed "megamergers": the merger, acquisition, or consolidation of already large corporations.[49] These corporate mergers have been increasing at an alarming rate: In 1982 alone, expenditures for megamergers totaled

$82 billion. A few examples during the 1980s: duPont bought Conoco for $7.4 billion; General Motors acquired Electronic Data Systems for $2.5 billion; U.S. Steel bought Marathon Oil for $6.2 billion; Texaco acquired Getty Oil for $10.1 billion; and Chevron bought Gulf Oil for $13 billion. Giant General Electric merged in 1986 with giant RCA at a cost to General Electric of $6.4 billion.

In 1988, a wave of super megamergers hit the financial world. For example, Philip Morris completed a $13.1 billion acquisition of Kraft to make it the largest of any non-oil merger. It created a food giant more than double the size of the next largest similar American producer, Procter and Gamble. In addition to a lengthy list of well-known cigarette brands such as Marlboro, Benson and Hedges, and Parliament, Philip Morris makes Miller Beer and a huge line of General Food Corporation products ranging from Maxwell House coffe and Jell-O to Kool Aid and Bird's Eye frozen foods. Kraft makes a large line of food products, including Velveeta and Philadelphia cheese, Parkay margarine, Seven Seas salad dressings, Sealtest ice cream, and Miracle Whip topping.

Governmental limitation of the size of the giant corporations appears to be the only practical means of checking their runaway size and power. Public opinion polls consistently show that Americans largely believe that corporations are becoming too large and too powerful for the welfare of the country. A survey conducted in 1979, for example, reported that 70 percent of the respondents felt that the size of big business enabled it to wield great power over the government itself.[50] The top 400 U.S. corporations presently control half of the nation's economy, while the top 50 non-financial firms have total assets almost as large as the next 350. Not only does corporate power increase with the size of corporations, but the fear of corporate power itself grows stronger. The excessive economic and political power that these corporations have amassed is an even more serious threat to the country than their monopolistic pricing practices. The mushrooming growth of already large firms through acquisitions and mergers raises concern that they will become even more disproportionately powerful in an American society that has been based fundamentally on diversity and decentralization of power. Kenneth Davidson, a specialist on megamergers, has pointed out that "such large corporations could disrupt the balance of our political system and blur the distinctions between private decisions and public policy."[51]

Megamergers tend to weaken competition and thus to drive out small competitors. As a result, consumers face even higher prices: Large mergers in the coffee and beer industries, for example, have not meant lower consumer prices for these products. On the other hand, megamergers can have positive effects as corporations cut certain administrative expenses and spread out advertising costs, which supposedly enables these giants to compete more successfully with other giants.

There must be a more direct and effective limitation of corporate size.

No specific U.S. laws now prohibit large corporate mergers except where the government can invoke the antitrust laws to prevent them. The use of antitrust laws to prevent mergers rests on the discretion of the particular political administration in the White House. The Reagan administration, for example, only gave lip service to the basic purpose and provisions of U.S. antitrust laws. During the years of the Reagan administration, critics often assailed the antitrust division as being "permissive" and its enforcement efforts as virtually "nonexistent." The Department of Justice challenged only 29 of 8,000 mergers submitted to it for review: More than 1,300 mergers, each valued at over $100 million, took place. The administration allowed the 18 largest mergers in history to go through without a challenge. There is need for a law that forbids any firm with sales or assets of, for example, $2 billion to merge with another, regardless of how diverse their business lines might be. Such a law would require corporations to prove that a proposed merger would greatly improve their efficiency or enhance competition.

INTERNATIONAL CONTROL OF TRANSNATIONALS

The control of transnationals at the international level, particularly their relations with the Third World, requires a coordination of efforts and policies of individual countries through programs devised by the United Nations or other international organizations. At present, if a transnational corporation should break the laws of one country, it can simply move its products into the markets of others. Hazardous products banned in the United States, for example, are dumped in countries where laws are less strict. In order to halt this practice, new mechanisms must be devised. The United Nations has proposed a transnational operational code, as well as voluntary consumer guidelines for member nations. The United Nations consumer code embodies the right to be protected from the marketing of hazardous goods, from fraudulent, deceptive or restrictive business practices, the right to information necessary to make informed choices, and the freedom to organize consumer groups. Transnationals have the power to co-opt Third World governments, and only a strong international code will help prevent unethical practices. Further studies of the world's legal systems are also needed so that the various countries can more effectively deal with the complexities of modern transnational corporations, coordinate enforcement activities and exchange information about enforcement actions taken against transnationals.

If corporate abuses continue to become more serious, more rather than less government regulation will be required. Stricter enforcement of existing regulations is a prime requisite. Former administrator of the National Highway Traffic Safety Administration, Joan Claybrook, has pointed out that corporations welcome government with open arms when it is a subsidizer, guarantor and lender of last resort, as in the $250 million government bail-out of Lockheed in 1971 and the $1.5 billion government loan to Chrysler in 1979 when both were about to go under. "But when Uncle Sugar becomes Uncle Sam, people protector of last resort, the corporate tiger bares its teeth and snarls."[52] Above all, greater responsibility to the nation and to its democratic system of government must accompany the awesome power that corporations have amassed.

NOTES

1. THE ABUSE OF CORPORATE POWER

1. Adolf A. Berle and Gardiner C. Means, *The Modern Corporation and Private Property* (Chicago: Commerce Clearing House, 1932); and Jordan A. Schwartz, *Liberal: Adolf A. Berle and the Vision of the American Era* (New York: The Free Press/Macmillan, 1987).

2. Peter F. Drucker, *Concept of the Corporation* (New York: Mentor, 1972), p. 18.

3. John Kenneth Galbraith, "Power and the Useful Economist," *American Economic Review*, 63 (March 1973): 6.

4. Brooks Jackson, *Honest Graft: Big Money and the American Political Process* (New York: Knopf, 1988).

5. Richard B. McKenzie, ed., *Plant Closings: Public or Private Choices?* (Washington, D.C.: Cato Institute, 1982); and Richard B. McKenzie, *Fugitive Industry* (San Francisco: Pacific Institute for Public Policy Research, 1984).

6. Graef S. Crystal, "Seeking the Sense in CEO Pay," *Fortune* (June 5, 1989): 96, 104.

7. Ralph Nader, ed., *The Consumer and Corporate Accountability* (New York: Harcourt, Brace, Jovanovich, 1973).

8. *Wall Street Journal*, May 11, 1989.

9. *Wall Street Journal*, August 1, 1989.

10. Russell Mokhiber, *Corporate Crime and Violence: Big Business Power and the Abuse of the Public Trust* (San Francisco: Sierra Club Books, 1988), p. 4; see also Brooks Jackson, *Honest Graft: Big Money and the American Political Process* (New York: Knopf, 1988).

11. Marshall B. Clinard and Peter C. Yeager, *Corporate Crime* (New York: The Free Press, 1980), pp. 113, 118.

12. For example, Edwin H. Sutherland, *White Collar Crime* (New York: Green-

wood Press, 1983); and John Braithwaite, *Corporate Crime in the Pharmaceutical Industry* (London: Routledge and Kegan Paul, 1984).

13. Clinard and Yeager, *Corporate Crime*, p. 113.

14. Irwin Ross, "How Lawless Are Big Companies?" *Fortune*, December 1, 1980, pp. 57–64.

15. "Corporate Crime: The Untold Story," *U.S. News and World Report* (September 6, 1982): 25–30.

16. John Woodmansee, *The World of the Giant Corporations: A Report from the GE Project* (Seattle: North Country, 1975).

17. Marvin Wolfgang, "Crime and Punishment," *New York Times*, March 2, 1980.

18. F. T. Cullen, B. G. Link, and C. W. Polanzi, "The Seriousness of Crime Revisited: Have Attitudes Toward White-Collar Crime Changed?" *Criminology* 10, no. 1 (May 1982): 83–103.

19. *The Washington Spectator*, 15, no. 14 (August 1, 1989).

20. See "Johnson & Johnson and the Tylenol Crisis," in W. C. Frederick, K. Davis, and J. E. Post, eds., *Business and Society: Corporate Strategy, Public Policy, Ethics*, 6th ed. (New York: McGraw-Hill, 1988), pp. 487–501.

21. Christopher Stone, *Where the Law Ends: The Social Control of Corporate Behavior* (New York: Harper and Row, 1975), pp. 24–25.

2. DETROIT ROULETTE

1. Harvey A. Farberman, "A Crimogenic Market Structure: The Automobile Industry," *Sociological Quarterly* 16 (August 1975): 438–57.

2. Patrick J. Wright, *On A Clear Day You Can See General Motors: John De-Lorean's Look inside the Automotive Giant* (New York: Avon Books, 1979), p. 72.

3. Marshall B. Clinard and Peter C. Yeager, *Corporate Crime* (New York: The Free Press, 1980), pp. 119–22.

4. *Wall Street Journal*, November 8, 1979.

5. *Wall Street Journal*, December 10, 1987.

6. Francis T. Cullen, William J. Maakestad, and Gray Cavender, *Corporate Crime under Attack: The Ford Pinto Case and Beyond* (Cincinnati: Anderson, 1987), pp. 190–92.

7. Morton Mintz and Jerry S. Cohen, *America, Inc.* (New York: Dial, 1971), p. 260.

8. Joel W. Eastman, *Safety vs. Styling: The American Automobile Industry and the Development of Automotive Safety, 1900–1966* (Lanham, Md.: University Press of America, Inc., 1984).

9. David Halberstam, *The Reckoning* (New York: Morrow, 1986), p. 437.

10. Eastman, *Safety vs. Styling*, p. 42.

11. *Crashes That Need Not Kill*, a film produced by the Insurance Institute for Safety, 1976.

12. Peter Collier and David Horowitz, *The Fords: An American Epic* (New York: Summit Books, 1987), p. 52.

13. *Wall Street Journal*, May 4, 1989.

3. THE GREAT OIL RIP-OFF

1. Anthony Sampson, *The Seven Sisters: The Great Oil Companies and the World They Shaped* (New York: Viking, 1975), pp. 6–7, edited quote.

2. Marshall B. Clinard and Peter C. Yeager, *Corporate Crime* (New York: The Free Press, 1980), pp. 119–20.

3. Sampson, *The Seven Sisters*, pp. 37–38.

4. James McGovern, *The Oil Game* (New York: Viking Press, 1981), p. 124.

5. Peter C. Yeager, "Analyzing Corporate Offenses: Progress and Prospects," *Research in Corporate Social Performance and Policy*, 8 (1986): 113.

6. *Wall Street Journal*, December 17, 1984. This lengthy article contains a detailed examination of the California case.

7. *Multinational Monitor*, 2 (April 1981): 4.

8. *Wall Street Journal*, May 14, 1985, and May 15, 1985.

9. McGovern, *The Oil Game*, p. 159.

10. *Wall Street Journal*, October 2, 1986.

11. *The New Mexican* (September 21, 1988): 1.

12. *Multinational Monitor*, 3 (July 1982): 4.

13. Matthew Rothschild, "Massive Oil Thefts from Federal and Indian Lands Are Charged," *Multinational Monitor*, 2 (December 1981): 31.

14. Clinard and Yeager, *Corporate Crime*, p. 121.

15. Stuart L. Hills, ed., *Crime, Power, and Morality: The Criminal-Law Process in the United States* (Scranton, Pa.: Chandler, 1971), p. 196.

16. *Wall Street Journal*, July 29, 1978.

17. Robert Sherrill, "The Case against the Oil Companies," *New York Times Magazine*, October 14, 1979.

18. *Wall Street Journal*, August 29, 1979.

19. McGovern, *The Oil Game*, p. 121.

20. Robert Sam Anson, "The American Petroleum Institute," *Common Cause*, 6 (October 1980): 25–31.

21. Edward Roeder, "Lubricating Congress," *Sierra*, March/April 1980, pp. 6–11.

22. Anson, "The American Petroleum Institute," pp. 25–31.

23. Quoted in ibid., p. 26.

4. THE DRUGMAKERS

1. Marshall B. Clinard and Peter C. Yeager, *Corporate Crime* (New York: The Free Press, 1980), pp. 119–22.

2. Quoted in Joel Kaufman, Linda Rabinowitz-Dagi, Joan Levin, Phyllis McCarthy, Sidney Wolfe, and Eva Bargman, *Over the Counter Pills That Don't Work* (Washington, D.C.: Public Citizen Health Research Group, 1983), p. vii.

3. Ibid.

4. *Wall Street Journal* (May 13, 1987): 35.

5. John Braithwaite, *Corporate Crime in the Pharmaceutical Industry* (London: Routledge and Kegan Paul, 1984), p. 204.

6. Hugh D. Walker, *Market Power and Price Levels in the Ethical Drug Industry* (Bloomington: Indiana University Press, 1971).

7. Quoted in Braithwaite, *Corporate Crime in the Pharmaceutical Industry*, p. 216.

8. "Prescriptions for Profit," Public Broadcasting System's "Frontline" special, March 29, 1989.

9. Kaufman et al., *Over the Counter Pills*, p. iii.

10. Ibid.

11. Sydney M. Wolfe, Christopher M. Coley, and the Health Research Group founded by Ralph Nader, *Pills That Don't Work: A Consumers' and Doctors' Guide to Over 600 Prescription Drugs That Lack Evidence of Effectiveness* (New York: Farrar, Straus & Giroux, 1981).

12. *Wisconsin State Journal*, December 5, 1972.

13. Braithwaite, *Corporate Crime in the Pharmaceutical Industry*, p. 149.

14. Braithwaite, *Corporate Crime in the Pharmaceutical Industry*, p. 80.

15. Keith Schneider, "Faking It: The Case against Industrial Bio-Test Laboratories," *The Amicus Journal* (Spring 1983): 14–26.

16. Russell Mokhiber, *Corporate Crime and Violence: Big Business Power and the Abuse of the Public Trust* (San Francisco: Sierra Club Books, 1988), pp. 289–99.

17. Braithwaite, *Crime in the Pharmaceutical Industry*, p. 78.

18. *Multinational Monitor* 6, no. 11 (August 15, 1985): 5.

19. Clinard and Yeager, *Corporate Crime*, p. 121.

20. Milton Silverman and Philip R. Lee, *Pills, Profits and Politics* (Berkeley: University of California Press, 1974), pp. 140–41.

21. *Wall Street Journal*, April 22, 1987.

22. Braithwaite, *Corporate Crime in the Pharmaceutical Industry*, p. 162.

23. *Wall Street Journal*, April 22, 1987.

24. Braithwaite, *Corporate Crime in the Pharmaceutical Industry*, p. 202.

25. *New York Times News Service*, September 28, 1989.

26. *Wall Street Journal*, September 13, 1989.

27. Kaufman et al., *Over the Counter Pills*, p. vi.

5. THE "PATRIOTIC" DEFENSE INDUSTRY

1. *Wall Street Journal*, October 12, 1988.

2. *The New Mexican*, April 14, 1988.

3. *Wall Street Journal*, May 17, 1985.

4. *Wall Street Journal*, May 13, 1985.

5. Norman Cousins, *The Pathology of Power* (New York: W. W. Norton and Co., 1987), pp. 29–30.

6. *Washington Spectator*, January 15, 1986.

7. *Washington Spectator*, June 15, 1985.

8. *Washington Spectator*, June 15, 1985.

9. *Wall Street Journal*, April 29, 1986.

10. Phillip J. Senior, "Profiting from Uncle Sam," *Common Cause*, 13 (May/June 1987): 20–22.

11. *The New Mexican*, June 26, 1988.

12. Cousins, *The Pathology of Power*, p. 159.

13. John Hanrahan, "Fat City," *Common Cause* (May/June 1983).

14. Marshall B. Clinard, *Corporate Ethics and Crime: The Role of Middle Management* (Beverly Hills: Sage Publications, 1983), p. 46.

15. Quoted in Ernest Fitzgerald, "The Pentagon as the Enemy of Civilization," *World*, February 27, 1973, p. 21.

16. *Wall Street Journal*, April 29, 1986.

17. Patrick Tyler, *Running Critical: The Silent War, Rickover and General Dynamics* (New York: Harper and Row, 1986).

18. Ibid.

19. *Senator William Proxmire News Letter*, May 1985.

20. *Business Week*, June 3, 1985, p. 43.

21. Ibid.

22. *The New Mexican*, May 20, 1987.

23. *Wall Street Journal*, June 22, 1987.

24. *The New Mexican*, December 5, 1985.

25. *Wall Street Journal*, September 27, 1989.

26. *Wall Street Journal*, September 5, 1989.

27. *Wall Street Journal*, April 6, 1988.

28. Ibid.

29. Cousins, *The Pathology of Power*, p. 100.

30. *Wall Street Journal*, November 23, 1984.

31. Clinard, *Corporate Ethics and Crime*, p. 38.

32. *Wall Street Journal*, October 4, 1982.

33. Andrew C. Revkin, "A War over Military Chips," *Science Digest*, 93, no. 7 (July 1985): 56–59, 79.

34. Cousins, *The Pathology of Power*, p. 144.

35. Florence Graves, "The Runaround," *Common Cause* (June 1982): 18–23.

36. "Furor on Pentagon's Revolving Door," *U.S. News and World Report*, April 29, 1985.

37. *U.S. News and World Report*, April 29, 1985, p. 28.

38. Ibid., pp. 7–28.

39. *Washington Spectator*, April 15, 1985.

40. *U.S. News and World Report*, April 29, 1985, p. 27–28.

41. Ibid.

42. Ibid., p. 30.

43. "William Proxmire Reports to you from Washington," *Newsletter*.

6. CORPORATE VIOLENCE

1. Nancy Frank, *Crimes against Health and Safety* (New York: Harrow and Heston, 1985), p. 84. See also Stuart L. Hills, ed., *Corporate Violence: Injury and Death for Profit* (Totowa, N.J.: Rowman and Littlefield, 1987); and Russell Mokhiber, *Corporate Crime and Violence: Big Business Power and the Abuse of the Public Trust* (San Francisco: Sierra Club Books, 1988).

2. Rachel Scott, *Muscle and Blood: The Massive, Hidden Agony of Industrial Slaughter in America* (New York: Dutton, 1974), p. 293.

3. Morton Mintz and Jerry S. Cohen, *Power, Inc.* (New York: Bantam, 1976), pp. 335–36.

4. Christopher Stone, "A Slap on the Wrist for the Kepone Mob," in Hills,

Corporate Violence, pp. 121–132; and Mokhiber, *Corporate Crime and Violence*, pp. 248–57.

5. Daniel J. Berman, *Death on the Job: Occupational Health and Safety Struggles in the United States* (New York: Monthly Review Press, 1978), pp. 49–53.

6. Joan Claybrook, *Retreat from Safety: Reagan's Attack on America's Health.* (New York: Pantheon Books, 1984) p. 78.

7. Dorothy Melkin and Michael S. Brown, *Workers at Risk* (Chicago: University of Chicago Press, 1984).

8. Berman, *Death on the Job*, p. 5.

9. Neil J. Mitchell, *The Generous Corporation: A Political Analysis of Economic Power* (New Haven: Yale University Press, 1989).

10. Berman, *Death on the Job*, p. 5

11. Ibid.

12. Marshall B. Clinard, *Corporate Ethics and Crime: The Role of Middle Management* (Beverly Hills: Sage Publications, 1983), p. 113.

13. *Christian Science Monitor*, September 2, 1988.

14. *Wall Street Journal*, December 14, 1988.

15. *Wall Street Journal*, April 2, 1986.

16. Berman, *Death on the Job*, pp. 1–4.

17. Paul Brodeur, *Outrageous Misconduct: The Asbestos Industry* (New York: Pantheon Books, 1985).

18. Quoted in Mokhiber, *Corporate Crime and Violence*, p. 280.

19. Samuel S. Epstein, Lester O. Brown, and Carl Pope, *Hazardous Waste in America* (San Francisco: Sierra Club Books, 1982), p. 78.

20. *Christian Science Monitor*, October 3, 1988.

21. *Wisconsin State Journal*, January 26, 1979.

22. *Wall Street Journal*, August 4, 1989.

23. *Wall Street Journal*, September 1, 1988.

24. *Multinational Monitor*, 9, no. 12 (December 1988): 17.

25. Morton Mintz, *At Any Cost: Corporate Greed, Women and the Dalkon Shield* (New York: Pantheon Books, 1985).

26. *Wall Street Journal*, March 14, 1988.

27. *Wall Street Journal*, July 25, 1989.

28. *The New Mexican*, June 22, 1981.

29. Robert H. Miles, *Coffin Nails and Corporate Strategies* (New York: Prentice Hall, 1982); Peter Taylor, *Smoke Ring: The Politics of Tobacco* (New York: Pantheon Books, 1984); Larry C. White, *Merchants of Death: The American Tobacco Industry* (New York: Beechtree Books, 1987).

30. Burt Schorr, "Should Cigarette Warnings Be Even Tougher?" *Wall Street Journal*, May 11, 1982.

31. William L. Weis and Bruce W. Miller, *The Smoke-Free Working Place* (Buffalo, N.Y.: Prometheus Books, 1985).

32. Tobacco Institute, "Answers to the Most-Asked Questions about Cigarettes," 2d ed. (Tobacco Institute, 1982).

33. *Christian Science Monitor*, November 25, 1987.

34. *Wall Street Journal*, April 29, 1987.

35. *Wall Street Journal*, April 22, 1988.

36. *Christian Science Monitor*, October 4, 1988.

37. Ellen Goodman, "Smokeless Tobacco Advertising Eats into the Health of Young People," *The New Mexican,* June 13, 1986.

38. *Wall Street Journal,* October 4, 1985.

39. Marshall B. Clinard and Peter C. Yeager, *Corporate Crime* (New York: The Free Press, 1980), p. 120.

40. *New York Times,* September 8, 1989.

41. Neil Orloff, "Climbing the Pollution Curve," *Wall Street Journal,* November 5, 1985.

42. Communication from the Material Resources Defense Council.

43. Internal memorandum of the Environmental Action Foundation, Washington, D.C.

44. *Wall Street Journal,* September 20, 1988.

45. Michael Brown, *Laying Waste: The Poisoning of America by Toxic Chemicals* (New York: Washington Square Press, 1981); and Epstein, Brown, and Pope, *Hazardous Waste in America.*

46. *Wall Street Journal,* February 16, 1989.

47. *Wall Street Journal,* May 21, 1985.

48. Russell Mokhiber, "Agent Orange: Bringing the Battle Home," *Multinational Monitor,* 8 (April 1987): 11–13.

49. Mokhiber, *Corporate Crime and Violence,* pp. 78–82.

50. *The New Mexican,* May 7, 1984.

7. CORPORATE BRIBERY

1. Quoted in Adam Myerson, "Social Responsibility," *Wall Street Journal,* October 6, 1980.

2. Neil H. Jacoby, Peter Nehemkis, and Richard Eells, *Bribery and Extortion in World Business* (New York: Macmillan, 1977). Also see, particularly for a detailed discussion of methods of bribery payments and concealment practices, Marshall B. Clinard and Peter C. Yeager, *Corporate Crime* (New York: The Free Press, 1980), pp. 168–80.

3. John Braithwaite, *Corporate Crime in the Pharmaceutical Industry* (London: Routledge and Keegan Paul, 1984), p. 12.

4. *Wall Street Journal,* September 22, 1983, and *Wall Street Journal,* November 21, 1983.

5. *Multinational Monitor,* 3 (January 1982): 35.

6. Leon Jaworski, *The Right and the Power: The Prosecution of Watergate* (New York: Pocket Books, 1977).

7. *Wisconsin State Journal,* November 14, 1975.

8. Hoerner Waldorf Report to the SEC, Amended Form 8K, April 1977.

9. Michael W. Reisman, *Folded Lies: Bribery, Crusades and Reforms* (New York: The Free Press, 1979).

10. Yerachmiel Kugel and Gladys W. Gruenberg, *International Payoffs: Dilemma for Business* (Lexington, Mass.: Lexington Books, 1977), p. 36.

11. *Wall Street Journal,* August 26, 1980.

12. *Wall Street Journal,* March 17, 1978.

13. Lee Iacocca, *Iacocca, an Autobiography* (New York: Bantam Books, 1984), pp. 113–14.
14. Quoted in Reisman, *Folded Lies*, p. 46.

8. THE RAPE OF THE THIRD WORLD

1. Dan Kurzman, *A Killing Wind* (New York: McGraw Hill, 1987); and David Weir, *The Bhopal Syndrome* (San Francisco: Sierra Club Books, 1987).
2. See Russell Mokhiber, *Corporate Crime and Violence: Big Business Power and the Abuse of the Public Trust* (San Francisco: Sierra Club Books, 1988) pgs. 86–96.
3. Mokhiber, *Corporate Crime and Violence*.
4. Amie Street, "Nicaragua Cites Pennwalt," *Multinational Monitor*, 2 (May 1981): 25; and Bob Wyrick, "Chemical Plant's Poison Inflames a Nation," *Newsday*, December 21, 1981.
5. Bob Wyrick, "How Job Conditions Led to a Worker's Death," *Newsday*, December 17, 1981.
6. Herman Rebhan, "Labor Battles Exports," *Multinational Monitor* (March 1980): 6.
7. Bob Wyrick, "Asbestos Plant Imperils Village in India," *Newsday*, December 16, 1981.
8. Wyrick, "Asbestos Plant Imperils Village."
9. Amy Goodman, "The Case Against Depo-Provera," *Multinational Monitor* (February/March 1985): 3–15.
10. John Braithwaite, *Corporate Crime in the Pharmaceutical Industry* (London: Routledge and Kegan Paul, 1984), pp. 257–65.
11. Milton Silverman, Philip R. Lee, and Mia Lydecker, *Prescriptions for Death: The Drugging of the Third World* (Berkeley: University of California Press, 1982), p. 10.
12. Silverman, Lee, and Lydecker, *Prescriptions for Death*.
13. Cited in James E. Coleman, *The Criminal Elite: The Sociology of White Collar Crime* (New York: St. Martin's Press, 1985), p. 46.
14. Silverman, Lee, and Lydecker, *Prescriptions for Death*, p. 108.
15. *Wall Street Journal*, May 15, 1986.
16. Mokhiber, *Corporate Crime and Violence*, p. 185.
17. David Weir and Mark Schapiro, *Circles of Poison: Pesticides and People in a Hungry World* (San Francisco: Institute for Food Development and Policy, 1981), p. 77–78.
18. Ibid., p. 11.
19. "Pesticides and Pills: For Export Only," Public Broadcasting System radio broadcast, October 5 and 7, 1982.
20. Weir and Schapiro, *Circle of Poison*, p. 17.
21. Weir and Schapiro, *Circle of Poison*, p. 29.
22. *Multinational Monitor*, 9, no. 9 (September 1988): 4.
23. Susan George, *How the Other Half Dies: The Real Reasons for World Hunger* (Totowa, N.J.: Rowman and Allanheld, 1977), p. 146.
24. Ellen Hosmer, "Paradise Lost: The Ravaged Rainforest," *Multinational Monitor* 8, no. 6 (June 1987).

25. Sandra Postel, "Protecting Forests," in Lester R. Brown, et al., *State of the World, 1984: A Worldwatch Institute Report on Progress Toward a Sustainable Society* (New York: W. W. Norton, 1985), pp. 74–79.

26. Paul Ehrlich and Anne Ehrlich, *Extinction: The Causes and Consequences of the Disappearance of Species* (New York: Random House, 1981), pp. 163–64.

27. Rachel Grossman, "Bitter Wages: Women in East Asia's Semi-Conductor Plants," *Multinational Monitor*, 1 (March 1980): 9.

28. Annette Fuentes and Barbara Ehrenreich, *Women in the Global Factory* (Boston: South End Press, 1984), p. 21.

29. Wyrick, "How Job Conditions Led to a Worker's Death."

30. Allan Ebert-Miner, "How Rawlings Uses Haitian Women to Spin Profits Off U.S. Baseball Sales," *Multinational Monitor*, 3 (August 1982): 11–12.

31. Grossman, "Bitter Wages."

32. Matthew Rothschild, "Women Beat Up at Control Data, Korea," *Multinational Monitor*, 3 (September 1982): 14–16.

33. Fuentes and Ehrenreich, *Women in the Global Factory*, p. 35.

34. *Christian Science Monitor*, February 2, 1989.

35. John Cavanagh and Joy Hackel, "Turning the World into 'Marlboro Country,' " *The Guardian*, April 13, 1983.

36. Paul Sigmund, *Multinationals in Latin America: The Politics of Nationalization* (Madison: University of Wisconsin Press, 1980).

37. Quoted in the *Washington Spectator*, January 15, 1988.

38. *Fortune*, April 24, 1989.

9. WHAT CAN BE DONE

1. James E. Inman, *The Regulatory Environment of Business* (New York: John Wiley and Sons, 1984), p. 627.

2. John Braithwaite, "Enforced Self-Regulation: A New Strategy for Corporate Crime Control," *Michigan Law Review*, 80 (1982): 1470–71.

3. M. Cash Mathews, *Strategic Intervention in Organizations: Resolving Ethical Dilemmas in Corporations* (Newbury Park, Calif.: Sage Publications, 1988).

4. Donald R. Cressey and Charles A. Moore, *Corporation Codes of Ethical Conduct* (New York: Peat, Marwick and Mitchell Foundation, 1981).

5. See Marshall B. Clinard, *Corporate Ethics and Crime* (Beverly Hills, Calif.: Sage Publications 1983), p. 153.

6. Marshall B. Clinard and Peter C. Yeager, *Corporate Crime* (New York: The Free Press, 1980), p. 304.

7. Irving Kristol, "Ethics and the Corporations," *Wall Street Journal*, April 16, 1975, p. 18.

8. Winston Williams, "White Collar Crime: Booming Again," *New York Times*, June 9, 1985.

9. Penina Migdal Glazer and Myron Peretz Glazer, *The Whistle Blowers: Exposing Corruption in Government and Industry* (New York: Basic Books, 1989).

10. Quoted in Marie Ragghiant, "The Reward is One's Own Dignity," *Parade Magazine*, March 22, 1987, p. 5.

11. John Hanrahan, "Whistleblower," *Common Cause*, 9 (March/April 1983): 16–23.

12. Clinard, *Corporate Ethics and Crime*, p. 125.

13. Clinard and Yeager, *Corporate Crime*, p. 60.

14. Clinard, *Corporate Ethics and Crime*.

15. Gilbert Geis, "White Collar Crime: The Heavy Electrical Equipment Anti-Trust Case of 1961," in Marshall B. Clinard and Richard Quinney, *Criminal Behavior Systems: A Typology* (New York: Holt, Rinehart and Winston, 1967), pp. 144–47.

16. Quoted in Clinard and Yeager, *Corporate Crime*, pp. 64–65.

17. Report to the Securities and Exchange Commission, Lockheed Aircraft Corporation Internal Audit Form 8K, May 1977.

18. Mark Green and John F. Berry, *The Challenge of Hidden Profits: Reducing Corporate Bureaucracy and Waste* (New York: William Morrow and Co., 1985).

19. Michael L. Benson, et. al., "District Attorneys and Corporate Crime: Surveying and Prosecutorial Gatekeepers," *Criminology*, 26 (August 1988): 505–18.

20. *The New Mexican*, June 19, 1988.

21. *Wall Street Journal*, December 16, 1985.

22. Joan Claybrook, *Retreat from Safety: Reagan's Attack on America's Health* (New York: Pantheon Books, 1984); Susan S. Tolchin and Martin Tolchin, *Dismantling America: The Rush to Deregulate* (New York: Oxford University Press, 1983).

23. Michael Pertschuk, *Revolt against Regulation: The Rise and Pause of the Consumer Movement* (Berkeley: University of California Press, 1982).

24. Clinard and Yeager, *Corporate Crime*, pp. 122–29.

25. Russell Mokhiber, *Corporate Crime and Violence: Big Business Power and the Abuse of the Public Trust* (San Francisco: Sierra Club Books, 1988), pp. 8–9.

26. Clinard and Yeager, *Corporate Crime*, pp. 125–26.

27. Newsletter, "William Proxmire Reports to You from Washington."

28. Brent Fisse, "Community Service as a Sanction against Corporations," *Wisconsin Law Review* (1981): 970–1017.

29. William F. Blundell, "Equity Funding: It Did It for the Jollies," in Donald Moffitt, ed., *Swindled! Classic Frauds of the Seventies* (Princeton, N.J.: Dow Jones Books, 1976).

30. Clinard, *Corporate Ethics and Crime*, pp. 71–74.

31. After he left office, Atkins was arrested and charged, in 1988, with taking part in a scheme to sell to Iran, for $600,000, confidential Ashland Oil documents dealing with a large Iranian 1979 oil contract dispute, which was finally settled by Ashland in 1989 for $325 million. Four of his closest associates at Ashland were shocked by his disloyalty to his former corporation. Atkins pleady guilty in 1989 to 2 counts of conspiracy and wire fraud.

32. Clinard and Yeager, *Corporate Crime*, p. 272.

33. Bureau of National Affairs, *White-collar Justice: A BNS Special Report on White-collar Crime* (Washington, D.C.: Bureau of National Affairs, 1976), p. 15.

34. *Wall Street Journal*, August 10, 1989.

35. Newsletter of Senator William Proxmire (D-Wis.), May 1985.

36. Quoted in "White-Collar Justice," Bureau of National Affairs, April 13, 1976.

37. Quoted in Clinard and Yeager, p. 291.

38. Mokhiber, *Corporate Crime and Violence*, pp. 28–29.

39. Geis, "White Collar Crime," p. 140.

40. R. Nathan, "Coddled Criminals," *Harper's Magazine*, January 1980, pp. 30–35.

41. Clinard and Yeager, p. 295.

42. Gilbert Geis, "Deterring Corporate Crime," in Ralph Nader and Mark J. Green, eds., *Corporate Power in America* (New York: Grossman, 1973), p. 194.

43. S. N. Brenner and E. A. Molander, "Is the Ethics of Business Changing?" *Harvard Business Review* 55 (January-February, 1977): 59–70.

44. Brent Fisse and John Braithwaite, *The Impact of Publicity on Corporate Offenders* (Albany: State University Press of New York, 1983).

45. Sandra S. Evans and Richard Lundman, "Newspaper Coverage of Corporate Price-Fixing: A Replication," *Criminology*, 21 (November 1983): 541.

46. Clinard and Yeager, *Corporate Crime*, p. 319.

47. Mokhiber, *Corporate Crime and Violence*, p. 35.

48. Ralph Nader, Mark J. Green, and Joel Seligman, *Taming the Giant Corporations* (New York: Norton and Company, 1976).

49. Kenneth M. Davidson, *Megamergers: Corporate America's Billion-Dollar Takeovers* (Cambridge, Mass.: Ballinger Publishing Company, 1985).

50. Yankelovich, Skelly, White, "Report to Leadership Participants on 1979 Findings on Corporate Priorities," (mimeo, 1979), as quoted in Davidson, p. 365.

51. Davidson, *Megamergers*, p. 335.

52. *Wisconsin State Journal*, January 14, 1979.

SELECTED REFERENCES

Andrews, Kenneth R. *Ethics in Practice: Managing the Moral Corporation*. Boston: Harvard Business School Press, 1989.

Berman, Daniel J. *Death on the Job: Occupational Health and Safety Struggles in the United States*. New York: Monthly Review Press, 1978.

Bradshaw, Thornton, and David Vogel, eds. *Corporations and Their Critics: Issues and Answers to the Problems of Corporate Social Responsibility*. New York: McGraw-Hill Book Company, 1981.

Braithwaite, John. *Corporate Crime in the Pharmaceutical Industry*. London: Routledge and Kegan Paul, 1984.

———. *Crime, Shame and Reintegration*. Cambridge: Cambridge University Press, 1989.

Brodeur, Paul. *Outrageous Misconduct: The Asbestos Industry*. New York: Pantheon Books, 1985.

Brown, Michael. *Laying Waste: The Poisoning of America by Toxic Chemicals*. New York: Washington Square Press, 1981.

Carson, Rachel. *Silent Spring*. Boston: Houghton-Mifflin, 1962.

Claybrook, Joan. *Retreat from Safety: Reagan's Attack on America's Health*. New York: Pantheon Books, 1984.

Clinard, Marshall B. *Corporate Ethics and Crime: The Role of Middle Management*. Beverly Hills, Calif.: Sage Publications, 1983.

Clinard, Marshall B., and Peter C. Yeager. *Corporate Crime*. New York: The Free Press, 1980.

Coleman, James W. *The Criminal Elite: The Sociology of White Collar Crime*. New York: St. Martin's Press, 1985.

Cousins, Norman. *The Pathology of Power*. New York: W. W. Norton and Co., 1987.

Davidson, Kenneth M. *Megamergers: Corporate America's Billion-Dollar Takeovers*. Cambridge, Mass.: Ballinger Publishing Co., 1985.

Eastman, Joel W. *Safety vs. Styling: The American Automobile Industry and the Development of Automotive Safety, 1900–1966*. Lanham, Md.: University Press of America, Inc., 1984.

Englebourg, Saul. *Power and Morality: American Business Ethics, 1840–1914*. Westport, Conn.: Greenwood Press, 1980.

Ermann, M. David, and Richard J. Lundman. *Corporate and Governmental Deviance: Problems of Organizational Behavior in Contemporary Society*, 3d ed. New York: Oxford University Press, 1987.

Fisse, Brent, and John Braithwaite. *The Impact of Publicity on Corporate Offenders*. Albany: State University Press of New York, 1983.

Fisse, Brent, and Peter A. French, eds. *Corrigible Corporations and Unruly Law*. San Antonio, Tex.: Trinity University Press, 1985.

Fitzgerald, Ernest. *The Pentagonists: An Insider's View of Waste, Mismanagement and Fraud in Defense Spending*. Boston: Houghton Mifflin, 1982.

Frank, Nancy. *Crimes against Health and Safety*. New York: Harrow and Heston, 1985.

Frank, Nancy, and Michael Lombness. *Controlling Corporate Illegality: The Regulatory Justice System*. Cincinnati: Anderson Publishing Co., 1988.

French, Peter A. *Collective and Corporate Responsibility*. New York: Columbia University Press, 1984.

Fuentes, Annette, and Barbara Ehrenreich. *Women in the Global Factory*. Boston: South End Press, 1984.

George, Susan. *How the Other Half Dies: The Real Reasons for World Hunger*. Totowa, N.J.: Rowman and Allanheld, 1977.

Glazer, Penina Migdal, and Myron Peretz Glazer. *The Whistle Blowers: Exposing Corruption in Government and Industry*. New York: Basic Books, 1989.

Green, Mark, and John F. Berry. *The Challenge of Hidden Profits: Reducing Corporate Bureaucracy and Waste*. New York: William Morrow and Co., 1985.

Halberstam, David. *The Reckoning*. New York: Morrow, 1986.

Hills, Stuart L., ed. *Corporate Violence: Injury and Death for Profit*. Totowa, N.J.: Rowman and Littlefield, 1987.

Hochstedler, Ellen, ed. *Corporations as Criminals*. Beverly Hills, Calif.: Sage Publications, 1984.

Jacoby, Neil H., Peter Nehemkis, and Richard Eells. *Bribery and Extortion in World Business*. New York: Macmillan, 1977.

Jaworski, Leon. *The Right and the Power: The Prosecution of Watergate*. New York: Pocket Books, 1977.

Kaufman, Joel, et al. *Over the Counter Pills That Don't Work*. Washington, D.C.: Public Citizen Health Research Group, 1983.

Kugel, Yerachmiel, and Gladys W. Gruenberg. *International Payoffs: Dilemma for Business*. Lexington, Mass.: Lexington Books, 1977.

Kurzman, Dan. *A Killing Wind*. New York: McGraw-Hill, 1987.

Lash, Jonathan, Katherine Gillman, and David Sheridan. *A Season of Spoils: The Reagan Administration's Attack on the Environment*. New York: Pantheon Books, 1984.

McGovern, James. *The Oil Game*. New York: Viking Press, 1981.

Mathews, M. Cash. *Strategic Intervention in Organizations: Resolving Ethical Dilemmas in Corporations*. Newbury Park, Calif.: Sage Publications, 1988.

Melkin, Dorothy, and Michael S. Brown. *Workers at Risk*. Chicago: University of Chicago Press, 1984.

Miles, Robert H. *Coffin Nails and Corporate Strategies*. New York: Prentice Hall, 1982.

Mokhiber, Russell. *Corporate Crime and Violence: Big Business Power and the Abuse of the Public Trust*. San Francisco: Sierra Club Books, 1988.

Nader, Ralph, and Mark J. Green, eds. *Corporate Power in America*. New York: Grossman, 1973.

Nader, Ralph, Mark J. Green, and Joel Seligman. *Taming the Giant Corporations*. New York: Norton and Company, 1976.

Pertschuk, Michael. *Revolt against Regulation: The Rise and Pause of the Consumer Movement*. Berkeley: University of California Press, 1982.

Reisman, Michael W. *Folded Lies: Bribery, Crusades and Reforms*. New York: The Free Press, 1979.

Sampson, Anthony. *The Seven Sisters: The Great Oil Companies and the World They Shaped*. New York: Viking, 1975.

Silverman, Milton, and Philip R. Lee. *Pills, Profits and Politics*. Berkeley: University of California Press, 1974.

Silverman, Milton, Philip R. Lee, and Mia Lydecker. *Prescriptions for Death: The Drugging of the Third World*. Berkeley: University of California Press, 1982.

Snoeyenbos, Milton, Robert Almeder, and James Humber, eds. *Business Ethics: Corporate Values and Society*. New York: Prometheus Books, 1983.

Stone, Christopher. *Where the Law Ends: The Social Control of Corporate Behavior*. New York: Harper and Row, 1975.

Taylor, Peter. *Smoke Ring: The Politics of Tobacco*. New York: Pantheon Books, 1984.

Tolchin, Susan S., and Martin Tolchin. *Dismantling America: The Rush to Deregulate*. New York: Oxford University Press, 1983.

Tyler, Patrick. *Running Critical: The Silent War, Rickover and General Dynamics*. New York: Harper and Row, 1986.

Vaughan, Diane. *Controlling Unlawful Organizational Behavior: Social Structure and Corporate Misconduct*. Chicago: University of Chicago Press, 1983.

Weir, Daniel, and Mark Schapiro. *Circles of Poison: Pesticides and People in a Hungry World*. San Francisco: Institute for Food Development and Policy, 1981.

Weis, William L., and Bruce W. Miller. *The Smoke-Free Working Place*. New York: Prometheus Books, 1985.

White, Larry C. *Merchants of Death: The American Tobacco Industry*. New York: Beechtree Books, 1987.

Wolfe, Sydney M., Christopher M. Coley, and the Health Research Group founded by Ralph Nader. *Pills That Don't Work: A Consumers' and Doctors' Guide to Over 600 Prescription Drugs That Lack Evidence of Effectiveness*. New York: Farrar, Straus & Giroux, 1981.

INDEX

About the Author

MARSHALL B. CLINARD is Emeritus Professor of Sociology at the University of Wisconsin, Madison. He is the author of eleven books, including *Illegal Corporate Behavior, Corporate Crime,* and *Corporate Ethics and Crime: The Role of Middle Management.* He has received two grants from the U.S. Department of Justice to study the Fortune 500 and has been the recipient of the Edwin H. Sutherland Award for Distinguished Contributions to Criminology.